The Care Crisis

The Care Crisis

*What Caused It and
How Can We End It?*

Emma Dowling

VERSO
London • New York

For all who care

First published by Verso 2021
© Emma Dowling 2021

1 3 5 7 9 10 8 6 4 2

Verso
UK: 6 Meard Street, London W1F 0EG
US: 20 Jay Street, Suite 1010, Brooklyn, NY 11201
versobooks.com

Verso is the imprint of New Left Books

ISBN-13: 978-1-78663-034-6
ISBN-13: 978-1-78663-037-7 (US EBK)
ISBN-13: 978-1-78663-036-0 (UK EBK)

British Library Cataloguing in Publication Data
A catalogue record for this book is available from the British Library

Library of Congress Cataloging-in-Publication Data

Names: Dowling, Emma, author.
Title: The care crisis : what caused it and how can we end it? / Emma
  Dowling.
Description: First edition paperback. | London ; New York : Verso, 2021. |
  Includes bibliographical references and index. | Summary: 'Emma Dowling
  examines the care crisis in the UK, looking at the changes to the care
  system over the last decade. Dowling gives an account not only of the
  impact of austerity measures on care provision in the UK but also of the
  underlying logic of neoliberalism driving the crisis' – Provided by
  publisher.
Identifiers: LCCN 2020041746 (print) | LCCN 2020041747 (ebook) | ISBN
  9781786630346 (paperback) | ISBN 9781786630377 (ebk)
Subjects: LCSH: National Health services – Great Britain. | Health care
  reform – Great Britain.
Classification: LCC RA395.G6 D69 2021 (print) | LCC RA395.G6 (ebook) |
  DDC 362.10941 – dc23
LC record available at https://lccn.loc.gov/2020041746
LC ebook record available at https://lccn.loc.gov/2020041747

Typeset in Sabon by MJ & N Gavan, Truro, Cornwall
Printed in the UK by CPI Group (UK) Ltd, Croydon CR0 4YY

Contents

Introduction

Open the papers on any day in Britain and you will find articles about the crisis in social and health care: an ageing population and the increase in dementia without the necessary care facilities or resources to deal with it; reduced mental health services; fragmenting community services; the abandonment of refugees; the lack of nursery schools; cuts to disability care budgets; overworked doctors and nurses; stressed children; cuts to education maintenance allowances. The list goes on. Since the financial crash of 2008, the toxic cocktail of recession and austerity has seen those who rely on disability payments suffer inordinately.[1] Elderly people feel lonely and isolated, while their carers are overburdened and underpaid.[2] Record numbers of people in the UK are using food banks due to a combination of financial vulnerability and welfare reforms.[3]

On top of cuts and economic hardship, societal care needs are actually increasing, due to demographic changes. From 2012 to 2022 the number of seventy-five-year-olds will have increased by over one million, from 5.1 to 6.6 million. This is a rise of more than 20 per cent and is exacerbated by a shrinking younger working population.[4] According to reports by the charity organisation Age UK and the Care Quality Commission, the public body that inspects and regulates health and social care in Britain, one in seven older people (1.4 million) were not receiving the care they needed in 2018.[5] The Care Quality Commission also reported in 2019 that the number of children with mental health disorders accessing social services had increased by 50 per cent in four years.[6] In the area of mental health, the care system severely struggles to keep up with demand.[7]

At the same time, precariousness and insecurity continue to rise. Since 2008, insecure self-employment has grown considerably in the UK and the number of agency workers has increased by nearly 50 per cent.[8] There has been a veritable explosion in zero-hours contracts. These are contracts that do not guarantee working hours, while requiring availability; zero-hours-contracts also exclude sick pay, holiday pay and entitlements to employer pension schemes. They are particularly prevalent in the health, education and hospitality sectors, but it is domiciliary care workers who are most affected. Between 2008 and 2012 there was a 40 per cent increase in home care workers paid at or below the national minimum wage who were on zero-hours contracts.[9] Zero-hours contracts are becoming the norm in the homecare sector.

Zero-hours contracts are said to give workers the flexibility to work when it suits them, particularly those with caring responsibilities.[10] While precariousness refers to employment status in the first instance, it also has an emotional dimension. Not knowing where the next paycheck is going to come from, not knowing what may happen in the longer term, not having adequate sick pay or a pension – this produces feelings of insecurity. The promises of flexibility and freedom – often wrapped up in notions of 'doing what you love' (on a project by project basis) or the convenience of 'working when you want to' – are exposed as myths when they meet the daily grind. In reality, zero-hours contracts are the opposite of self-determination. They require someone to be available even though they might not be given work. Having to make yourself available without knowing whether you will even be called on (and therefore be paid) is more anxiety-producing than it is conducive to greater freedom. And being under pressure to turn up for work even when, say, you are unwell, for fear of not getting any more shifts, compounds the emotional burden. Not to mention that designating caring responsibilities as something that people do in their own time, as their own responsibility, constitutes part of the logic of relegating care work to the unpaid realms of the personal.

All the while, a wellbeing industry is booming for those who can afford it. Proliferating too is the advice literature on self-care alongside a concomitant insurance industry, start-ups for new care technologies, along with personalised care services, from care budget planners to cuddle therapists. The crisis of care does not affect everyone in the same way: as care becomes more and more commodified, access to care becomes more and more dependent on what you can pay. Moreover, one person's care needs are often played off against another's, separating and dividing people and putting their needs in competition with one another in a context of manufactured scarcity, producing significant care inequalities. All too often this arises from political decisions about whose care decision-makers consider dispensable and whose they do not.

Needs are also played off against one another when care workers are pitted against those they care for, or vice versa. When junior doctors went on strike in the UK in 2016 over changes to their contracts which would make them work even more hours, with less access to training and less pay, the then health secretary Jeremy Hunt positioned himself as championing the interests of patients against the actions of junior doctors he branded 'irresponsible'.[11] No matter that the proposed changes would be to the detriment of junior doctors' welfare and would increase the safety risks resulting from understaffed hospitals with overworked personnel.

The evident failures of the privatisation of health and social care services are part and parcel of the current crisis of care. For example, in 2019, all four of Britain's biggest residential care home providers were up for sale owing to financial difficulties.[12] How have care home companies managed to rack up such inordinate debts – to the tune of hundreds of millions of pounds – which inevitably entail sizeable interest payments to their creditors? How come the responsibility for ensuring the wellbeing of the elderly, vulnerable and frail is being handed to private equity companies, US hedge funds and international real estate investors, whose entire raison d'être is to operate with the kinds of high-risk financial practices designed to maximise financial returns on investment? Such warning signals, however, have not propelled a rethink of privatisation, marketisation and financialisation. Instead, spending cuts have turbo-charged these trends and, indeed, created new opportunities: where cuts have hit, they have created funding gaps to which further privatisation and outsourcing, marketisation and financialisation are considered to be the solution.[13]

The restructuring of welfare states in Europe and North America is but one facet of a manifest global care crisis, in which a growing number of the world's population cannot access the care and support they require.[14] For this crisis affects access to care, as well as the work that goes into its provision. To get a sense of the dimensions of the global need for care: in 2015 there were an estimated 2.1 billion people worldwide in need of care, predominantly children (the overwhelming majority) and the elderly. By 2030, the total is expected to reach 2.3 billion.[15] However, care for these recipients is increasingly difficult to ensure.

While the number of the world's population unable to satisfy basic care needs grows, so too does care inequality not just within, but across, societies. Where Global North countries display dramatic disparities in access to care, developing countries face a situation where a lack of health-care infrastructure exacerbates the challenges of chronic illness and epidemics, natural disasters and political conflicts.[16] The crisis of care also includes the plight of refugees in countries along the borders of the European Union, countries already struggling with depleted social infrastructure while having to respond to the needs of migrants fleeing war, persecution and penury. According to the United Nations Refugee Agency, in 2016 there were an unprecedented 65.6 million people forced from their homes worldwide, over half of whom were under the age of eighteen.[17] When refugees – adults and children – drown in the Mediterranean, powerful voices in prospective host countries dare to suggest that they should not be rescued, lest it motivate more people to come.[18]

Too often the problems we face as a society are couched in economic terms, with all else appearing as secondary: get 'the economy' back on track, facilitate economic growth – that is how to solve the pressing issues of our time, be they climate change and environmental degradation or social inequality, exclusion and want. However, were we to change our view and look at the economy from the perspective of care, our debates about the problems we face and the solutions to them on a local and global scale would also change.

When we think of care we usually think of individual sentiments or behaviours – the feeling of caring *about* someone or the act of caring *for* someone, or even caring about the state of the world. Yet individual intentions and actions appear inadequate in the face of the overwhelming problems of our time. It feels so futile – naïve, even – to believe in the possibility of everyone being more considerate of each other so as to bring about a better world. It is painfully obvious that massive economic disparities and major political power imbalances are the root of our present predicament. Can something so seemingly fragile as care be powerful enough to transform such forces? Acts of kindness may make us feel better, but can they really be both the means and end for change? And it is not just the cynics who are suspicious of the imposition of an imperative to care. Ways of caring can also be patronising and confining. Immediately, the questions arise: who defines? Who decides? Who enforces? And how?

The Framing of Crisis

Everyone should be able to live a materially secure and meaningful life premised on emotional wellbeing, physical health, fulfilling social relationships and maintenance of the ecological environment. Deprived of the means, time and capacity to care for ourselves and one another, we struggle to maintain not only physical but also mental health, straining to hold on to a sense of self-esteem in the face of multiple pressures. A crisis of care means that more and more people are unable to do these things or to get the help they need. A crisis of care also means that those who provide care to others are unable to do so satisfactorily and under dignified conditions. To speak of a crisis of care is to speak of the changes to the material conditions for the provision of care – whether within households and families, in communities, by public or social services or through the market, private corporations and agencies. To speak of a crisis of care is to point to the growing gap between care needs and the resources made available to meet them.[19] To speak of a crisis of care is also to look closely and critically at the kinds of ideological assumptions about human nature that inform not only policies, but also dominant economic theories. In an unequal world, no crisis affects everyone equally. To speak of crisis is thus to ask the question, *a crisis for whom?* It means to highlight class and inequality in the way the crisis is experienced, and in the way that care is organised to entrench division and pit us against one another. It means asking: who is cared for and who is not?

Nevertheless, to speak of crisis – any kind of crisis – is to join a litany of crisis lamentations that crowd the public sphere and make us numb to its urgency. We no longer know whether the language of crisis is just another overused hyperbole or whether the crises – economic, social, political, environmental – are so entrenched that they have simply become normalised. Feelings of disempowerment, hopelessness and insecurity converge in a kind of diffuse despair that – not unlike the air pollution that shrouds our cities – leaves a toxic film all around, barely visible, but certainly perceivable.[20] Like a kind of inverted fairy dust, this despair has us all in a painful hiatus, not knowing how to impel change and unable to imagine a different future, let alone bring it about.

Despite this cacophony of crisis, to name it as such is to affirm that *something is amiss*, that *what is happening is not OK*. The sociologist Michel Wieviorka suggests that, while a crisis has real effects, it also reveals things about our situation that have been kept out of sight, and forces certain truths about social, political and economic life into our awareness.[21] Consequently, the task at hand is not merely to take crises at face value, but to drill down into those problems and questions that were kept out of sight.

Brexit brought the calamitous consequences of austerity, rising inequality and neoliberal failure to the fore. The coronavirus pandemic made it even more difficult to ignore the crisis of care and the consequences of an underfunded health and social care system. Brought into view were the lack of resources and equipment available to health and other care workers, as were issues of understaffing, long hours and low pay in the care sector. The situation in care homes for the elderly has been especially troubling.[22] During the lockdown, families had to turn their homes into offices, nurseries and schools, with an uneven burden of the work involved falling on women. And not everyone was able to find a safe haven in lockdown, whether that was because they had to continue travelling to work, because they were driven out of the home by domestic violence, or because they did not have a home in the first place.

Exposure to the economic consequences of the coronavirus crisis has not been the same for everyone and has been more intense for precarious workers. Indeed, the consequences of contracting the virus have been unequally distributed: in addition to factors such as age or pre-existing health conditions, socioeconomic status and ethnicity have also been shown to be significant factors.[23] All in all, the desperate shortcomings of a 'just-in-time' economy with few reserves were made evident.[24] However, the kind of recovery that would end the care crisis is by no means a given.

Yes, crises can be instrumentalised.[25] Nonetheless, to frame crisis as a starting point is to insist on the possibilities for change that still glisten through the dust of despair in the everyday struggles, social movements, experiments, commitments and conversations of all of us around the world who refuse to be blackmailed, who believe in alternatives to the present situation that are grounded in social and environmental justice. Now, if 'crisis' suggests an aberration, a departure from a norm, what do we mean by 'crisis of care'? What is the norm from which we have veered? If we look back in time, we see that the status quo of care has never been up to standard. The current care crisis, then, does not demand a return to a better past, but rather a struggle for a better future.

Individualism Revisited

It has become commonplace to attribute the very cause of the 2008 Global Financial Crisis to a lack of 'care'. We are familiar with the caricature of the banker, out for a big fast buck, in cahoots with wilfully negligent politicians who indulged rampant speculation and lack of regulation in the financial sector. When the Greek crisis came to a political head vis-à-vis the European Union in the summer of 2015, the German government and the institutions of the European Union were criticised for being more concerned to recover their money and appease investors than about the desperate situation of the Greek people. German tabloids stoked resentment with their drip-feed messages about 'lazy Greeks'.[26] On either side, phenomena of political, social and economic inequality were recast as matters of individual responsibility.

Margaret Thatcher, along with Ronald Reagan, is said to have cemented the individualism that has become a central pillar of Anglo-American neoliberal ideology. But when she famously exclaimed that there was 'no such thing as society', she went on to say something else that is less often quoted:

> There is a living tapestry of men and women and people and the beauty of that tapestry and the quality of our lives will depend upon how much each of us is prepared to take responsibility for ourselves and each of us prepared to turn round and help by our own efforts those who are unfortunate.[27]

Clearly we *are* supposed to care for one another, after all. However, we are supposed to care in ways that align with neoliberal doctrine. It is this part of Margaret Thatcher's interview that serves as a reminder of how the key factor of the whole construct is not individualism per se, but private or personal responsibility. This private or personal responsibility can be individual, but it can also be mindful of others. The point is that helping others must be voluntary and informed by an ethics of charity or other forms of moral obligation, such as those conferred by kinship. What it must not be is public – that is, organised, managed and funded collectively, on the basis of solidarity, and enshrined in the rights of citizenship (or residency).

If this project of retrenching the state's material responsibility for social welfare has been the key project of neoliberalism, the cementing of care as a private or personal responsibility is scarcely less important. In part, this feeds off the idea of individualism as the concern we have with and for ourselves and the maximisation of our own self-interest: the ability to demand a good price for our labour power when we take it to market (what is now ubiquitously known as our 'human capital').[28] But it also reinforces the idea that our responsibility for ourselves and others is a private, voluntary matter. Here the promise of freedom sits alongside the prospect of abandonment, to be merely mitigated by commodities and (financial) markets, or offset by the compassion of others. That Margaret Thatcher should have made her remarks regarding society's non-existence in a women's magazine seems particularly jarring, given the role that women have played in keeping society going with their caring labour. This is labour that continues to be performed, against the idea that we have been reduced to selfish, fearful and competitive beings. And so, her outright denial of the existence of society only served to – once again – render all this work economically and politically invisible and insignificant. At the same time, the very welfare-state retrenchment Margaret Thatcher oversaw relied significantly on this unpaid care work, often against the odds, in increasingly difficult conditions.

Globalisation's Care Fix

The Global Financial Crisis was not the beginning of the care crisis, yet it has been the catalyst of its worsening through the combined effects of recession, austerity and an economic recovery that has been regressive in its effects. Prior to the Global Financial Crisis, academics, practitioners and activists were already urging concerted action against the ways in which changing demographics and the neoliberal reconfiguration of care were exhausting societal care resources in ways that were placing undue burdens on carers, producing significant deficits for those needing care.[29]

The combination of lower birth rates and increasing life expectancy means more people are living longer, often with complex care needs, with the prospect of fewer resources to help meet those needs. The changing age composition of the population also has a geographical component, with implications for care. Younger people are more likely to live in cities and urban zones, whereas rural and coastal areas attract a greater concentration of older people.[30] Furthermore, families today are more dispersed; people have fewer children; more people live alone.

There has been a recorded 20 per cent increase in female labour-force participation in OECD countries over the last thirty years.[31] The majority of these women found work in the public sector or the expanding service sectors that required skills associated with femininity, including caring.[32] Without a concomitant transformation in the social division of unpaid reproductive labour, the significant increase in the female labour-force participation left many women doing double or even triple shifts, caring for offspring, relatives and neighbours, or volunteering for charities that provide care for those in need, with many households struggling to meet care needs when all efforts were geared towards working outside of the home to bring in income.[33] Political theorist Nancy Fraser paints a picture of capitalism as an economic system that if left to its own devices – its systemic logic of constant market expansion in pursuit of profit – 'eats its own tail' by devouring the social capacities needed to sustain the economy, with no view to maintaining or replenishing them.[34]

In the wake of the Global Financial Crisis, Britain has undergone a deep restructuring, most visible in the extensive austerity measures supposedly geared to enabling economic recovery. The austerity measures implemented post-crisis offloaded more of the cost of care from the state onto individuals, households and communities. There is an emotional dimension to austerity, too. The implementation of such measures affects how people think of themselves and of others and how they seek to act in the world. Austerity measures serve to convince individuals that the only person they can truly rely on is themselves, supported, at best, by their family, and implying a greater reliance on informal support and charity provision.[35] Yet the crisis obscures as much as it allows us to see: austerity measures that offload the cost of care onto the shoulders of the most disadvantaged in society are fuelled less by necessity than by an ideological agenda.

Both the formal care sector and informal care settings have been of great interest to capital in the reorganisation of the economy in the aftermath of the financial crisis. However, this interest did not start then, even if it has intensified since. Already in the late 1970s and 1980s, the 'shrinking' of the state opened the door to the outsourcing of public services to multinational corporations. The extreme austerity of the last decade now poses limits to erstwhile business models of privatisation, largely because the guaranteed revenue streams of public funding for privatisation are significantly diminishing. Nonetheless, as I will explore, new business models are once more being developed, as are new financial products and services. In addition, a heightened emphasis on personal responsibility for care is part of the search for profitability through the further commodification of care.[36] Despite the keen emphasis on social values and on local, community-orientated solutions, market logics are driving these developments, deepening the orientation towards profitability, financial returns on investment and upward redistributions of wealth.

Mobility and migration play a significant role in current debates about care. The vicissitudes of the Brexit referendum are an expression of the contradictory concerns brought to light. There has been a political backlash resulting from the way that migrant workers and non-migrant workers are pitted against one another, with migrant workers scapegoated for the ongoing economic crisis. And this despite the fact that the contribution of migrant workers from other countries within the European Economic Area – not just to the economy in general but to the health and social sector in particular – far outweighs their consumption of care resources, including public benefits.[37]

The entwined processes of globalisation (the capacity of capital to move production to parts of the world where labour is cheaper and there are fewer regulations) and financialisation (the pursuit of profits through rent and interest, as opposed to productive activity) means that the forces of capital have become less interested in the reproduction of any particular national labour force. This in part explains the retrenchment of public services. Yet this does not mean that care needs diminish. While it may have been possible for capital to move the production of commodities to wherever labour is cheaper and regulation weaker, care still has to be performed in the places it is needed in more or less direct contact with the people who require it.[38] The last thirty years have seen the proliferation of 'global care chains'.[39] This term gives a name to the phenomenon of migrant women (and, to a significant although lesser degree, men) from Global South countries and from Eastern Europe plugging care gaps in the Global North that have arisen due to the entry of many women into the labour market over the last thirty years, without a fundamental change in the sexual division of labour.

In other words, when it comes to care, production does not move to where labour is cheaper; instead, those workers from parts of the world where labour is cheaper move (or are actively recruited) to where the care work is needed. They take up positions as nannies, au pairs or other kinds of domestic workers in the home, or as nurses and other kinds of health and social care workers in hospitals, hospices and eldercare homes. A central pillar of the neoliberal configuration of care has been the fact that many (often white and middle-class) women have offloaded their caring and reproductive responsibilities onto the shoulders of migrant workers from Eastern European or Global South countries.

Consequently, class hierarchies among women have become further entrenched and care deficits merely displaced elsewhere. But the enhanced autonomy that many middle-class women have achieved brings its own set of problems once freedom is equated with productivism, competition, consumption and continuous self-optimisation. For such women, this means juggling the obligations of work and family or deciding in favour of one or the other.[40] For migrant care workers it can mean leaving behind families and children whose care needs go unmet or have to be fulfilled by adolescent sisters, aunts or grandmothers.[41] In other words, there is an exacerbation of care deficits in countries of origin through global care chains, while ethnicity and migration background are conduits to lower status in the labour market. Christa Wichterich uses the term 'care extractivism' to highlight the ways in which unpaid and underpaid care work is exploited in contemporary capitalism.[42]

The Dynamics of the Care Fix

This reorganisation of care work is an example of what we may call a 'care fix'. In the face of crisis and in light of the limits or impasses it faces, one mechanism available to a capitalist economy is to reorganise to overcome crises of profitability. Scholars such as the geographer David Harvey or the sociologist Beverly Silver, terming such forms of reorganisation a 'fix', have analysed the ways in which capitalist production undertakes spatial, technological, organisational or financial 'fixes' to solve the pressures of maintaining profitability.[43] This can very well mean that the underlying problems which led to the crisis in the first place are not addressed, but merely displaced. For example, as aforementioned, with globalisation a good deal of the production of goods was moved from countries such as the UK and US to parts of the world offering cheap labour and few regulations. This might have slashed production costs, but that does not mean that the market for the purchase of these goods is a given, nor that the workers will forever accept the conditions they are expected to work under. So, in the pursuit of profitability, capitalist production will again run into problems sooner or later. It is a bit like how we talk in everyday usage about 'getting a fix' – perhaps of our daily craving for chocolate, or of our favourite TV show. Once the hit wears off, the craving returns.

We can apply the analogy of the fix to the changing dynamics of care in society and the way that care is being reorganised in the face of both an economic and a care crisis. Changes in the ways in which goods and services are produced and consumed are linked to the ways in which care is provided – whether it be in families, partnerships, friendships, neighbourhoods and communities, by a (welfare) state, or through the market in commodified forms. A care fix entails the management of the care crisis in ways that resolve nothing definitively, but merely displace the crisis, thereby perpetuating the structural reflex of capitalist economies to offload the cost of care to unpaid sectors of society. Care fixes lie at the heart of the current reorganisation of the relations of production, reproduction and care.

This book examines the causes and manifestations of the growing care crisis and the emerging solution to it, in an investigation of the kinds of care fixes currently taking shape. Attended to are the ways in which care inequalities are rising, while the responsibility for caring is systematically handed down a societal care chain of paid, underpaid and unpaid caring labour based on a core structural feature of capitalist economies. This feature is the systemic imperative to expand markets in the pursuit of profitability, which goes hand in hand with a devaluation of the work of care, either by making this work invisible or by offloading its cost.

About the Book

The care contexts explored in the subsequent chapters are ones that have been at the forefront of the transformations prompted by austerity and the social and economic restructuring in Britain that followed the 2008 global financial crisis. My aim has been to uncover the invisible side of what is normally surveyed when we speak of economic crisis and 'the economy' – finance, GDP, growth, markets and so forth – to show how things appear quite different when we look at these phenomena through the lens of care. If austerity Britain is the book's backdrop, its broader context is the global economy.

The focus of the book is care work, both paid and unpaid, and the material conditions that enable or prevent caring from being carried out. I show how the affective dimensions of care, the emotions, feelings and relationships involved, play an important role in enabling the restructuring of care, where people's sense of compassion and responsibility are mobilised in attempts to compensate for or cope with the care crisis. At the same time, I point out how the domains of care are of particular interest for the production of economic value in contemporary capitalism. Overall, I identify key trends in the ways that the status, the provision and the work of care are changing, raising questions and points for discussion about the consequences entailed.

The book opens by looking at what we mean by 'care' and the lens of care work, before exploring different facets of what I am calling the care fix. Looking to the care fix of austerity, I show how cuts to the social security system, reductions to local authority budgets and attempts at making efficiency savings within the NHS exacerbated the care crisis. Large numbers of people face reduced access to care services, while the ability of individuals to care for themselves and for others has been undermined. Regressive changes to taxation have altered the nature of the tax base to the detriment of those on lower incomes, distributing wealth upwards. All the while, the anxious affect accompanying the justification of austerity as a necessary form of crisis management has merely served to deepen insecurity.

I investigate the precise nature of the care fix and seek to find out who exactly is picking up the tab for austerity and neoliberal restructuring in the realms of care. Political theorist Nancy Fraser, among others, has argued that the care crisis 'externali[ses] care work onto families and communities while diminishing their capacity to perform it'.[44] The question is, on whom exactly is care work offloaded? Whose feelings of responsibility for care and whose sense of compassion are mobilised in order to keep care infrastructures afloat under adverse conditions? In times of greater female labourforce participation and hence women's reduced availability for unpaid care work in the home, we need to investigate the gendered, racialised and classed dimensions of this externalisation and seek to locate the spaces and places to which care is relegated within households and beyond, be this in neighbourhoods and communities or within broader civil society.

In adult social care the crisis is particularly acute. In recent years care homes have been closing down and homecare providers have been handing back contracts to local councils.[45] The systematic underfunding of social care is long-standing and entrenched, and it has been exacerbated by austerity. However, attributing the problems in social care to the lack of public funding alone is not just insufficient, it is dangerously deflecting. I take a closer look at the adult social care sector in Britain to show how the privatisation of adult social care and the subsequent financialisation of parts of the sector are premised on a care fix that erodes pay and worsens conditions for care workers. From there, I turn my attention to the ways in which new kinds of financial instruments are being developed to mitigate the care crisis by ostensibly helping to reduce the cost of welfare, health and social care to the public purse through preventive measures. I then take a critical look at the ideas of the new, 'caring' capitalism purportedly emerging with the rise of social impact investing and the ideas of financial investment for the social good. Finally, I look at the rise of the self-care industry, its characteristics and ramifications, and its limitations as a solution to the care crisis. Having scrutinised the causes of the care crisis, I end the book with some proposals for actions to end it.

To write this book, I immersed myself in the theme of care. My key concern was to link up perspectives and experiences of care that are not usually thought about or presented together, while making sense of the dominant political-economic mechanisms at work in shaping the care crisis. I drew extensively on existing empirical research from across the social sciences in order to make my arguments and also examined governmental reports, reports published by multilateral organisations, publications of think tanks and non-governmental organisations, and press articles covering the period from 2010 to 2020.

In order to be able to include direct experiences of care work in the book, I talked to people across the board. I conducted twenty formal interviews in late 2015 and early 2016, in which I spoke with individuals in the fields of eldercare, community nursing, social work, psychotherapy, healthcare, domestic work, family caregiving, volunteering, political activism, trade union organising and journalism. I spoke with nurses and doctors, paid care workers and unpaid carers, professionals and non-professionals, men and women, people with migration backgrounds and people without. I used my existing networks to contact people in fields that were of interest to me, but I also contacted organisations and formally requested interviews.

These conversations on care served as explorations that helped guide further research and analysis, serving as background information that prompted me to take the research in one direction or another, and have informed what is presented in subsequent pages. Accounts of some of the interviews are included as illustrations in the book, appearing in the form of anonymised vignettes edited from the interview transcripts.

They are intended to convey experiences of caring and insights into what it means to care.

But I also had numerous informal conversations on the topic. Writing a book about something that touches everyone's life in one way or another means that everyone you meet and talk to has valuable insights to share, not just when you are consciously doing research, but also when going about everyday life. Often when I mentioned in conversation that I was writing a book about care, the person I was talking to would spontaneously offer their thoughts on and experiences of the matter. All these conversations helped me learn something about care. What became obvious in all of them was that most people felt that something was seriously amiss: almost everyone was critical of the status quo.

In addition, I attended public events and participated in workshops and discussions on the topic of the care crisis. I watched films and documentaries, read novels, went to exhibitions in museums and art galleries on the topic of care. Reflections based on my own experiences of care are included in my analysis, too. I also participated in the anti-austerity movements, went to the junior doctors' picket lines and visited the refugee camp in Calais. All research was undertaken between the autumn of 2015 and early 2020.

While informed by the rigour of academic research, I have written with a broad, non-academic audience in mind. The book is intended for readers who are not experts in these fields and who are not necessarily academics. My desire is to contribute to the political debate on the current crisis of care and what to do about it.

Brexit happened in the midst of the process, weighing on this book in terms of context, while not playing a direct role in the individual chapters. Not long after the referendum of 2016, I left England where I had lived for over fifteen years and moved to Germany. Unintentionally, I became an observer of the Brexit events from afar, often having to explain to people what on earth was going on in Britain, in so far as I myself could make sense of it. I also got to witness what was going on in these different places, and how the multifaceted political and economic crisis to which the care crisis pertains is playing itself out abroad as well. Then, as I was finalising the manuscript, the coronavirus pandemic broke out. The crisis of care that I had been writing about suddenly became headline news, thrusting the issues discussed in the chapters of this book firmly into the limelight.

The multifaceted crises we are living through make the conversation about care even more urgent. Without care we would not be able to live, let alone be economically productive. This essential characteristic of care is also the source of its exploitation. The reason why those who *do* care are locked into a sense of responsibility, especially in times of crisis, is because they fear what might happen to those they care for were they to stop caring. Yet, for all the talk of a care crisis, people often mean very different things when they talk about care. Any attempt to end the care crisis requires a clear understanding of what we mean by care.

1

What Is Care?

Throughout our lives we all require care, regardless of who we are or where we come from in the world. So too do animals, plants and other elements of the ecological environment that we are part of – something that societies are urgently having to acknowledge in the face of anthropogenic climate change. At certain points in time or due to specific life events, we may need more care than at other points, such as when we are children, when we are unwell, or when we are elderly. Moreover, human beings are diverse and have varying needs, capacities and capabilities involving differential levels of care needs, for example if we have a disability. We need care, not just to survive, but to live well, including when there is nothing 'wrong' with us as such.

In academic theories of care, care is conceived as all the supporting activities that take place to make, remake, maintain, contain and repair the world we live in and the physical, emotional and intellectual capacities required to do so.[1] In this sense, care is at the heart of making and remaking the world. The propensity to care and the work of caring are the lifeblood of our social and economic system. Care is central to the reproduction of society and thus one of its bedrocks, part of a fundamental infrastructure which holds society together. Without care, life could not be sustained.

According to the Oxford English Dictionary, the origins of the word *care* are not related to the Latin *cura* (to look after something or someone, to ensure their wellbeing). The word care stems from the Old English *caru*, which means sorrow, grief and even anxiety, or also 'burdens of the mind'. One only need think of the image evoked by the term 'carefree', being without a worry in the world. For sure, having to do the work of caring might weigh us down. Care can be burdensome, especially when the responsibility for caring is unevenly distributed, so that some within a family or a community find themselves having to do much more care work than others.

However, it is not just the work of care that can be burdensome; being in need of care can be difficult, too. When adults require care – whether temporarily or permanently, due to illness or disability – the condition of having to rely on others for help can bring with it difficult emotional and practical negotiations that arise in situations of dependency and vulnerability. Worry and stress can be just as much part of care as feelings of love and affection. Given the chores involved in the everyday routine of caring for someone, tasks performed as part of caring labour may at times feel like anything but care. Besides, care work in the real world is not always motivated by feelings of compassion, or by a calling to minister to others and alleviate distress. Care work is often undertaken out of the need for an income, or out of a sense of duty or obligation. Indeed, being torn between different kinds of feelings and commitments can make the work of care tormenting for all involved. Sometimes the anxiety is connected to the realisation that we really do need other people to live. Our lives are necessarily interdependent.

Constant Compromises

Interdependence was a point that came to the fore of my conversation with Liz and Mick, a couple in their early sixties caring for Mick's mother after his father had a stroke. Mick's mother is over eighty and now trying to cope on her own. Liz remarked that initially everybody had jumped up and done what they had to do, but then, as the weeks went by, the longer future had come into view. They felt they were able to provide good family support thanks to Liz, Mick and his two sisters. One of Mick's sisters lived locally, the other one lived quite far away. The one who lived further away had made an effort to come down, but she was a grandma too and had her life up where she lived. The couple's son had been very good at visiting, which had been a great support. On the one hand Liz and Mick wanted to do all they could to care for Mick's mother; on the other hand they felt they needed to have a life too. They talked about the 'constant compromises' occupying their minds. It was not the actual tasks, it was the fact that the day was curtailed. Sometimes it felt like the whole situation was taking over their lives. When they were feeling a bit down in the dumps, dissatisfaction loomed larger: Mick's mum had never really shown much interest in their lives, yet here they were, committing their time to her. Family relationships certainly can be complex.

Liz found herself thinking of the relationship she had with her children and what she wanted for them when she was in her eighties. If she had some money then, she would like to spend it on care rather than have her children care for her and Mick. She had told her two daughters who lived further away never to move back, so they wouldn't get dragged into caring for their parents. They should get on with their lives. She was quite happy to go into a care home. The whole thing with Mick's mum had really focussed her thinking. She didn't want her kids coming round with cooked dinners for her. She'd rather buy professional help and have her daughter sit down for a cup of tea and a chat with her. That's what she wanted for her children. Of course, you had to be able to afford professional help, she added. She would probably find it difficult herself to leave all the work to the professionals. She would prefer to pick and choose what bits she could do and what bits to leave. In any case, the way professional help was given was changing, due to budget constraints. They didn't do the old-fashioned meals on wheels anymore. She had a friend who organised food deliveries for herself, but not everyone could afford to do that.

If Mick's mum ever needed bathing or washing or that sort of level of care, Liz reckoned she probably wouldn't want Liz doing it for her. That would be the stage when they would need professional care. Mick's mum was very tidy, so if the house started to look a mess, they'd know something was wrong. Recently they had managed to get a few days away. They had never looked forward to a break as much as they had then. It was nice just to have some time together, something you really appreciated when there were such time pressures. Mick was anxious about leaving his mum on her own. He felt he had to face his anxieties and make a conscious effort to do something like take a weekend off.

Women and Care

Despite the fact that men like Mick *do* care, the Overseas Development Institute reports that 'in 2014, on average across 66 countries representing two-thirds of the world's population, women spent 3.3 times as much time as men on unpaid care.'[2] Time-use surveys show that today's men are increasingly involved with childcare at home, although mothers frequently retain the primary responsibility for the overall 'management' of childcare. Statistically, men are most active in the context of care when they are older (above the age of fifty) and caring for their partner.[3] The ratio varies by region, but everywhere in the world without exception, women do significantly more unpaid care work than men.[4] This unpaid care work breaks down into household work (81.8 per cent), direct personal care (13 per cent) and volunteering (5.2 per cent).[5] To give us an idea of the scale: the International Labour Organisation estimates that were we to put a figure equivalent to an hourly minimum wage on it, the total of unpaid care work would amount to 9 per cent of global GDP.[6]

Studies show that worldwide, mothers (but not fathers) experience income loss as a result of having children and the lack of (affordable) childcare is often a reason why mothers (especially with young children) are not engaged in paid employment or work part-time.[7] A survey carried out across EU countries in 2016 found that among respondents, 44 per cent of women and 30 per cent of men found it difficult to combine paid work with caring responsibilities.[8] Feminist economist Nancy Folbre calls the economic disadvantages that arise from caring a 'care penalty'. They can include loss of earnings due to caring responsibilities, but also low earnings and low job quality due to working in the low-paid care sector. Given that more women than men are in caring roles, this care penalty is higher for women.[9] According to the International Labour Organisation, women with caring responsibilities tend more often to be employed informally or in self-employment. Therefore they are less likely to be able to pay into social security, or are deterred from taking jobs that demand long or irregular hours.[10] When it comes to paid care work in areas such as education, health and social care, women are the majority. Care work makes up 19.3 per cent of global female employment and 6.6 per cent of global male employment.[11]

Given the socially ascribed role of women as carers, feminist activists have thought a great deal about the nature of care, claiming care as the prerogative of a specifically *feminist* care ethic. A feminist ethics of care insists that we live interdependent lives and emphasises how the motivation to care stems from feelings of reciprocity and responsibility. Caring here involves the consideration of others and their wellbeing. Care is understood as the opposite of aggression, exploitation and oppression. Instead, care is generative and life-affirming in its orientation.[12] Such a feminist ethics positively affirms the importance and the value of care as a regulative ideal for society, while it also pushes for a more equitable sharing of care responsibilities.

Care Goes Unseen

While everyone needs a nurturing and caring environment throughout their lives, caring activities are some of the most undervalued and invisibilised activities of all, while those who perform them are some of the most neglected and unsupported people in our societies. Despite the importance of care, on the surface it appears to have very little value. We show scant appreciation of just how crucial care work is in providing the very conditions for us to live, at least when measured by the dominant standards of income or social status. Here, then, we come full circle to the issue of recognition: who has not wondered why it is that carers, nurses, teachers and child minders, despite the immensely important work that they do, are some of the lowest-paid workers? If all this caring for and about others still gets done day in and day out, it seems it is being done against the odds.

Care work is either unpaid or paid, and, more often than not, under-paid.[13] Care work takes place in homes, in neighbourhoods, in community contexts, in networks of families and friendships, in publicly funded institutions and commercial organisations. Care work is undertaken for those who need help because they are unable to take care of themselves – whether fully or in part, temporarily or permanently – to ensure that their basic physical needs are met; a person should have an acceptable level of comfort or be assisted to function at an acceptable level of capability. Agreement on what constitute acceptable standards of care is a profoundly social, cultural and political matter. It is the result of historically contingent customs, negotiations and struggles.[14]

Care work is commonly done, too, for people who certainly *would* be able to care for themselves but who choose to employ others to care for them or their dependents, freeing up their time to do other kinds of work, pursue careers, follow interests or develop hobbies. The upper classes have long upheld the tradition of domestic servants and service personnel as the condition of possibility of a care-free life. The affordance of care here is a luxury, for the burden of work is passed down to others. The anthropologist David Graeber has made the point that not needing to care about what others are thinking or feeling is a marker of wealth and power, with members of an inferior class paid to do the caring.[15]

The idea of care as that extra treat that you get if you (can) pay for it also weaves its way through contemporary consumer culture. At one end of the spectrum there are up-market restaurants that will provide you with a dining experience to make you feel truly cared for, or supermarket brands that cost more because of the customer care they promise. At the other end there are the 'no-frills' airlines that will fly you from point A to point B but not much else. For example, low-budget airline Ryanair caused an outcry when it was reported to be planning the introduction of a £1 fee for the use of aircraft lavatories, although this was never actually implemented.[16] While the PR cultures of care in branding are ostensive, a component element of the assistive labour of care is that it is – if done properly – positively *supposed* to go unseen. As one 'modern-day butler' explains: 'In the corporate world you strive for recognition. In the private service world, your goal is invisibility. When things are going very, very smoothly and they do not notice you, then you're successful.'[17]

In this sense, care is assisting others to live well. While the butler above is probably paid quite handsomely for his ability to appear invisible, a lot of care work – especially when unpaid – happens in the unseen and unacknowledged interstices of everyday life, based on the societal and cultural expectations around whose role it is to care. Very often, what looks like an individual's achievement could actually never have been accomplished without the support and assistance of a network of others, whose efforts remain unseen and with whom little glory is shared. In psychological theories of child development, a mother contains the infant by means of both encouragement and frustration, thus providing the conditions through which the infant comes to possess a sense of self and a feeling of their own agency.[18] Mothers are left to do a lot of the invisible work to help children grow and develop, yet these efforts are rarely valued as they deserve. Instead, motherhood comes shrouded in moralism, whereby Western culture iconises the 'good mother' and blames the purported 'bad mother' in equal measure.[19] Nonetheless, it is usually the mother who still cares when everyone else has gone, for which she does not always receive the necessary support.

Caring No Matter What

Sue has an adult son who suffers from both mental ill-health and addiction, in a health and social care system whose support is becoming more and more rudimentary. Even the Care Quality Commission reports that, when people seek access to the right mental healthcare in England, they often end up in inappropriate parts of that system, including living in unsuitable housing, becoming homeless, presenting at an A&E department or being picked up by the police.[20] Sue told me that she felt responsible for her son. If he had cancer, nobody would think she was doing the wrong thing; but, she explained, the nature of his condition made it harder to deal with. She felt embarrassed. And she felt she was being blamed by society twice over: once for causing the problem and again for not sorting it out. Sue used to attend a meeting for carers, where she got help filling in forms to apply for benefits. There was also a self-help group that she participated in. But the group check-ins were so difficult, when she had to say who she was caring for and what the problem was. Sue described her son's condition as 'not very glamorous' and admitted that she hated having to say what it was, explain and half excuse herself. She never felt like she got a lot of sympathy anyway. People would tell her he should just stop and sort himself out. But, of course, that was not as straightforward as some seemed to think. She has been told he has to hit rock bottom, but she fears that's dangerous, too.

She tried to get him into a private hospital. He would have gone there, but the starting price was £20,000. At that kind of cost, it was not really an option. Her son went to the GP every so often. The doctors knew about his situation. The nurse tended to see him once a year. He didn't always make it to the appointments, although he could phone up for his medication. What could they do? He was an adult, after all. Sometimes Sue and her son spent a nice day together. 'When he was in a good mood,' she added. Then they went to the café by the market. But his mood could change swiftly and he could get terribly upset. He was not working, and he hadn't any friends. Sue handled his money. She paid his bills. She paid them out of her money because he never had any. She just didn't know what to do, or how to do it.

Sue thought she led a very odd life. She didn't see her friends very often and they certainly didn't want to get involved. On Tuesday nights she went round to her friend's house for dinner. They had known each other since they were at school. Her friend was aware of the situation, although she hadn't been all that sympathetic at first. With time she had become more so. When Sue visited, her friend chatted to her and the husband did the cooking. It was something different one night a week. Aside from those Tuesday outings, Sue did an art class on Thursday mornings at the local church hall. She felt it focussed her when she was there. The most difficult thing in a way was the fact that she hadn't got a life, and she had no support. Support for *her* life. Her husband had passed away when her boy was young. No other family members lived close by. There was nobody to say, 'I'll get up there and change that light.' Just those small things. Nonetheless, she would never be able to stop caring for her son.

Putting the Needs of Others First

The situation for Sue and her son could be very different if there were more joined-up support for both of them and less stigma. For many, not unusually women, their caring duties and expectations often see them putting the needs of others before their own. They prioritise not *their* care but the care of others. People in caring professions and those who have caring responsibilities for children and relatives know a lot about putting others' needs first, having to shoulder grave responsibility and be the container for others' woes – sometimes even at the expense of their own wellbeing, resulting in burnout, stress or compassion fatigue. Burnout might be more familiar as a stress-related condition that results from overextension in working life. Compassion fatigue is a stress-related condition that results, more specifically, from overextension in the context of working with especially vulnerable or traumatised people.[21] Against the idea of the autonomous individual whose concerns revolve around himself and is always hailed as the epitome of social progress and individual freedom, we can ask what this celebration of individual autonomy obfuscates: who does the work to allow for that individual to emerge and thrive? On whose assistive labour does this depend? How and why is this assistive labour so often rendered invisible?

The Lens of Social Reproduction

Bow Quarter in East London is a gated community of expensive luxury flats and one of the first gentrification projects of the 1980s. For about a century, between the 1870s and 1970s, the Bryant & May factory workers produced matches here. The factory is known for the matchwomen's strike that occurred in July 1888, when women working at the factory demanded safer working conditions and better pay. Historian Louise Raw draws attention to the often-forgotten presence of a female labour force in the factories of Victorian England, emphasising these women's active role in labour struggles of the period. She also shows how dominant ideas about female domesticity and women's rightful place in the home became a barrier to alleviating the dire working conditions in factories. Rather than work in squalor in the factory, working-class women were encouraged to return to the home, where they would be sheltered from poverty and all social ills, and where they could fulfil their roles as devoted wives and mothers.[22]

Not far from Bow Quarter is the Victoria and Albert Museum of Childhood with its collection of historical children's toys, some of which tell stories about societal gender roles past and present. One of the exhibits is a set of toy home appliances. Beautifully stencilled in intricate Edwardian curlicue above the image of a blonde little girl in an apron with flowers at her feet, the inscription *Happiness is having someone to care for* adorns a toy ironing board. Produced between the years of 1970 and 1980, the set also includes a stove, a sink and a cookery set. The feminised imagery of the girl, along with the pastel colours and floral motifs, reinforced for new generations of little girls the notion that such activities constitute the very core of female happiness.

Around about the same time as Chad Valley Toys were mass-producing these kitchen sets in their factory in Birmingham, feminists were penning quite different thoughts. In a 1975 pamphlet entitled *Wages Against Housework*, Silvia Federici wrote:

> They say it's love. We say it is unwaged work ... we are all housewives because no matter where we are they can always count on more work from us, more fear on our side to put forward our demands, and less pressure on them for money, since hopefully our minds are directed elsewhere, to that man in our present or our future who will 'take care of us'.

Taking care in order to be cared for, that was the heteronormative reproductive deal of the post-war era. The Fordist–Keynesian era, which many still regard as the 'golden years' of capitalism, looks different when seen from the perspective of Global South countries, of women, of queer communities, of people of colour.[23] It was an arrangement premised on the unpaid caring capacities of women. Female labourforce participation outside the home was not zero; in fact, in many industrialised countries it approached 50 per cent in the 1970s (with the exception of countries such as Spain and Italy, where the figure is closer to 30 per cent).[24] Indeed, as the Victorian matchwomen of Bryant & May attest, the fact is that women have always worked outside their own homes – not just in factories and offices, but in other people's homes as domestic servants. Moreover, women's lived experiences are varied and differ depending on class, ethnicity, migration status and location in the world.[25] However, these social relations do not merely sit alongside one another. They are interlinked in relations of inclusion and exclusion and stratified by hierarchies of power and relative autonomy – over one's time, one's body, one's feelings, and one's work. The housewife might not have been every woman's reality, but she was the benchmark against which all women (and womanhood) was measured. The housewife in the heteronormative family was the paradigmatic figure of womanhood in the Fordist–Keynesian period.

Overall, the feminist analysis of social reproduction that began to be developed in the 1970s sought to show that huge swathes of gendered unpaid *reproductive* labour have long been the key condition for the creation of what we consider economic value in our society. Therefore, the home, the family, the neighbourhoods and communities that comprise society were intimately connected to the realm of production where commodities were made and traded. Not just as spaces for the consumption of commodities bought into the home with the wage, but as settings for the unpaid labour of social reproduction.

The analysis of social reproduction developed in the 1970s focussed on unearthing the specific social and economic experiences of women and the spheres they occupied. The goal was to expose the hidden, unacknowledged and unpaid caring work and housework predominantly carried out by women. Unwaged housewives responsible for housework and child-rearing were dependent on and thus subordinate to male partners who earned the 'family wage' (Silvia Federici termed this the 'patriarchy of the wage').[26] The political struggle was for the liberation of women from isolation in the home and from economic dependency on a husband as the 'breadwinner' and head of the household. Overall, the purpose was to challenge and modify the standard female role, but also to change the status of reproductive labour and its organisation.

At the heart of the analysis lay a concern with questions of *power*: the power of women to challenge their situation and transform society, and the power that resides within the sphere of social reproduction, given its importance for the functioning of the economy. The concern was with the analysis of the situation of those (unpaid or underpaid) workers whose labour created and maintained the conditions for the production of value in the capitalist economy, as well as with questions of political organisation in order to achieve change.

Set against the notion that workers find commonality with other workers in their workplace, enabling them to exchange experiences and organise collectively, the Fordist–Keynesian household was a different kind of workplace, usually containing only one worker, the housewife, who was alone and thus quite isolated in her experience. The aim of feminist activists and scholars was to politicise the sites where unpaid reproductive labour was performed, that is, in the household, at the kitchen sink, in the bedroom and in the wider community. The conceptual struggle was to show how the institution of the family and the gendered division of labour that occurred within it had a double ideological function. One, it served to reduce the cost of labour given the reliance on the free or low-cost feminised labour in the home. Two, it absolved employers (and governments) from having to foot a large part of the bill for all this housework and caring work. The feminist analysis of social reproduction sought to link capitalist exploitation to what *appear* as forms of oppression independent from it (such as forms of sexism and women's oppression), enabling an understanding of how this economic system was premised upon utilising, reinforcing and thus shaping forms of oppression that do not take place directly within the wage relation as such.

Gender, Race and Class

By drawing attention to the specific experiences of women, feminist theorising of social reproduction contributed to the efforts to decentre the white, male industrial worker as the only, or most important, subject of social and political transformation – the assumption of large swathes of the labour movement of the twentieth century in the Global North. Not all experiences of working people are the same. Not only do wage hierarchies shape the composition of class relations, so too do divisions between waged and unwaged work. Together with Black, anti-racist and post-colonial scholars who focused their analysis on the oppression and exploitation of people of colour and their labour, the feminist analysis of the link between gendered forms of oppression and exploitation contributes to the analytical toolkit for making sense of the hierarchies and divisions *within* the global workforce, along with different bargaining positions within the capitalist organisation of work.[27]

Silvia Federici makes this point with regard to her activism within Wages for Housework (an international movement founded in 1972). The organisation was inspired by the struggles led by African American women as well as by anticolonial thinkers and activists. The latter were particularly important for understanding how parts of the world (such as former colonies) or parts of the society (such as households) were not separate from capitalist production but in many ways provided the conditions for its functioning in terms of resources or unpaid labour.[28] Women, people of colour and colonised peoples had different experiences of and access to power; their labour was valued (and not valued) differently to that of the white working-class male subject in the core countries of industrial capitalism. Following on from this, we can see how not all women's experiences were or are the same, either. This point is at the heart of feminist theories of intersectionality and pertinent to understanding today's social division of care work in terms of gender, class, ethnicity and migration background.[29]

Constitutive Contradiction

The lens of social reproduction, as developed with and through feminist struggles, helped to identify a whole sphere of unpaid human activity as pertinent for the production of economic value in a capitalist economy. Without the unpaid reproductive work of cooking, cleaning and caring, there would be no workers to make the goods and perform the services that lie at the heart of the production of value in capitalism and create the very conditions for the economy to function. The perspective of social reproduction draws attention to the fact that these different spheres of labouring activity co-exist alongside each other, with one of them serving the other. Put in conceptual terms, we can say that the sphere of production and the sphere of reproduction are 'co-constitutive', they go hand in hand and depend on each other. The sphere of production requires unpaid reproductive labour, yet the household is not an autonomous entity; it cannot survive on unpaid reproductive labour alone: it also requires an earned monetary wage to access the sustenance that only exists in commodified forms, such as food, clothing, energy, furniture, technical appliances, housing and so forth. Concretely, while the sphere of reproduction and the sphere of production may co-exist as interdependent spheres, they are not equal: the sphere of reproduction is subordinated to the sphere of production, existing to satisfy the needs of production. Think only of the ways in which what you eat, who you meet, how often you exercise and even the things you do for recreation are increasingly geared to considerations of your present or future productivity.

The key analytical point to take away from the study of the relationship between housewives and their working husbands under current conditions of Fordism–Keynesianism is that unpaid reproductive labour is rendered invisible by its appearance as non-work or as unskilled/low-skilled work, warranting that it either not be paid at all, or paid very little. In a capitalist economy, the reproduction of labour power is a cost to capital that must be offloaded (or externalised) in order to maintain profitability.[30] Political theorist Kathi Weeks puts this more succinctly: namely, that there is a contradiction between capital accumulation and social reproduction that runs through capitalist economies of any kind:

> Capital requires, for example, time both to 'consume' labor power and to produce (or re-produce) it, and the time devoted to one is sometimes lost to the other. The competing requirements of creating surplus value and sustaining the lives and socialities upon which it depends form a potential fault line through capitalist political economies.[31]

How this occurs depends on particular socio-cultural and politico-economic circumstances that require an examination of the function of families, friendships, homes, neighbourhoods and communities and to the mediations between capital and labour performed by the welfare state. Important, too, are the struggles of social movements who demand that costs be borne by capital, meaning employers, or that social reproduction no longer be subsumed under the interests of capitalist production and the imperatives of profitability and economic growth.

Care and Social Reproduction

What is the relationship between care work and reproductive labour? Do they describe the same phenomena, or are they different? In my understanding, care work is one aspect of the labour of social reproduction. Care in the sense of *caring activity* refers to the labour process itself: caring as the act of tending to the emotional and physical needs of others. Many a time care is the modus operandi of social reproduction and sometimes also its product, when certain actions – whether in themselves caring or not – lead to others experiencing a sensation of being cared for and about. Care is often also the motivating force propelling someone to carry out reproductive labour: we care *about* others, therefore we may care *for* them. Indeed, this motivation can be bound up with ideologies of caring that draw precisely on the affective register in order to harness, direct and make use of it (hence the preponderance of women as carers). What distinguishes the two concepts in essence, then, is that the term 'care' has an explicit qualitative meaning. Care (work) is an *ethical* social relationship based on both feelings of affection and a sense of service, both requiring *and* producing sympathetic attachments with bonds that tie us to others, whether weak or strong.[32] In contrast, 'social reproduction' is a functional economic category – a category used to describe the institutionalised separation between productive and reproductive activities and their arrangements within capitalist economies.

Care has often been considered something that is 'provided', meaning it is given by one person to another for free or is bought and sold as a commodity. But care need not merely be thought of as a resource, nor does care simply go one way. Care is a social relation that manifests itself in thoughts, words, gestures, as well as priorities and commitments. Therefore, care is best understood as a particular configuration of social relationships that are politically and economically – and hence historically – conditioned, with all of the gendered, racialised and classed implications of power relations, as well as considerations of vulnerability, need, ability and disability.

Caring for the Market

What happens to affective relations and caring activities when they are subsumed under market forces and turned into services that are sold? As ever more areas of social life and work are directly commercialised, the affective investments of care come into conflict with logics of measure, profitability, time constraints, cost reduction, standardisation, and economies of scale in multiple ways. For example, the imperative to display or communicate certain feelings – say of happiness or excitement or, indeed, care for the other – when one might not necessarily be feeling them, prompts concerns about the emotional or psychological cost of producing inauthentic affect in order to maximise revenue for one's employers. Arlie Hochschild poignantly analysed the effects of such 'emotional labour' in the case of female airline stewards in the 1970s.[33]

Furthermore, carrying out care work both in its emotional and physical dimensions requires time. Consequently, attempts to routinise, standardise and even rationalise care for the purposes of increasing productivity and saving costs and time end up jeopardising the very ability to provide that care. This can also lead to a sense of alienation, if the actions and words of those doing the care are scripted or streamlined in order to measure and enhance productivity, or simply made to wrap up in less time than it takes to really connect with a person and enable them to feel valued and cared for. For care workers it can be distressing if their capacities to care adequately are undermined due to lack of time, or high staff–client/patient ratios, or lack of resources.

Nonetheless, it is often the emotional investment placed by affective labourers in clients or patients that makes the work bearable and worthwhile. The commitment to other people, or simply the emotional connection experienced at work, can serve as the basis for experiencing fulfilment at work. Yet, it can also be the basis for continuing to work in the face of inadequate working conditions, bad pay or even no pay. Against the odds, caring for and about what one does and the people one does it for (paradoxically) becomes a way of protecting oneself from feelings of alienation or despondency. However, it is precisely that sense of commitment and responsibility for those cared for by those who care for them that can be exploited in order to keep a modicum of care in place in the face of adverse conditions, including underfunding.

Commodification continues apace, not only drawing in emotional and affective components of social life but also capturing the household through increased consumption and financialisation. Nonetheless, even if people are buying more commodities or taking out insurance, unpaid, non-commodified activities in homes and communities – the many forms of reproductive labour – have by no means disappeared.[34]

The Welfare State

Care is not confined to the unpaid spheres of social reproduction, nor is it simply a commercialised service. Care work is also carried out in the context of the welfare state that plays a significant, albeit conflicting role with regard to the provision of care and social reproduction. The idea that the state should be actively involved in the social reproduction of a country's workforce is relatively recent. It is a phenomenon that entwines the history of industrialised capitalism, from the late nineteenth century onwards, with the demands for social protection made by those who had to sell their labour power to its factories. Yet, even in its purported post-war heyday up until the early 1970s, the contours of the welfare state rested on a number of exclusions and marginalisations. Those affected have struggled to transform them, with varying degrees of success – notably women, people of colour, migrants, LGBTQIA communities and service users organised in mental health or disability rights movements.[35]

What propelled the idea of the welfare state in the past was the role of the state in the reproduction of labour power and the assurance of a modicum of social cohesion and infrastructure for the accumulation of wealth in a capitalist economy. While welfare has certainly been geared, in part, towards helping those in need, its mainstay has been the maintenance and augmentation of the productivity of the labour force. The combination here is one of investment in the productivity of the workforce through, say, healthcare and education, but also the provision of care services that enable people who *can* work to do so, for example by providing institutional childcare or eldercare.

Yet, as the feminist concept of social reproduction sought to make visible, this investment in the reproduction of labour power did not happen off the back of the welfare state alone. Instead it was routed through the unit of the nuclear family and its household, relying on the unpaid feminised labour that goes on within it, traditionally through the figure of the housewife. The nuclear family – and a moral interest on the part of the state in how the family was organised – provided the counterpart to the male breadwinner model, mirrored in post-war Keynesian welfare state policy. This was a welfare state that provided for some aspects of care through public services and benefit payments to those unable to work, albeit with a view to a 'male breadwinner', since married women were considered mere dependants, like their children, and access to welfare and public services was routed through the male head of the household.[36] Feminist movements challenged the construction of 'welfare dependency' in order for women to gain direct and independent access to the welfare state as citizens and workers, fully included in their own right.[37]

The combination of a variety of struggles in the 1970s with the entry of many more women into paid employment meant a dilution of the post-war reproductive deal. The current public provisions of childcare and the shift from a male breadwinner to a dual-earner model in Britain and elsewhere are geared towards enabling both adults in two-parent families to work, especially where households on the whole are no longer able to survive on one wage alone as might have been the case in the past. Gendered roles may have been somewhat transformed, yet neither the link between gender and unpaid reproductive labour, nor the central role of the family, have disappeared.

Using case studies from the US context, Australian social and political scientist Melinda Cooper has demonstrated more recently how social conservatism and with that the hetero-normative nuclear family remain an important undergirding principle of neoliberal ideology and policymaking.[38]

In addition, since the 1970s, the welfare state has increasingly incorporated the demands of private capital and the tenets of the capitalist market, as services have been sold off and public–private partnerships have come into vogue. Ideas of competition, innovation and efficiency have seeped into the so-called New Public Management, a term that first appeared in the 1980s in the Anglo-American context to describe the way that public sector bodies were being reorganised to 'bring their management, reporting and accounting approaches closer to ... a particular perception of business methods [and] making the public sector less distinctive as a unit from the private sector'.[39] This has profoundly affected service provision and access, and in particular has transformed the working conditions of care workers employed across the health and social care sector, a topic I will return to in more detail in later chapters.

Ethnicity, citizenship and migration background have also been a constitutive factor in post-war welfare state arrangements in countries such as Britain.[40] Since its inception in 1948 to the present, the institution of public health and social care in Britain, the National Health Service, has drawn heavily on migrant labour – initially in the 1950s employing many workers from the Caribbean, subsequently attracting staff from Asian, African and Eastern European backgrounds.[41] In the last twenty years, there has been a significant increase in migrant labour across the care sector. Here, the link between low pay and precarious working conditions in the care sector and migration background or status is key to understanding how the capitalist economy relies on not just *un*paid, but also *under*paid labour. Moreover, citizenship, migration and residency status have constituted the basis for legal entitlements and exclusions from the welfare state. While appeals to nationhood or contributions to the national economy inform normative constructions of entitlement and exclusion, sociologist Gurminder Bhambra insists that we acknowledge the injustices of colonialism on which the wealth of European nations and the US is based, and overhaul the narrow confines within which claims on the welfare state are made.[42]

Ideologies of Caring

Care is deeply enmeshed within power relations, but these often disappear behind what kind of caring, and by whom, is considered normal. An important element of the women's movements of the 1970s was taking apart the ways in which the social role of women as carers was intimately linked with the idea that women – as mothers, wives and nurses – were intrinsically suited to nurturing. Feminists ferociously deconstructed the ideologies of caring that kept many women subordinated within the nuclear family (and elsewhere), performing housework and care work – the 'labours of love' that were mystified as a natural female vocation.[43] New ideologies of caring often emerge precisely in the context of crisis in order to justify and facilitate certain crisis management strategies. One current ideology of caring is what Christa Wichterich has termed a 'smokescreen of culturalisation', in which migrant workers are designated as especially suitable carers for the elderly because they hail from 'other' cultures, which unlike Western individualism show deep respect for the elderly and attending to them is considered a prestigious activity.[44] The idea of the 'Big Society' floated in Britain in 2009 is another example of an ideology of caring, vehemently denounced in many quarters as nothing but a smokescreen for austerity measures that cut community services while piously invoking civic engagement and social action.[45] Ideologies of caring also play a role in the designation of who receives care and who does not within a society, reviving ideas of the deserving and undeserving poor. Moreover, ideologies of caring have lately re-emerged in a new guise in the current imperative for self-care.

A further ideological aspect is brought to the fore by mental health and disability rights movements who have been vocal about the needs, wishes and desires of care recipients, fighting the stigmatisation of disability, as well as demanding adequate care.[46] It is also within disability rights movements that the narrow focus on care as a purely positive form of affection has been problematised, highlighting another issue – not just the unequal distribution of care burdens, but the patronising aspects of care within unequal power relations. Disability rights activists have voiced caution at the 'custodial overtones' of care and pointed to how, for people with disabilities, the reality of their exposure to existing care regimes has included restrictions to their autonomy.[47] This may happen when others take charge of their care, or when carers' views are given priority over the views of those who are cared for. The relationship between interdependence and autonomy is one that posits the two as opposites and prioritises the former over the latter. With their interventions, disability rights movements contribute yet another important angle on the kind of care that is needed to challenge, rather than entrench, inequality and discrimination.[48] We must not lose sight, therefore, of the structural conditions that impede or facilitate the availability of and access to sufficient care. Against paternalism, we must 'turn on its head the model that disabled people can only passively receive care, not give it or determine what kind of care we want', as the Canadian poet, writer and activist Leah Lakshmi Piepzna-Samarasinha has argued.[49]

The point here is that when it comes to care and the crisis, we are never dealing with a black-and-white situation premised on the simple presence or absence of care. Instead, we need to look at how care, compassion and responsibility are mobilised in particular ways in particular contexts – sometimes for, sometimes against certain groups. Ideologies of caring are also used to assign the task of caring to particular social groups or classes, while different historical periods come to rely on different ideologies of caring, not least those through which labour power is reproduced. An attention to ideologies of caring helps make sense of the kinds of care fixes I analyse in subsequent chapters.

Fault Lines of Care

Care is not reducible to the concepts of emotional or affective labour and to concerns over the commodification of feelings in service work. Care is also not reducible to the labour of social reproduction. Using the term 'care' invokes the relational and affective, but also the ethical dimensions of looking after ourselves and others. Essentially, care is about the maintenance of life *for* itself. Care is therefore *more* than the necessary labour of reproducing a healthy workforce. Caring for ourselves and for others can be about clawing back time and space beyond the logic of productivity and economic growth that dominates our lives and is destroying the planet. Caring for ourselves and others also means tending to the needs of the elderly, the sick or people with disabilities – even if, or rather precisely when, someone is not or is no longer economically productive. The concern with care is a reminder that productivist arguments for investing in care are not sufficient to capture what is at stake – namely, the possibility of leading a meaningful life beyond being merely instruments of labour.

Care reveals to us how our lives are not reducible to bare functionality or mere necessity. There is a difference between bathing and clothing an elderly person so that they can survive, and the act of doing so carefully, which means taking time, acting attentively, with affection and concern. The latter makes life worth living, but it may also very well prolong the cared-for person's life. Hence, caring affects are not optional, they are not an added bonus or a luxury that can be siphoned off or treated as secondary. Instead, those more fragile dimensions of care – love, concern, regard, attention, affection – are just as crucial for human flourishing. The inseparability of care's material and immaterial dimensions reveals a precious interplay between care's practical elements and care's affective dimensions, two sides of the proverbial coin. Care encompasses the physical activities of taking care, as well as affective relationships involving emotions, feelings and ethical concerns. The two dimensions cannot really be separated, although all too often in practice they get blown apart. Indeed, their separation is indeed a very real source of crisis.

The current care crisis is intricately linked with the Global Financial Crisis and its aftermath. We were told that austerity was necessary to rebuild confidence in national economies, to attract investment and create jobs.[50] The evidence so far confirms what most already suspected: that austerity has not achieved its stated aims.[51] For those at the receiving end, this has not been abstract conversations about gross domestic products, rates of inflation, stock and share prices or the relative values of currencies or public deficits. The combined effects of recession, austerity measures and economic restructuring – aimed for the most part at the stabilisation of the incomes of the upper echelons of society – precipitated a landscape of uneven recovery and ongoing crisis. Who has ended up paying for all this, and to what end?

2

Paying for the Crisis

Linda is a social worker working in child protection. The first thing Linda mentioned to me when we met was a recently aired episode of the Channel 4 programme, 'Dispatches', about social work and local authorities, which had angered her. The producers had slipped an undercover social worker into a city council. Linda hadn't thought that was very ethical to begin with. The programme portrayed the council in a very negative light, exposing all the things that were wrong. The government were saying the council was inadequate and failing, but they were not offering any practical help – as if their agenda was to no longer be accountable for the section of society that relied on social services. The morning after the programme aired, an article in the paper announced that the children's services were being handed over to a voluntary trust. To Linda, these developments felt like the government wanted to see them all fail, so as to bring in more private companies and the voluntary sector. She saw no sign of interest in helping social workers to change things. Instead, it was all about whether you were fitting into certain criteria and outcomes. This saddened Linda; she felt very strongly about the work she and her colleagues did, yet struggled to keep up her morale in the face of all the negative portrayals in the media. Working with some of the most vulnerable people in society, she felt she was being undermined.

In her view, austerity measures meant that the demand for services was going up, but the very services that were needed didn't exist anymore, because they had been cut. Why were they getting more referrals of children at risk of significant harm? What was going on in society, that people were not coping? Why were early intervention services being taken away, allowing problems to escalate to the point of a crisis? These were the questions Linda was asking. Poverty or unemployment were stresses that significantly impacted on families. There were housing issues, too: overcrowding, the threat of eviction or just bad quality of housing. Linda didn't think that councils were bothering to maintain estates where they had a plan to demolish them. To her mind, this affected people's wellbeing. There was a lot of depression, and neither adults nor children were able to access the support they needed. There was a real crisis in mental health. For many minors there were not enough opportunities in employment and education. Linda had recently spoken with a young man whose academy had changed all their rules and made things a lot harder for him. Then they chose his options for him, when he had wanted to choose them for himself. He was really unhappy. People felt like things were out of their control and they didn't have a lot of voice or power to do anything about it.

Families were very isolated. Society had changed, people moved around a lot more today and therefore didn't always live near their extended families. Often relatives had their own difficulties and weren't able to offer support. Economic decline meant people had to move to big cities to get jobs. Childcare was a real difficulty for people because it was so expensive. Recently, Linda had visited a family living in an overcrowded flat. The mother had learning difficulties and was not getting any support from adult services. That impacted on the care of the children. Linda feared the council would have to remove the children and put them into foster care. She didn't think it would need to get to that if they could put the necessary resources and support in place – like carers for the children, or additional services for the mother. In her view, it was the many cuts to services that were making things escalate towards court proceedings. Linda's message was clear: the cutting of so many crucial services needed to stop.

In Austerity's Wake

Austerity is a mode of governing in the future perfect: it hails a day in which its goals *will have* been achieved that never comes to pass. It is a temporality that entirely suits the logic of financialised capitalism: a mode of accumulation based on expectations, projections and speculations of future gains or losses and the management of financial risk based on such predictions.[1] As a rough outline, the forces of capital attempt to overcome their anxiety around sluggish economic growth by seeking assurances from governments that they will remain a priority for policymaking in the future. In turn, politicians reassure market participants, while making the precarious feel still more so. Governing in the future perfect in this way only perpetuates the general sense of insecurity.

To justify this policy, the crisis scenario was exaggerated.[2] Capitalist economies have long operated with high debts and deficits, which prior to 2008 were never deemed a problem.[3] There was little outside pressure for austerity, no need to deal with worried creditors, for example – unlike Greece at the time, which was forced by the European Union to structurally adjust.[4] Moreover, the link between high public deficits, reduced economic growth and heightened risk of crisis was based on economic research that has since been refuted. Economists Carmen Reinhart and Kenneth Rogoff, invoked by former chancellor George Osborne to justify the need to reduce the public deficit, demonstrated a significant correlation between levels of public debt above 90 per cent, low economic growth and a heightened risk of crisis. However, their research was shown to contain methodological errors.[5] Even researchers associated with the International

Monetary Fund – a long-standing champion of neoliberal globalisation and structural adjustment policies demanding austerity – has conceded that austerity does not necessarily provide the desired economic boost, pointing to evidence of shrinking economic output, increased unemployment, heightened welfare costs and sharpening inequality.[6] Instead, the austerity measures implemented by the UK government in the wake of the Global Financial Crisis simply served to consolidate the power of the very forces that caused the Global Financial Crisis in the first place, by fostering conditions for financialised capitalism to thrive while continuing to propagate the myth that economic growth under conditions of financialised capitalism benefits everyone.[7]

Since 2016 and the Brexit vote, austerity measures have no longer been central to government rhetoric. The Spring Budget Statement of 2019 praised fiscal consolidation efforts and the successful reduction of the budget deficit, while maintaining the same course on policy – even if the necessity of austerity measures, now hugely unpopular, was played down.[8] Nonetheless, the Institute for Fiscal Studies has warned that although the 'end of austerity' for public services has been heralded, in such uncertain political and economic times this is more likely to represent a pause than an end.[9] Whatever the future, the cuts are celebrated as a success by the UK Government, while their calamitous effects continue to be felt by those paying for the ongoing crisis. While the promise of a stable economy is permanently pushed into the future, this future has become far from perfect for many people, as the effects of fiscal consolidation take their toll.

Costing the Cuts

Most of the planned cuts have now been implemented. Total departmental budgets were cut by 12 per cent between 2009 and 2017, and in 2019 day-to-day spending per person was 9 per cent lower than it was in 2010, according to the Institute for Fiscal Studies.[10] The Centre for Welfare Reform puts the total cuts at 13.5 per cent of expenditure, or £94 billion.[11] The effects of austerity are not, however, fully grasped by tallying up aggregate figures, but rather by understanding the consequences of regressive changes to taxation, funding and services that have an impact on people's daily lives. The most concentrated austerity measures have been enacted in two key areas pertinent to the care crisis, which has left more people struggling to meet their needs. One of these areas is the social security system. Under the guise of consolidation and simplification, many of the changes were to means-tested benefits and tax credits, especially direct spending cuts and restrictions to eligibility criteria, as part of the 2012 Welfare Reform Act and the roll-out of Universal Credit. By 2021, the government will have shaved £37 billion off its annual social security spending.[12] Another area is local authority funding, responsible for community and social care services. The roll-back of central government grants means local councils have lost 60p off every £1.[13] Taken together, cuts in these two areas have compounded their effects. Due to loss of benefits, people have found themselves in greater need of the services of local authorities, only to find that these services are not available because they, too, have been cut.

Indeed, half of the British population receives benefits or tax credits at some point in their lives, and a cross-section of society makes daily use of the services provided by local authorities.[14] Nonetheless, austerity measures have not affected everyone in the same way. While those at the very top of society have managed to immunise themselves from the economic crisis, those at the lower end have been exposed to increased precarity and insecurity. Terms such as the 'squeezed middle' or the 'just-about-managing' mark a new dividing line that also reaches into the middle class, affecting parts of the population who once considered themselves relatively secure.[15]

The Centre for Welfare Reform has reported that the poorest 10 per cent of families have had their incomes cut by 9 per cent.[16] As a result of reforms, 2017 saw 1.5 million more children in Britain living in poverty than in 2010, and child poverty was predicted to rise further.[17] According to a report published in 2017 by the Runnymede Trust, there has been an average drop in living standards of around 17 per cent among the poorest households, with lone mothers (92 per cent of all single parents) facing a decrease in living standards of 18 per cent. Figures also show that lone women pensioners have been particularly affected by recession and austerity.[18] Cuts disproportionately take their toll on Black and Minority Ethnic women, too, since they are disproportionately likely to be living in poverty – in part due to institutionalised racial and gender discrimination in the labour market, and/or because they are living with dependent children.[19] Poverty in the UK has long been significantly racialised. According to the Joseph Rowntree Foundation, all Black and Minority Ethnic groups in Britain are more likely than the White population to be living in poverty. Figures released in 2020 put the percentage of White British families living in poverty at 19 per cent, with 42 per cent of Black-African/Caribbean families and 50 per cent of Pakistani and Bangladeshi families living in poverty.[20] Overall, 14 million people in Britain – that's 22 per cent of the population – are living in poverty.[21] In 2017, 1.5 million people were destitute.[22]

People with disabilities have been inordinately affected by the cuts. Nearly half of those living in poverty in the UK live in households with a disabled person.[23] Changes to disability allowances have resulted in a reduction of support, especially for the most severely disabled. Overall, by 2022, disabled households will have lost 14 per cent of their income.[24] What is more, extreme poverty is prevalent among people reliant on disability support. For example, in 2015 the Disability Benefits Consortium found that a third of recipients of disability support were struggling to pay for food.[25]

While punitive sanctions against job-seekers have left many without the benefit payments they rely on to survive, in-work poverty continues to rise, exacerbated by measures such as the reduction to the amount of hours one can work while in receipt of Universal Credit.[26] The Department for Work and Pensions (DWP) reported in 2014 that 10 per cent of Jobseeker's Allowance claimants no longer receive their full entitlement for periods that can add up to a year.[27] A 2018 report by the UK Equality and Human Rights Commission found no evidence to support the idea that cuts or financial incentives exerted any direct effect on increasing employment. Instead they have contributed to increasing in-work poverty.[28]

The most disadvantaged in society lose the most, because they have fewer resources to buffer the effects of cuts and are less able to compensate for loss in income and access to services. Yet, the unequal effects of austerity are not limited to such a simple knock-on effect. Even more egregiously, the specific austerity measures have in and of themselves been regressive. The UK Equality and Human Rights Commission demonstrates that this is the case even when progressive reforms such as the National Living Wage and increased thresholds for income taxation are taken into account. The commission concludes that such regressive reforms were by no means a necessity, stating that 'the precise mix of reforms implemented *was not inevitable*, nor was the impact on vulnerable protected groups that ensued'.[29] In other words, those in most need of care or those who provide care themselves are bearing the brunt of austerity, and have been all but abandoned.

Upwardly Mobile Wealth

While the restructuring of the welfare state through austerity measures and further labour-market deregulation have led to lower living standards and heightened insecurity for many, monetary policies have led to rising asset wealth for a minority, contributing to what political economists Jeremy Green and Scott Lavery have called a 'regressive recovery'.[30] These policies included Quantitative Easing, the practice of introducing new cash into the money supply on the decision of a central bank. In theory, this is supposed to address a lack of liquidity. Since 2009, therefore, the Bank of England has held a share of Britain's public debt in order to increase the money supply, with the aim of stimulating the economy through encouraging investment. However, Quantitative Easing leads to asset price inflation, favouring those who own financial assets.

In addition, tax cuts have helped the wealthy to keep more of their money. Increases to personal tax allowances as well as higher rate tax allowances benefit affluent citizens, because less of their income is taxed. Conversely, the increase in Value Added Tax (VAT) from 17.5 per cent to 20 per cent in 2010 places a greater burden on lower-income groups, who spend more of their income on VAT-rated goods.[31] VAT has now overtaken income tax as a major source of government revenue; at the same time, continued reductions in corporation tax are making taxes on business less and less relevant.[32] Corporation tax cuts between 2010 and 2016 are estimated to be worth at least £16.5 billion a year.[33] Corporation tax receipts are forecast to amount to a mere 2.3 per cent of national income by 2021–22, whereas prior to the Global Financial Crisis and the ensuing recession, these receipts amounted to 3.2 per cent of national income – nearly 1 per cent higher.[34] The Institute for Fiscal Studies calls these corporation tax cuts 'some of the largest giveaways' since 2009.[35] The Runnymede Trust calculates that, up to 2020, benefits and tax credit cuts cost poor people £37 billion, while the £41 billion of tax cuts implemented since 2010 mainly advantaged the better-off.[36] Overall, two significant shifts in government revenue-raising are occurring: from the wealthier to the poorer and from businesses to individuals.[37]

Cornered Councils

A second area in which cuts have been particularly severe is local authorities. Aside from services such as road maintenance, refuse collection, housing support, libraries and community centres, one of the most central functions of councils is to provide a wide range of social care services for both adults and children.[38] These services include long-term care and support for the elderly, the disabled and those with mental health needs; support in the case of substance abuse; children's centres and youth clubs; day centres for people with learning disabilities, and women's refuges. Moreover, local authorities are tasked with helping people temporarily in acute need through emergency welfare assistance, including the prevention of homelessness.

Historically, local authorities were funded by central government grants supplemented by income from Council Tax and Business Rates. But between 2010 and 2020, local authority funding was cut by an astonishing 60 per cent.[39] What is more, during this time new responsibilities in public health were shifted from central government to local authorities, even as a further 14 per cent reduction to public health funding was made.[40] The biggest consequence of funding cuts is to force local councils across the country to reduce services, tighten criteria for assistance, limit hours and staff and generally do more with less. The *Local Government Chronicle* tallies redundancies at 222,000 between 2010 and 2018.[41]

Cuts to adult social care have been the most severe of all. According to the Centre for Welfare Reform, the number of adults receiving social care is now 50 per cent lower than in 2009.[42] The services that have been most affected by austerity include youth services, women's refuges, Sure Start Centres and a variety of community development initiatives, seriously diminishing the quality of life on a local level and often leaving those who use these services without alternatives.[43] Feminist economist Ruth Pearson explains that roughly 1,000 Sure Start Centres have been closed since 2010 and the remainder have increasingly focused on 'problem families', as opposed to being spaces for families from all sorts of backgrounds to converge.[44] Between 2010 and 2017, more than 75 per cent of England's local authorities cut their spending on domestic violence refuges by 24 per cent. Between 2010 and 2014, 17 per cent of specialist women's refuges had to close and by 2019, a third of all referrals could not be dealt with due to lack of capacity.[45] Moreover, emergency assistance for people in need, including people facing homelessness, has also been curbed. In 2013 the government abolished Community Care Grants and Crisis Loans, with food banks, credit unions and other charities stepping in to provide what help they can.[46]

Alongside cuts, a major factor in the restructuring of funding is the phasing out of central government grants. If we consider that, concurrently, the amount of revenue from business rates that local authorities are allowed to keep has been increased from half to three quarters, the intended direction of travel becomes evident. There is to be a greater reliance on private sources of funding.[47] While councils cannot (yet) set their own business rates, they will become much more dependent on attracting businesses to their boroughs and ensuring they pay their taxes, a problem exacerbated in a digital economy in which tax avoidance among internet-based companies is widespread.[48] Local councils are effectively left to their own devices and heavily dependent on local income streams. In the short term, this means propping things up with local reserves or introducing additional charges for certain services; in the medium term it means selling local assets and looking to outsourcing and privatisation, while also raising taxes to generate revenue. Already, changes to council tax rates have taken their toll on poorer residents who now have to contribute more.[49]

Poorer councils in particular are least likely to be able to make up funding shortfalls by raising council tax or turning to other income streams.[50] These are councils in deprived London boroughs and in those parts of England affected by deindustrialisation, which have also been hardest hit by cuts.[51] Social geographers Mia Gray and Anna Barford coined the term 'territorial injustice' to describe the growing dependence of citizen access to public services on the health of the local tax base and the diminution of basic infrastructure in poorer boroughs and regions, driving a wedge between those cities and regions that can afford services and those that cannot.[52]

Big Society Inc.

Cuts to local authority funding have been accompanied by a rhetoric of community empowerment that frames a diminished budget as a boon for council freedom and autonomy. Syncing with popular grassroots calls for devolution, localism and democratic participation, the narrative of the first austerity-related government Spending Review in 2010 was that political power and financial control would be transferred to the local level, so that councils could set their own priorities, depending on the needs of the communities they served, including the 'greater personalisation' of services and the greater involvement of voluntary and community organisations.[53] The short-lived concept of the Big Society that accompanied the austerity agenda from the start encapsulated these ideas of civic virtue and community empowerment.

According to the conservative ideology of the Big Society, not only was Britain 'broken' and mired in moral decline, it was also burdened by the albatross of 'big government'. The Big Society was about devolving power from the state. Specifically, citizens caring about and for one another were expected to be more involved in the organisation and delivery of previously public services. To this end, the Big Society's biggest advocate, former prime minister David Cameron, proclaimed that the 'emphasis on responsibility [was] absolutely vital'.[54]

Three decades after Margaret Thatcher's assertion that there is no such thing as society, David Cameron was embracing what seemed, at least on the surface, to be the opposite: an intense belief in the importance of society and the social, and the need to harness the potential of civic action that would allow British society to once again 'flourish' through an ethic of care.[55] This was accompanied by a series of policy measures opening up local service provision to accelerated privatisation under the mantle of community empowerment. The voids created by austerity became opportunities for commercial expansion. New 'community business models' popped up whose very names and designated purposes made this link evident. For example, 'public asset managers' take public assets into private ownership; 'business savers' step in where cuts threaten the closure of public services and social goods such as libraries, clubs and swimming pools; and the burgeoning industry of community business and social enterprise models is a symptom of the further withdrawal of government-funded welfare and social service provision.[56]

Participatory Austerity

Long after the clarion call of the Big Society has faded, what's left is reality. This reality is that local authorities face huge shortfalls in funding. The Local Government Association has predicted a funding gap of £7.8 billion by 2025 – and this only reflects the funding needed to maintain spending levels, without accounting for increased requirements in local communities.[57]

Whether out of conviction or desperation, the restructuring of local council funding has generated some bizarre participatory methods as cornered councils attempt to respond to the challenges. For example, since 2014, Camden Council in London has been running campaigns publicising the 'tough choices' they have to make in the face of cuts, offering consultations and inviting the democratic participation of local residents in deciding what cuts to make, so that residents can 'have their say' about which services should go and which should stay. Even the tropes of social movement activism are invoked, hailing the history of this London borough as a place where communities have regularly come together to bring about social change. This kind of participatory austerity accepts austerity as an immutable fact: local residents are supposed to come together to enact regressive social change and support the euphemistically entitled 'financial challenge', while the legitimacy of the kinds of austerity measures and funding restructuring that deepen care inequalities are in no way questioned, at least not in the official publicity materials.[58]

Disfiguring the Welfare State

In November 2018, Philip Alston, the United Nations' special rapporteur on extreme poverty and human rights, visited Britain on a fact-finding mission to ascertain the impact of austerity on human rights. His verdict on the British government's responsibility for the implementation of the austerity regime was damning. Alston concluded that the austerity measures in Britain were a form of 'radical social engineering', premised on cost-saving, limits to government support, the idea of individual responsibility and a focus on getting people into employment no matter how. According to Alston, the mentality motivating this retrenchment of Britain's social safety net was 'punitive, mean-spirited and callous' and 'designed to instill discipline and enforce blind compliance.'[59] This echoes the observation of sociologist William Davies that neoliberalism has become increasingly punitive and vindictive.[60] Social policy expert Peter Taylor-Gooby has repeatedly warned that the post-2008 austerity regime in the UK undermines common social provision. In Taylor-Gooby's view, the British welfare state has performed a veritable volte-face, becoming an 'engine of social division' as opposed to supporting and enabling social cohesion, which is what welfare states are supposed to do – at least in principle.[61]

These developments go hand in hand with alarmist portrayals of 'welfare dependency', which have long been a standby of the neoliberal insistence on individual achievement and personal responsibility. With the renewed rounds of austerity post-2008, such derogatory imaginaries were reinvigorated and extended. 'We're Closing in on Benefit Thieves', a government campaign announced in 2012. The images superimposed military target symbols on darkened images of individuals supposedly representative of the average benefit claimant, looking like they could be your next-door neighbour – if you were lower-class, of course. The posters gave a hotline number and asked members of the public to report anyone they might suspect of unduly claiming welfare benefits. Big Brother's little brothers and sisters. For some months in 2012–13, it was impossible to walk past a telephone box without being confronted with the suggestion that someone you knew might be a fraudster. There were also posters that warned how surveillance cameras, tracking technologies and undercover fraud investigators were in operation to find culprits. The cynicism of this campaign was astounding: not only were the images incredibly violent, with the use of the military target symbol suggestive of shooting and killing, they also promoted suspicion and hostility among members of the public, luridly linking welfare recipients with criminal activity. Contrary to the hype, benefit fraud is actually a relatively minor problem. The DWP estimates that 1 per cent of benefit payments are made on fraudulent claims, while scarcely more than 1 per cent of overpayments are due to errors, including errors on the part of officials. Moreover, a further 1 per cent of claimants are actually *under*paid, due to errors. All in all, the estimated annual net loss is of 1.6 per cent. This adds up to £2.8 billion.[62] To put the issue in perspective: HM Revenue and Customs estimates the combined annual loss of tax income due to tax evasion, tax avoidance and a number of other reporting errors to be £34 billion.[63] That's twelve times as much.

Sociologists Imogen Tyler and Tracy Jensen have researched the role of stigma in the construction of negative portrayals of welfare recipients and asylum seekers. Tyler and Jensen argue that the negative caricatures are created to do the ideological 'dirty work' of reinforcing ideas of personal responsibility and individual blame.[64] I find this observation particularly poignant, given how much of society's actual dirty – and extremely arduous – work is done by the very groups caught in the net of vilification, namely people on low pay and in precarious conditions, often forced to claim because their job fails to provide them with a secure and adequate income in an increasingly deregulated labour market. Academics David Etherington and Anne Daguerre surmise that the shaming of benefit claimants serves as a device to discipline the whole of society.[65] A general mindset is encouraged in which welfare per se becomes something to stamp out. An ideological wedge is driven between allegedly good and bad members of society, painting a pernicious picture: on the one side is society proper, made up of those who are hard-working, economically productive, self-sufficient and morally virtuous. On the other side are the lazy, depraved and undeserving who take more than their share and contribute nothing to the collective good. The social policy professor John Hills identifies in these developments a new welfare myth of 'them and us', whereby the welfare state is conceived as unaffordable and supporting people who do not genuinely need or deserve that support.[66] Important here too, in my view, is the imperative to internalise an anti-welfare stance: no self-respecting person should sink so low as to have to rely on the welfare state.

The reality is, of course, very different. As aforementioned, half of the British population receives benefits or tax credits at some point in their lives, and a cross-section of society makes daily use of the services provided by local authorities. But not because they are bad people – in fact someone's personal moral conduct quite rightly has nothing to do with it – but because public provision of services in accordance with differential need is part of collective solidarity and common social provision in a civilised society. In fact, 42 per cent, or nearly half, of Britain's welfare expenditure goes on pensions.[67] The erosion of a societal agreement on the need for common social provision fuses with the abandonment, punishment and stigma the welfare system foments to reinforce the idea of personal responsibility, quite literally through the material effects of austerity, but also through caricatured negative portrayals of welfare recipients.[68]

The Recovery Industry

Private companies are heavily involved in administrating different aspects of the new measures, for example in conducting evaluations of people's mental and physical condition and fitness for work. In 2014 the UK government contracted Health Management Limited, part of the Maximus group, to conduct occupational health assessments when employees reach, or are expected to reach, more than four weeks' sick leave, and to devise a return-to-work plan that is shared with their employer and GP.[69] Critics and campaigners have questioned both the ethics and effectiveness of their practices, but less attention has been focused on the dynamics of profitability that surround them.[70] Private companies have been involved with identifying and implementing 'cost' and 'efficiency' savings in the public sector. In effect, this turns the punitive restructuring of society and the anxieties and psychological hardships generated by austerity into a lucrative opportunity. Part of the dynamics of profitability is an outcomes-based, payment-by-results approach, in which commercial providers are rewarded for getting people into paid work.[71] There are obvious dangers to linking the successes of job placement or work assessments deeming people fit for work to financial rewards.

A further example is fostering services, which have also seen an increase in interest on behalf of private companies listed on the stock market, including private equity. Over the last ten years the numbers of children placed in care have increased, for example by 3.7 per cent between 2012 and 2013. The *Financial Times* reported that fostering was becoming a growth market:

> As benefit cuts pile the pressure on struggling families and children with severe disabilities are given life-prolonging medical treatment ... private equity and other companies have been attracted to the sector, largely because they can see the potential for cost savings and economies of scale, particularly in administration and training, through consolidation and by increasing the volume of cases on their books.[72]

In addition, there is the wholesale move to online administration of welfare assistance. Among the efforts to expand online public service delivery since 2010, Universal Credit is the first government service in Britain that is 'digital by default'.[73] This means Universal Credit applications are to be fully processed and managed online. UN Special Rapporteurs Philip Alston and Christiaan van Veen have warned that this kind of 'Digital Welfare State' risks 'replacing the rule of law with the rule of web design', because of the difficulties claimants face in identifying, understanding and challenging the decisions that for the most part have ceased to be made by real people. Instead they are made by algorithms, via digital infrastructures provided by private tech companies that profit from (and so have an incentive to push for) broad-based implementation.[74] Here it seems the difficulties that claimants face are the price paid for the profits that can be made by the companies providing the digital infrastructures.

Burdening Professionals

Not only do the combined effects of recession and cuts to the benefits system create more unmet care needs, they also create extra burdens on the services that continue to exist and those who provide those services. This is a point that social worker Linda emphasised in her conversation with me. In her experience, social workers were rushed off their feet. There was very little time to actually spend with the children and their families. Most of the time she was on autopilot, going from one thing to the next and then rushing back to type something up, going to the next thing. She had friends who had been off sick with stress, but assessment referrals took two or three months to come through. In the meantime, they had to pay privately for counselling. Some social workers she knew were doing agency work. If they signed up to an agency, they could take three or four months off if work got too overwhelming. They might be a little bit better off financially, and agency workers had the flexibility of knowing that they could leave with one week's notice, but really all it meant was losing their benefits as a permanent worker. Plus, paying agencies was costing councils huge amounts of money. To do social work success-fully meant building relationships with families and children over time, rather than just dipping in and out of people's lives and fighting fires. However, under current conditions there just was not enough time to spend with people. Social workers were often exposed to people's trauma; it could be really difficult work. There was very little within the system that recognised the arduous job that social workers did and provided her and her colleagues with the support they needed. According to Linda, anyone looking after other people needs to be looked after, too.

Compensating for Cuts

What is going on when voluntary precarity (as in agency work) seems a price worth paying to regain a modicum of control? Providing care under duress or in overburdening and insecure working conditions erodes a person's ability to care for other people. Austerity measures attack from every side, as social and other community workers are exposed to the deteriorating living conditions of others while also dealing with the deterioration of their own working conditions. Research has shown that local council and third sector employees have found themselves having to 'mitigate', 'ameliorate' and 'compensate' for the effects of the cuts.[75] Investigating the responses to budget cuts of workers in frontline service delivery across community-orientated social work and third sector occupations, a study conducted in the North East of England explored the emotional costs to these important public service workers as they found themselves having to compensate for deleted posts, cuts to service provision and curtailed hours.[76] The study describes how respondents felt overwhelmed, drained and exhausted to the point of near-burnout, and points to how such an affective state was becoming the norm for people working in these fields. The study explains how employees do the best they can against the odds and work harder to deliver the services. Their ethical and political commitment to the communities they serve means they continue regardless, often having to stretch the human and financial resources they have and going beyond the call of duty, even taking on extra tasks unpaid.

What this means is that responsibility is placed onto the shoulders of individuals who must develop personal coping strategies in order to keep going. In the aforementioned study, such coping strategies are termed 'practices of resourcefulness', to show not only that feelings of care, compassion and responsibility are being drawn on as if they were a resource, but also that workers must develop resourcefulness in the sense of having the skill to be creative in the face of scarcity, do more with less and find ways to compensate for the cuts.[77] The propensity to care and feelings of responsibility are mobilised, becoming what enables people to carry out their jobs under increasingly difficult conditions, precisely *because* they care. Compassion and commitment are the fuel that enables people to continue despite their frustration and alienation. When affective resources are overexploited in this way, they do not simply deplete in the sense of diminishing. Instead the situation takes its toll, emotionally and physically.

Displacement Effects

Of course, cost-cutting in one area means additional resources are required elsewhere. Following cuts to social care services, hospitals have witnessed a rise in the use of Accident and Emergency facilities, especially by older members of the population. The Institute for Fiscal Studies has reported that a 30 per cent reduction to social care spending for people over the age of sixty-five, between 2009 and 2016, led to a significant rise in visits to A&E by the same cohort, signalling increased costs for hospital emergency departments.[78] Among the very oldest members of the population, these effects are obviously the most pronounced, since their care needs tend to be greater.[79] Year on year, acute hospital admissions and the use of emergency departments are rising, showing clearly that these parts of the healthcare system are bearing the brunt of the lack of services elsewhere.[80] Consequently, it becomes more difficult for emergency services to function, while waiting times at A&E departments get longer and longer.[81] This shows that the costs of care are not necessarily reduced by austerity: they merely reappear elsewhere in overstretched care infrastructures.

Hidden Austerity

For one day in January and one day in April 2016, Britain's junior doctors went on strike. All across England there were picket lines in front of hospitals. Stalls were set up and junior doctors, many wearing their typical green scrubs, stood handing out leaflets and engaging with passers-by, carefully and patiently unpacking the details of their dispute with the government, countering misinformation and clearing up misunderstandings as they sought to convey their perspective. Their strike wasn't only about saying 'enough is enough'. By spilling out of their hospitals and into the streets, the junior doctors created spaces for discussion, debate and exchange with the people they served, whether those coming in and out of the hospitals, or casual passers-by who would also be reliant on medical and health services at past or future moments in their lives.

The 2016 action was triggered by a regressive restructuring of employment contracts. Junior doctors went on strike because of the changes to their contracts, but they were also drawing attention to the long hours and numerous consecutive shifts they were already working – all too often without a break, because things were so busy, and frequently having to do extra shifts to cover for staff shortages. In 2016 they were already exhausted, providing healthcare against the odds of an ailing infrastructure and the systematic depletion of the resources needed to maintain the wellbeing of their patients. And yet they were portrayed by the government as reckless and selfish for not accepting contractual changes that would see them working even longer hours, with less access to the training they needed to be good doctors. The strike was a battle for the hearts and minds of the public, who were being told by politicians and some of the media that the new contract was a great deal.

To all intents and purposes, funding for the National Health Service was protected from austerity measures. Nevertheless, the dispute over the junior doctors' contracts is an example of how the logic of efficiency savings was also applied to areas of the public healthcare system that were less directly affected by cuts. In the name of consumer choice and improved service provision, the 'seven-day NHS' was the idea of extending services so that patients would be able to see a GP seven days a week, and hospitals would offer the same services at the weekend as on weekdays. This plan was widely criticised by healthcare professionals and a number of major healthcare trusts and foundations for failing to allocate sufficient funds to make it work.[82] Central to the dispute over the contracts was the proposal that the standard working week would be increased by thirty hours to include Monday to Saturday, 7 a.m. to 10 p.m. The government proposed to take away pay for unsociable hours while providing an ostensible 11 per cent pay rise. According to the striking doctors I met on the picket line, this amounted to a 30 per cent pay cut. It wasn't that they were against a 'seven-day NHS' – just that it had to be properly funded. Like most other people, they wanted to be appropriately remunerated for their work and earn enough to cover the cost of living.

The junior doctors' strike was a struggle against hidden austerity. At the heart of the restructuring was a care fix that relied on the devaluation of the junior doctor's labour through changes to her pay structure and working conditions. The same fix encompassed cuts to training funds, for example abolishing the training bursaries for nurses and midwives in 2017.[83] While overworking people is a problem in itself, it also raises serious safety concerns. The more safeguards are taken out, the more the quality of healthcare is impaired. The 'seven-day NHS', which was supposed to be an offering to the electorate to improve healthcare provision, played off exhausted healthcare staff against the people they cared for in the name of customer service. There is an emotional component to this kind of devaluation of labour: feeling disheartened, unappreciated and disrespected is demoralising. If it goes on for long enough, it eats into anyone's self-esteem and goodwill.

Fixing Financialised Capitalism

Looking back on a decade of austerity, what do we see? Low taxation, low interest rates and low inflation were supposed to attract investment into the British economy and generate economic growth.[84] Austerity measures were part of a policy agenda that sought to communicate to financial actors that their interests were paramount, inviting the very actors responsible for the financial crisis in the first place to enter further into the economy. Austerity has been discredited as a strategy, even if it has not been discarded as a policy. Not just in Britain, but globally, economic growth remains sluggish and with investors reluctant to invest.[85] In austerity's wake, government spending in Britain as a percentage of national income is much the same as it was before the crisis. In other words, the public deficit has not been reduced in real terms in any significant way, although it has not risen much either.[86] Despite cuts, social security spending has continued to increase. On the one hand, this has to do with rising economic inequality and regressive recovery. For example, expenditure on housing benefits is higher due to the rising costs of housing, while more is spent on in-work benefits due to low wages. On the other hand, it has to do with current demographic developments, which mean that there are increasing numbers of people of pension age and more people claiming disability and incapacity benefits.[87] Yet, despite this rise in spending, the austerity measures that have been implemented continue to take their toll on the people affected by them, amidst a hostile environment for the very existence of a collective responsibility for care.[88]

Accompanying austerity comes a specific ideology of caring – or rather *uncaring* – that seeks its legitimation through a denial of the structural reasons why people need welfare in the first place, while further undermining the idea that care should be a collective responsibility. In the process, some of the central functions of the welfare state, such as social security, have been weaponised. They become the very tools with which to reduce access to welfare. As benefits and services are cut, a coercive, punitive environment is deployed as a deterrent to even applying for them. In the meantime, tax revenues have actually risen by nearly 2 per cent over the last decade.[89] However, this 2 per cent has in effect been taken from those who are least able to afford it. Regressive changes to taxation, including the reduction of corporation tax, have altered the nature of the tax base to the detriment of those on lower incomes, distributing wealth upwards and deepening social divides.

At the same time, more opportunities have been created for the logics of financial wealth extraction to penetrate deeper into the social fabric and into the realms of care and social reproduction. Reforms actively invite the financial industry into the realms of welfare and public services, creating opportunities for generating profits, while austerity also leaves a void at local authority level and at the level of the household that can be filled by private finance. The anxious tension accompanying the story of crisis management and the constant projection into the future of the achievement of stability create a climate of legitimacy for drastic measures, keeping everyone on edge. This is the affective state into which the divisions of Brexit inserted themselves. Austerity was portrayed as an urgent matter of collective survival, all the while relying on those who do care to continue doing so, putting the population at the service of entrenching financialised capitalism and reorganising the relations between state, market and society along the way. Nonetheless, the kind of financialised accumulation that is promoted in this fashion cannot create the desired stability, for it simply exhausts the very sources it seeks to profit from.

3

Who Cares?

Amita is a junior doctor working at a hospital. On strike in 2016, she faced a care crisis at work and a care crisis at home. One of her central concerns was the knock-on effect of the contracts for unpaid care in the home. Her worry was that the new junior doctor contract would especially affect people with caring responsibilities, because of the way it devalued out-of-hours time. Night duties or weekend duties were to become part of the normal working week. In other words, out-of-hours time would become plain time, which meant that Amita and her colleagues would be expected to do more out-of-hours. That would be hard on anyone with caring responsibilities, many of whom were women. During evenings, nights and weekends there were no formal care structures, plus it was more expensive to pay people to provide care from 5 p.m. to 9 a.m. than from 9 a.m. to 5 p.m. So, if you had children and could no longer care for them yourself at that time because you had to work, you would have to find someone else to care for them. If that carer wasn't a family member or friend who would do it for free, then you had to pay them.

Amita felt it was almost as though someone was saying: 'Well, you chose to have children, so you'll just have to cope.' If out-of-hours time were to be paid less, it would also mean less money to pay someone to take care of the children if she had to go to work. Amita worried to what extent the changes to the junior doctors' contracts would make it harder for women in particular, because women still bore most of the responsibility for care at home. Some women ended up paying more in childcare than they earned working. They also put up with a lot of trouble and hassle. Amita wondered how many more women would decide it wasn't worth it and stay at home.

The new contracts were implemented in October 2016. However, concerns over the gendered effects of the contracts remain, because the changes posed a particular problem for those who worked part-time and had caring responsibilities.[1] In 2018, a new agreement was reached that included a weekend allowance uplift and an enhanced rate of pay for late shifts.[2]

As so often with the issue of care, we are missing a crucial part of the picture if we do not take account of the interdependence of the spheres of production and reproduction. The restructuring of the employment contracts for junior doctors had repercussions on the resources of time and money available for childcare. While Amita wanted to resist being pushed out of her job and back into the home, the alternative was that someone else, who would earn less and work the unsociable hours, would need to step in and take care of the children. Thinking across production and reproduction allows us to get a handle not just on the distribution of paid work and unpaid care work, but on the hierarchies that persist between women. Where Amita faced discrimination at work due to the care penalty in her employment contract, one of the privatised options she had – namely to buy herself and her partner out of the care work – offloaded that care work onto someone else who would in all likelihood be female, lower-class and quite probably with a migration background.[3] This is just one example of the many chain reactions (and privatised cost considerations) that link up the spheres of production and reproduction, as well as hierarchies based on the intersections of gender, ethnicity and class.

Although incomes and services have been eroded by cuts, the needs they met have not vanished into thin air. Central to the dynamics of the care fix are the ways in which caring is reconfigured, how care is (re)distributed and under what conditions care takes place. This includes the people and places to which care is displaced. We often hear that the public today suffers from compassion fatigue, having become desensitised in light of so much bad news and reports of suffering and crisis.[4] But as we deplore heightened individualism and competition, along with the negative effects that these have on people's lives and their willingness to care, there is a tendency to overlook the fact that we *do* look out for one another, we *do* help one another, we *do* care. Why? Because we feel a sense of responsibility or duty towards others on the basis of social ties or kinship; because we feel compassion for and empathy with others; or because we hold certain ethical or political principles of mutual help or solidarity. Writer Rebecca Solnit has shown how, particularly in times of crisis, people come together. For example, she recalls how in the aftermath of Hurricane Katrina in New Orleans in 2005, people did not turn against one another. Instead, the overwhelming majority engaged in compassionate social action and mutual aid.[5] However, with regard to caring, we see time and again that not *all* people necessarily come together in equal measure in the wake of disaster and tragedy. In reality, some people are more compelled than others to care. Plus, what people care about and who people care for is shaped by the broader social and economic context of care across the spheres of production and reproduction.

Triple Privatisation

A major consequence for care of fewer public services and more privatisation, marketisation and financialisation is what feminist scholarship has termed 'double privatisation'.[6] Double privatisation for households means that a greater share of personal income goes to buy the increasingly commodified and marketised products, services and insurances that enable people to maintain their livelihoods. However, it also signifies an increase in unpaid care work for those who cannot afford marketised services. Hence, double privatisation has a clear class dimension, something that all too often is simply taken for granted. For example, the UK Office for National Statistics explains that

> many households are reliant on unpaid household services because they can't afford to contract them out. On the other hand, some households prefer to carry out their own childcare as they see their own service as superior to a market equivalent. There may be many reasons for households carrying out service work for themselves, not least the saving of disposable income which can then be spent on other goods and services of their choosing.[7]

This unqualified juxtaposition of affordability and choice does not get at the social and economic hierarchies that inform the basis of the decisions that are made within households. It is one thing to have the means and thus the freedom to ponder what bits of the work of care and social reproduction you would like to do yourself, because you enjoy them, find them rewarding or in some other way meaningful. It is a very different scenario if you are under pressure to weigh up what you can afford, or what you have to give up doing yourself although you would rather not, while you juggle the multiple commitments and time constraints of work and family life, exhausted and teetering on the verge of burnout.

Feminist scholarship has shown that, due to the persistence of gendered societal expectations based on ideologies of caring, it is predominantly women who step in to provide unpaid or underpaid reproductive labour in the wake of austerity.[8] The neoliberal care fix of re-privatising social reproduction is thereby exacerbated.[9] This happens due to the combined effects of welfare state retrenchment and marketisation of services, while greater female labour market participation has taken place without a significant overall transformation of the sexual division of labour.[10] While women's overall time in unpaid work has decreased and men's has increased, there is still a gender imbalance when it comes to the unpaid work of care and social reproduction. In aggregate terms, women carry out 60 per cent more unpaid domestic and care work than men.[11] Yet, as women have been further drawn into the waged labour force, their availability for care and reproductive labour has diminished. This calls for a better understanding of the complex shifts in the distribution of caring and reproductive labour. We must look closely: to whom exactly does the responsibility of caring fall today? What changes are currently taking place? To what effect?

While the (heteronormative) family still constitutes the basic unit of social organisation that informs much of social policymaking, not everyone lives in traditional nuclear family arrangements, receiving and/or providing care in this context. Over the last thirty years there has been a rise in single households (including single-parent households) and in childless families, but also in institutionalised living (such as care homes) and queer or other family and kinship relations of choice. Moreover, due to increased mobility, many more people live away from their families. Even in the context of the heteronormative family, friendship, neighbourhood and other informal community networks are part and parcel of the care infrastructure within which an individual is embedded. Here, support and mutual aid are activated through choice and on voluntary terms, founded on shared values and shared social experiences. While ties might be loose or quite close, a sense of interdependency and reciprocity informs them. Consequently, these everyday relations of friendship and mutual aid are important sites of care, too. Moreover, there is a vast amount of unpaid care work that is undertaken by activists and volunteers in public sector organisations, community groups, charities and other kinds of associations, particularly in times of crisis and situations of need. Under today's conditions of financialised capitalism, we are therefore seeing a 'triple privatisation' occur, where people are also providing unpaid care work outside the home.

The idea of the 'welfare mix' – a term used since the 1990s to describe the provision of welfare from a variety of sources, including public, private and familial – resonates here.[12] The welfare mix can include the harnessing of private capital to provide services, but there is also a conscription of unpaid reproductive labour from voluntary organisations and civic associations, that is, resources beyond the family and the household. As the figure of the housewife recedes, as people move around more for work and close friends and relatives end up living further afield from one another, as queer communities and friendship become more important, as cuts in services reinvigorate the need for charity, so do neighbours, communities, volunteers, NGOs, charities, churches – all with their own organisational and affective logics – come to inform the ways in which reproductive labour is carried out and for whom. The family may not be the only locale of unpaid reproductive labour, but the requirement of capitalism to draw on unpaid reproductive labour in different ways remains. This is key for understanding the ways in which the economy relies on unpaid reproductive labour, even when its specific configurations of care may change.

Home from Home

What goes on in households is notoriously invisible, because households are considered to be private spaces. Indeed, our homes are places of retreat from the world, where we seek privacy and claim the freedom to do what we want, when we want and how we want. And yet there is a reason why the slogan 'the personal is political' has been so important for the feminist movement in demanding that what happens in the 'private' spheres of social life should be of broader concern, thereby challenging women's economic dependence, demanding legislation and protection against domestic violence as well as calling into question the sexual division of labour.

A related aspect of the invisibility of households is paid domestic work and the twilight zone of informality that characterises it. This is a zone that domestic workers often inhabit because of casualised employment conditions resulting in a lack of social protection. Domestic workers constitute just over 2 per cent of the global workforce with over 70 million domestic workers employed in households worldwide, two-thirds of whom are female.[13] Figures for domestic workers in Britain are difficult to obtain precisely because of the informality that goes with the terrain. Employed within a private setting that is difficult to check up on, domestic workers experience some of the worst working conditions. Employment regulations do exist, but they are difficult to enforce. Moreover, domestic workers are often recruited from very precarious population groups, such as migrant workers, whose circumstances make them willing to work long hours – even 24/7 – with a high level of commitment at very low pay and with scant employment or social protections.[14]

Carola is a domestic worker from the Philippines who has been in the UK for ten years. She has spent the last twenty years looking after other people's children in various countries, having left her own three children back home. She cares about all the children she has looked after. She was with one family for more than ten years. She started out with that family when the children were born and helped raise them. Domestic work is not just about childcare, it is also about taking care of the household and doing the cleaning, cooking, laundry and ironing. These are tasks domestic workers often do when the children are asleep – unless they can find a way during the day to keep the children busy or have another adult to help, a grandmother, for example. Domestic workers must have the ability to adapt and be flexible, given the different kinds of families they work in. Helping children learn to read and write can be part of their responsibility, too. Some employers become completely dependent on their domestic workers, Carola explained.

The economic situation Carola was in back in the Philippines had forced her to leave, even though she hadn't wanted to. It was a good decision, but life wasn't necessarily better. Nobody wants to be away from their family. Her children are now adults, but she seldom saw them when they were growing up. Her letters took months to reach them. Many children back home relied on the income their mothers earned abroad, but leaving one's children meant a lot of worry over whether they would be OK. Carola knew of many English housewives who didn't even work but still wanted a nanny or a domestic worker, because of the status this afforded. Yet equally, she knew of lots of middle-class families who were not super-rich but employed domestic workers – particularly where women wanted to work, or where women were single mothers and needed to work.

Many employers were very good, but some did not treat domestic workers well: like they didn't need to sleep, like they didn't need to rest. Some domestic workers lived under appalling conditions, providing care for others while being neglected themselves. Having a social life could be quite difficult, because of the long hours. Carola worked from Monday to Saturday. Some of her friends who are also domestic workers worked on Sundays, too, because otherwise their earnings would not be enough. Domestic workers needed their labour rights to be respected and they needed assurances of a minimum wage. They too needed to be afforded dignity and respect, so that they could see their families and have equality as mothers and as women. Carola thought that domestic workers were great survivors. Other people could learn a lot from their experiences.

Organisations such as Kalayaan and the Voice of Domestic Workers campaign for the rights of migrant domestic workers and help them escape abusive situations.[15] Not all migrant workers in households first entered Britain with the families who employ them, on domestic worker visas (short-term visas that restrict holders to domestic work and which, prior to 2016, forbade the holder to change employer).[16] Nor do all migrant domestic workers find themselves in abusive situations. However, the informality of the household as a workplace, coupled with dependency on employers, can make migrant domestic workers especially invisible and vulnerable.

While we might think that household help was the pre-rogative of the upper classes of a bygone era, a combination of societal developments is actually facilitating the growing significance of paid workers within the home.[17] This care fix reflects the fact that the more affluent buy in domestic help, whether that's for housework, childcare or eldercare. The practice is not restricted to the especially wealthy. The personal and household services sector is the second-fastest growing sector behind information and communication technology in Europe, with demand expected to increase due to a combination of greater female labour market participation and ageing.[18]

Zooming Out on the Home

The last thirty years have seen a dilution of the nuclear family and the male breadwinner model. The assumption in policymaking and the reality for most families, aside from the wealthiest, is a dual-earner model where instead of one, main (male) breadwinner, both partners bring home a wage. Importantly, credit is now a central component of household income, with households taking out mortgages to cover housing, using credit cards for everyday requirements, taking out loans to pay for needs such as educational qualifications, or acquiring care-related insurance packages and financialised pension funds. Shortly before the Global Financial Crisis, overall household debt in the UK peaked at 93 per cent of GDP. In 2017, the figure had decreased somewhat to 87 per cent. By way of comparison: in 1980, overall household debt comprised just under 30 per cent.[19] The household is not only a site where labour power for production is nurtured and maintained; for finance capital, it is also a potential market for financial products, with households as customers.[20] The state has made concerted efforts to encourage personal responsibility for financial security by pushing individuals and households towards the financial services industry. For instance, recent pension reforms have actually cost the state more in the short term, yet they are in line with the vision of Britain as a finance-led economy.[21] Likewise the hikes in university tuition fees, which leave young people with tens of thousands of pounds of debt in the form of student loans.[22] These developments constitute a shift towards what is known as asset-based welfare – the idea that we should acquire assets to secure our livelihoods, home-ownership being an example. All in all, life has become much more directly connected to the financial services industry and exposed to the vicissitudes of global financial markets and risks of economic downturn.[23]

Households are important realms where we care and are cared for, where we maintain our livelihoods and replenish our capacities to live and to earn a living. Most of us do this using a combination of monetary income and unpaid reproductive labour. We buy food, furniture or electricity; we do all those household chores like cooking and cleaning and caring for ourselves and our partners, children or other members of our families who require assistance; we use technology in the form of computers and household appliances to help us with this work. With this basic premise in mind regarding the way households function in capitalist economies, we can start to unpack the specific configurations of care. We can examine household incomes, who is responsible for bringing them in, how they are made up, and what they are spent on. We can also look at the distribution of care and reproductive labour in the home and the conditions under which it occurs.

Cradle to Grave

For children below the age of three, the for-profit supply of childcare in Britain is almost exclusive, while for children above the age of three it lies at about 40 per cent.[24] Tax credits and tax breaks are supposed to help low-income and middle-class families to pay rising childcare fees. Ruth Pearson notes that childcare is more expensive in the UK than in other European countries, accounting for roughly 30 per cent of income for couples in which both partners work outside the home full-time, and roughly 20 per cent for couples in which one partner works full-time and the other works half-time outside of the home. In 2017 tax-free childcare was introduced and all parents currently receive an entitlement of fifteen hours a week free childcare for children below school age; low-income in-work parents can receive an extra fifteen hours a week. However, as Pearson points out, these benefits exclude the most disadvantaged households whose incomes are below the tax threshold, while Universal Credit does not cover rises in the cost of childcare.[25] The amount of time an average person spends doing unpaid care for a child increased by 1.5 per cent between 2000 and 2015. The proportion of childcare done by mothers is decreasing, but it still stands at 74 per cent. Overall, the average time spent on childcare by a parent has actually fallen, by almost 6 per cent, but the amount of time a child's siblings and grandparents devote to caring has increased.[26] Interestingly, the data differ for the different nations in Britain. In 2016, people in England were doing more informal unpaid childcare than people in Scotland, which the Office for National Statistics attributes to different levels of formal care provision.[27]

According to a poll conducted by the Trades Union Congress, nearly 7 million grandparents in the UK look after their grandchildren on a regular basis, mostly to enable both parents to work.[28] At the same time, these grandparents' own care bills are rising. Between 2009 and 2015, local authority–funded social care fell by 20 per cent, causing a surge in the self-funding of homecare in particular. Between 2005 and 2013, the percentage of older people receiving support from social services dropped from 15.3 per cent to 9.2 per cent, while the personal contribution individuals make towards the cost of care has increased by an average of £1,000 a year.[29] Moreover, while the number of adults receiving care has remained approximately the same for the years between 2005 and 2014, the total number of hours of unpaid caring rose by almost 25 per cent in this period of time. This reflects a significant rise in the amount of continuous care being provided at home.[30] A little more than half of this continuous adult care is provided by women (58 per cent). However, a good deal of this care work is also undertaken by men (42 per cent), many of whom are over the age of fifty and are caring for their partner.[31]

Informal Carers

Informal carers are people providing continuous care for a partner, relative or friend who needs assistance with personal care and everyday tasks and who cannot manage without this support. This may be because of old age, disability or illness, including mental health conditions and addiction. Someone might not identify as a carer, even though they effectively are.[32] It is not always straightforward to define what counts as informal care and what is simply part of being a partner, a daughter, a son-in-law or a good friend. Where exactly is the line drawn? The 2011 Census figures suggest that 12 per cent of the population provides informal personal care (assistance with washing, dressing or feeding) and practical care (help with mobility, or financial matters). However, if providing emotional support and arranging care for someone are included in the definition of informal care, the figure rises to 17 per cent.[33] With this in mind, Carers UK, a charity that supports informal carers, put the figure at an estimated 8.8 million people in 2019.[34] Most carers are providing more than fifty hours a week of unpaid care, with many providing more than double that.[35] At least two-thirds of informal carers are women. The Office for National Statistics puts the figure at 59 per cent for 2015/2016.[36] However, Carers UK stipulate that 81 per cent of the carers they surveyed in 2019 were female.[37]

The numbers of informal carers are rising due to a combination of increasing need and austerity measures.[38] For example, between 2011 and 2019, the number of informal carers over the age of sixty-five went up by 43 per cent.[39] Carers find themselves having to take on more caring, even undertaking tasks that would have previously been carried out by a healthcare professional.[40] Often, they have to find extra money to self-fund care services.[41] In addition, they face difficulties in getting the support they need, with reduced respite services and other kinds of assistance for carers.[42] Since 2014, carers are also entitled to their own needs assessments, but in a climate of underfunding, too often these needs go unmet. The outlook seems bleak: 45 per cent of those surveyed expect a worsening of the situation.[43]

In the conversations I had with informal carers caring for partners, parents or children with disabilities, illnesses or addictions, one wish came repeatedly to the fore: more support. This meant different things – more emotional support, better information, or more practical assistance with the job of caring – and corresponds to NHS survey data, which found in 2015 that 17 per cent of informal carers felt they had no support, while 43 per cent felt they had insufficient support. In other words, the majority of those surveyed in England were not receiving the support they needed.[44] It is important, too, that carers get occasional time off from what is otherwise a full-time, round-the-clock commitment.[45] According to research, less than 10 per cent of carers feel able to take a sufficient break from caring. When they do take time off, often this is not for recreation, but in order to see to other responsibilities or attend a medical appointment for themselves.[46]

Informal caring comes at a high economic cost to boot. In their 2019 survey, Carers UK found that nearly 40 per cent of their respondents were struggling financially. In other words, they were using up savings, getting into debt, or falling into arrears with utility or mortgage payments. Nearly 70 per cent of respondents were having to use up income and savings to pay for indispensable items such as nutritional supplements or mobility equipment. Even with Carers Allowance, currently just over £60 a week, it can be difficult to make ends meet. There has been an exponential rise in the number of people unable to manage work and care commitments simultaneously, and so having to give up their jobs.[47] This of course means loss of income. Some worry that all the government's talk of more support for informal carers is just a way of saving on paid professional care, while exploiting the unpaid work of families and friends.[48] In 2018 the government published an action plan for carers. Yet, beyond awareness-raising, support for volunteering and encouragement for employers to offer flexible working hours or recognise skills gained in caring, the plan does not really put in place the kind of meaningful material support that would prevent financial hardship, enable carers to take breaks and ensure support for care recipients and those who care for them.[49]

Children Who Care

In 2018, the *Independent* reported that the number of children and young adults with caring responsibilities in Britain had risen by more than 10,000 in four years.[50] Campaigners and children's organisations have been concerned that young carers are compensating for the cuts to disability benefits and adult social care services.[51] In 2013 there were already more than 166,000 children and young adults under the age of twenty-four in Britain caring for a chronically ill or disabled relative, with 41 per cent aged between ten and fourteen and 33 per cent aged sixteen or seventeen.[52] This is thought to be merely the tip of the proverbial iceberg, because many young carers are invisible to statistics and to authorities. Over two-thirds care for a parent, about a third are in charge of a sibling, while 4 per cent care for grandparents or other members of the community; 10 per cent care for more than one person.[53] The Children's Society reports that young carers are 'more likely than their peers to come from a poorer background, have a special educational need or a disability, and come from black, Asian or minority ethnic communities'.[54] They are twice as likely as their peers not to speak English as a first language.[55] In the older age brackets, young carers are much more likely to be female, especially if these girls and young women are caring longer hours.[56] Tasks can include housework, administering medication, washing and bathing someone, providing emotional care, translation or managing household finances.[57] Roughly two-thirds care an average of five hours a week, while one-third are caring up to fifteen hours a week and 3 per cent more than thirty hours a week. Young carers are often forfeiting time they could be spending with friends and peers or doing homework and attending school. They can find themselves under strain as they shoulder such responsibility. Indeed, academic research shows that many young carers experience poor physical or mental health.[58]

Calling on Volunteers

Households are not the only sites to which care work is externalised in the wake of austerity. In recent years, there have been a number of initiatives and legislative reforms that have increased the relevance and scope of volunteering in areas that relate to care.[59] Volunteering in the context of care means offering unpaid help to people who are not relatives, either informally (as in shopping for elderly neighbours) or formally (via a charity, social enterprise or hospital).[60] The Families and Children Act (2014), the Health and Social Care Act (2012) and the Care Act (2014) all seek to enhance the role of the voluntary, community and social enterprise sector (VCSE), while the 2019 NHS Long-Term Plan pledged £2.3 million for the development of volunteer programmes, aiming to double the amount of volunteers active in the NHS by 2022.[61]

Volunteering is becoming a panacea for an array of contemporary societal challenges. Volunteering is supposed to enable more citizen involvement in governance and service provision. Nowadays it is quite common for young people to volunteer or intern before entering salaried employment.[62] There is also a focus on encouraging volunteering among disadvantaged young people or the unemployed as part of programmes to integrate young people 'not in education employment or training' (so-called NEETs). The sociologist Kori Allen has argued that at a time of increasingly precarious labour markets, unpaid volunteering becomes a form of 'hope labour' for the precariously employed who are compelled to seek unpaid work as a way to gain work experience and skills and enhance their so-called employability, or their potential to acquire a job at a future date.[63] Working for free is made a condition for getting a job in the future. This is problematic in and of itself, but it is especially questionable when volunteering is by no means a guaranteed route into employment.[64] In health and social policy, volunteering is considered a remedy for isolation and inactivity in old age, preventing loneliness and ill-health.[65] Volunteering is even an element in the new trend towards 'social prescribing' in medicine, where involvement in social activities is recommended as a crucial contribution to the health and wellbeing of patients, especially with regard to mental health.[66]

The growing appeal of volunteering is occurring in the very particular context of the care crisis, which helps to explain both the interest in getting more people to volunteer and the criticism of deploying volunteers across local government and community services, social work, health and social care, where volunteers are called on to fill gaps left by cuts. The trend has raised concerns over the loss of paid jobs, the diminishing quality of services and even the safety of those who rely on such services when they are provided by untrained and unqualified laypersons.[67] Moreover, the availability of volunteers by definition of the term cannot be guaranteed, because volunteers are not contracted to fulfil duties in the same way that paid employees are. For example, befriending, mentoring or buddying programmes for people with mental health conditions are very unevenly distributed across the country.[68] In a climate of underfunding there may well not be the kinds of institutional infrastructures that would facilitate the involvement of volunteers and support their recruitment, training and supervision.[69] Consequently, volunteers may feel exploited or even overburdened by the expectations placed on them, even if some people may volunteer precisely because they feel they should help out in times of heightened need.

In a capitalist society marked by paid work that is often alienating, frustrating or in other ways unfulfilling, it can make total sense to want to find an antidote. Volunteering can be a way to gain insight into areas of social life which you might otherwise not have access to; you meet new people and learn new skills, even experience a sense of belonging. Helping others and actively contributing to society provides a sense of purpose and meaning. You feel you are doing something worthwhile that is really needed. This can be the case especially if you are not in paid employment, whether temporarily or long-term, due to illness or a disability, because you are retired or because the household income is earned by someone else, such as your partner. Formal volunteering remains overwhelmingly a middle-class activity.[70] This is because it requires time and means, and often the privilege of access to networks that can provide a way into volunteering. Women tend to volunteer more than men, especially in informal settings,[71] or when volunteering involves helping others in an extension of the traditional caring role that is socially attributed to women. Volunteering does not take place in a vacuum, but in context. It thus takes on specific functions, the effects of which call for closer scrutiny.

Institutionalised Foodbanks

Volunteer-run food banks proliferated across the country after the Global Financial Crisis. Their number continues to rise year on year due to the combined pressures of austerity and hikes in the cost of living.[72] It is breathtaking how quickly food banks have spread over the last decade: there are now over 2,000 food banks across the UK.[73] Even more astounding is how quickly they have been normalised. Should you need help, it is highly likely a statutory agency will direct you to a food bank and even give you a voucher confirming your eligibility – as if food banks were a regular part of the welfare state, as opposed to a charitable attempt to compensate for welfare state retrenchment and economic disparity. According to the charity organisation Trussell Trust, 30,000 professionals have referred people to food banks, over 50 per cent of whom were from statutory agencies. This means social workers, health visitors or school liaison officers are routinely directing people to food banks.[74]

For anyone in doubt about the relationship between regressive welfare reform and the rise of food banks in Britain, the Trussell Trust provides evidence.[75] In just over 30 per cent of cases, someone's income simply does not cover the cost of essentials; 20 per cent of food bank users struggle due to delays to benefits, especially the five-week wait associated with Universal Credit; another 17 per cent use food banks because of cuts to their benefits or crippling sanctions. In many cases, people are in work but still do not earn enough to live.[76] This includes when in-work benefits are cut due to sick leave, or during the winter months when heating costs are high. These are direct consequences of the austerity measures deemed necessary in the wake of the Global Financial Crisis.

Such stark realities, along with the structural reasons for poverty and food insecurity, are all too often kept from view, while negative portrayals of food bank users are rife. Food bank use has been linked to bad financial management or the inability to provide for oneself. Either someone is a victim to feel sorry for, or, less pitiably, they are incompetent, or feckless. Here accusations have ranged from the cynical (people use food banks because they have splashed all their money on cigarettes, alcohol and gambling) to the downright bizarre (poor people ruin themselves on expensive ready-meals because they do not know how to cook).[77] These fabrications serve to reinforce the idea that people only have themselves to blame if they find themselves in trouble.

However, while these hostile portrayals of welfare recipients may seek to legitimise the failures of a retrenched welfare state, they are also giving way to the idea of food banks as the emblem of a compassionate society ready to help the needy. Stigmatisation and victimisation are here played off against one another to reinforce the idea of a civic duty of care motivated by empathy or ethical values, as opposed to any entitlement to assistance on the basis of membership of the polity. Food banks have been celebrated as an expression of a compassionate society in which citizens actively help those in need, thereby deflecting responsibility for these needs arising in the first place. For example, Conservative politician Jacob Rees-Mogg claimed to feel 'uplifted' by the volunteering at food banks, as a demonstration of the kind of 'compassionate country' that Britain is.[78]

It is true, food banks do rely on the compassion of volunteers. These volunteers currently provide a staggering 4 million hours of unpaid support, distributing food, taking stock, fund-raising, picking up and delivering food as well as inputting data. If all the volunteers were paid the minimum wage instead of working for free, it would cost £30 million.[79] Where would we be without them? The problem is that food banks replace the social security net with charity, and informalise assistance as something predicated on the personal goodwill of others. In addition, it risks reinforcing hierarchies between those blessed with the time, means and inclination to help others, and those in need of help and obscurely ashamed of it, of having to be thankful that at least someone cares. Many if not all of the volunteers in food banks are retirees who have the time, means and inclination to help.[80] One might discern an intergenerational care fix here, with baby boomers able to retire early enough and healthy enough to engage in this activity. Current campaigns to lift the stigma from food bank use are necessary, for nobody should have to feel ashamed about experiencing poverty.[81]

Yet this must not detract from the fact that the root of the problem is growing poverty and inequality, not discrimination against those who are on the receiving end. No doubt, food banks themselves can become spaces of encounter because they enable people of different classes, ages and political persuasions to meet and mingle, exchanging experiences and viewpoints; food banks can even be spaces of political organising for social change.[82] However, none of that justifies the normalisation of their existence and thus the existence of poverty and destitution as an inevitable feature of contemporary capitalism – a capitalism that rests at the same time on the production of huge food surpluses which are then donated as alms to the poor, waste management rebranded as social responsibility.[83] Off the back of an economic system that produces destitution, the responsibility for alleviating need is outsourced to individuals who feel a personal sense of responsibility to care, for whatever reason. The increasingly critical stance taken by the Trussell Trust represents a timely refusal of the normalisation and thus institutionalisation of food banks.[84]

Keeping the NHS Going

A 2018 survey of hospital staff and volunteers by the King's Fund, commissioned by the Royal Voluntary Service and Helpforce, is exemplary in terms of illustrating the conflicting dynamics of volunteering in the context of care. The report describes how some staff expressed worries over job substitution and patient safety where laypersons take on tasks that should be done by professional staff, such as feeding patients or assisting with mobility.[85] However, of the nigh on 50 per cent of NHS staff who regularly came into contact with volunteers, 70 per cent felt very positive about their presence in the hospital.[86] In particular, staff felt that volunteers freed up their time by supporting patients. Volunteers also brought in new ideas and fresh perspectives on how to do things better (and sometimes more economically – a reflection of how deep the cost-saving mantra has penetrated the collective psyche).[87] The main recommendation of the report is role clarification, to enable more effective collaboration and assuage staff worries over volunteers taking their jobs.[88]

It is no secret that the backdrop to volunteering in the NHS is the funding shortfall. Everyone agrees in principle that volunteers should not be propping up ailing services by replacing professional health and social care workers, whether because that means they take away paid jobs or because they carry out tasks that they are not qualified for. At the same time, what seems to be welcomed is a new role for volunteers that redraws the boundaries between work time and non-work time in the context of scarce resources, pointing to a future scenario – one that we must take a closer look at.

According to the survey, volunteers predominantly do things like help patients find their way around the hospital; pick up medication from the pharmacy; assist with mealtimes by opening and positioning food and encouraging patients to eat; bring cups of tea; provide comfort and emotional support; alleviate boredom; collect patient feedback; alert staff to patient needs; facilitate peer-support and self-help.[89] The effects of these activities are at once assistive and affective: volunteers make a patient's stay in hospital more bearable or even pleasant. As one respondent put it, volunteers 'bring human kindness into busy hospital life.'[90] Already in 2013, the King's Fund suggested that hospitals could no longer cope without volunteers: 'The reality that must be confronted is that it may not always be possible to sustain high-quality services without involving volunteers and other sources of informal care.'[91]

In this function, it matters that the volunteer is not a paid member of staff. The volunteer is helping out because they *want* to, not because it is part of their job description. Their affective disposition is different: perhaps the volunteer is less rushed and more cheerful; maybe the volunteer is more attentive to the patient and makes the patient feel cared for. Some of the patient quotes in the report emphasise that, because the volunteer is unpaid, the patient feels that their relationship has a different ethical quality that is not informed by professional distance or monetary exchange. The volunteers 'add value' by 'enhancing the patient experience'.[92] The value they add lies precisely in the fact that the activity is voluntary and unremunerated.

We can see, then, how volunteers are operating in the interstices of clinical care. They are an affective force that enables the hospital to function more smoothly, infusing its day-to-day running with more care. In so doing volunteers occupy a space between staff on the one side and friends and relatives on the other. It might not always be clear who exactly they are substituting (if indeed they are substituting anyone). In many cases they might be doing things that a friend or relative might do, especially for patients who are lonely or isolated. At the same time they are actively easing the pressure on overstretched staff, freeing up their time and enabling staff to focus on the more specialised, medical tasks.

The distinction between the duties of specialised staff and those expected of volunteers has a lot to do with what is considered to constitute expertise and skill. Indeed, the kinds of things volunteers do are the kinds of things we think anyone can do, in that they demand basic social competencies of care. Yet, time is actually a key factor here, as is the propensity of the assistive and affective dimensions of care to be externalised when time is scarce. What staff lament is lack of time, the very thing volunteers are said to have in abundance: 'Volunteers have more time to devote to the caring role than [staff] do, giving patients high-quality time and attention in a way not possible for staff.'[93] Where caring affects are considered *assistive* as opposed to constitutive of a particular occupation, they easily become an add-on. We see here how a boundary is redrawn between paid and unpaid work. Hospital staff are paid to do the 'medical' and 'specialised' tasks, while unpaid volunteers take over the caring, relational elements of the job. Despite the emphasis on quality enhancement as opposed to cost reduction, in reality the issue is one of time as a scarce resource. A care fix is required to maintain standards of care on a tight budget. This care fix not only relies on recoding caring activities as unpaid work, it potentially transforms the nature of what staff do, by emptying their role of many of its caring dimensions.

Care Against the Odds

There are contexts where volunteering is politicised, crossing a line into activism by extending the remit of care to those who have been excluded, challenging the existing terms under which care is provided and demanding political change. Helping refugees where there is no other help available is one example of care against the odds. When Vera first started volunteering on Saturdays at the 'Jungle' camp in Calais, France, she expected charity organisations and UN refugee and children's organisations to have a presence. But they were not there. The other volunteers were people who just turned up, like her. The absence of the voluntary sector made her wonder. She was subscribed to a few charity organisations regarding different causes, but she'd never thought to question what they were doing when they sent emails saying they were 'working on the ground'. Like many members of the public, she presumed charity organisations to be helping on the spot. Now she was getting a different picture. Food and clothing were brought by grassroots volunteers. At first there was no registration of the children, so volunteers did a head count of all the young people who used the kids' space. There were over 500 children in the camp, many unaccompanied. Her feeling was that politicians and the public imagined the camp to be much more organised than it was.

Volunteers set up a community centre in the camp because they noticed there was very little information available to exhausted, fearful refugees who might be prepared to take desperate steps. There was simply no one to listen to them, to talk through their fears or offer support. In the Jungle Book, the kids' space run by volunteers, she and other volunteers organised basic activities like making kites, drawing and colouring, doing quizzes and puzzles. If it weren't for them, the children would have to occupy themselves. When the volunteers came on Saturdays, the children told them it was nice to speak to people from another culture, nice to speak to an adult. Every aspect of a person's everyday life in the camp was extremely arduous. After a three-hour queue for the shower in the morning, shower time was limited to three minutes. People often still had soap in their hair when they came out. That might not sound like a big deal, but it was just another degradation. Then it was a three-hour queue for food.

A lot of the food was given out for free. Recently, police had come into the camp and confiscated all the food. They said it was not fit for consumption, without providing an alternative. It was quite common for the police to take people's mobile phones and destroy them. Often the refugees had pictures of their families on there. That was all they had, Vera explained. It was as if the police had taken precious photograph albums and burned them. Children told her they'd been beaten by the police, and adults she spoke to mentioned tear gas.[94] Vera was shocked that people could be treated like that.

Vera kept asking herself what kinds of policies could possibly solve the refugee crisis. She spent a lot of time thinking about what countries needed to do. Finally, she realised that she had things back to front: if she wanted to help, she had to support an individual to improve their situation themselves. She had to assist them in building their self-esteem and finding their own solutions to their problems. It would be wrong to engage in a kind of 'false generosity'.[95] This was not about making herself feel good, while locking the person who was being helped in a relation of dependency. The external circumstances of refugees may be difficult to change, but it *was* possible to change the way that refugees were perceived and treated. She thought that the inevitable consequence of erecting fences, using tear gas and pretending refugees did not exist would be millions of displaced people. An altogether different approach would be to welcome people as contributors to society with a positive outlook on what they might bring, helping them so that they did not need help anymore. Even the term 'refugee' made people feel disempowered, as though they had nothing to offer.

For Vera it was important to get information out of the camp. If she were a refugee, she told me, she would want to be able to think that someone – sometime, somewhere – would find out about what had happened to her, even if it were in the future. [96] After all, refugees were people just like us.

Even as activists and volunteers try to forge solidarities and care against the odds, they run up against limits and are often struggling with ambivalences and contradictions, but also with the sheer magnitude of the change they are trying to enact in the world. Vera expected the camp to be evicted eventually (the Calais refugee camp was forcibly evicted in 2017, but a smaller camp has since been rebuilt). In the longer term she feared that refugee camps would become a permanent feature in Europe. Children would grow up in camps and have their own children there. Life as a displaced person living in a makeshift camp would become normalised – unless we said now that that was unacceptable.

Bringing in the Community

In local communities, volunteer networks of community care are increasingly expected to help integrate the different services used by a social care recipient, acting as a kind of connective tissue, taking on a bridging function between public services and the private sphere of the home.[97] Geographers

Andrew Hall and Ed Power have gone in search of new 'landscapes of care' in the everyday places where people gather. They argue that new caring practices point towards innovative relations of care emerging at the community level – in homes, in cafés, in community centres or gardens, in parks and arts spaces.[98] Feminist geographer Sarah Hall has also taken an interest in these sites. She explores what she calls 'everyday social infrastructures' where women in particular help each other out with care. This happens within families among sisters, mothers and grandmothers, as well as within the broader network of local communities, both on- and offline. Hall describes how women have set up playgroups, self-help groups or coffee mornings and shows how, in the face of the retreat of the state, many people become more dependent on the informal networks of family and friends as a direct result of cuts and diminished services. She, too, argues that this brings with it potential for renewing solidarity and conviviality. However, Hall also points to the persistence of gendered roles when it comes to caring: women are picking up austerity's tab. Moreover, she cautions that the new informalities bring challenges, too. Where negotiation with paid professionals is formal and based on explicit entitlements, the moral expectations that govern intimate and familial relationships are different. At times they remain implicit and can place strains on relationships. They can even jeopardise the care that someone might have come to rely on.[99]

Community care can accompany a radical politics that seeks to ensure people's access to care, especially those who might otherwise not have that access. Yet ideals of community care can also be a pretext for governments to blandish cuts to public expenditure, increasing isolation and vulnerability. Such conflicting meanings make the term 'community' a slippery concept to deploy. Indeed, any use of the term 'community' should come with a disambiguation notice, for it is apt to elicit more questions than definitive circumscriptions.

Who constitutes the community? Who is part of any given community and who is not? What norms and values govern a community? What relations of power inform its logics? Is there one community, or are communities multiple and even overlapping? 'Community' can be a term of exclusion as well as inclusion, according to whether the idea is to integrate individuals into a common cause or exclude some people from being part of a group. Referring to 'communities' is often a way of being vague, invoking commonality where there is little actual interaction between the supposed members of that community; even papering over neglect. In its most general sense, the term 'community' describes experiences and practices of interdependency on the basis of shared identity, sense of commonality or common cause.

In Britain, the concept of 'care in the community' arose partly in response to the struggles of the anti-psychiatry movements of the 1960s and 1970s, which sought the deinstitutionalisation of mental and physical healthcare and an end to stigma and isolation in psychiatric hospitals. These struggles chimed with government aims in the 1980s to save hospital care costs by enabling patients with long-term illnesses and disabilities, including the elderly, to live in their own homes while undergoing treatment or receiving care. The conjoining of these two aims always balanced uneasily between empowerment and abandonment. For while it gave in-patients freedom from institutionalisation, it also relied on the capacity of families, neighbours and social services to step in, with some patients falling through the societal net and not getting the care they needed. Already then, critics saw in the rhetoric of community care simply a smokescreen for cuts that passed responsibility on to families, friends and volunteers, who would in all likelihood be women.[100] In the poignant formulation of activists at the time: 'Hospital closures do not mean more people dying in the street, they do mean more domestic work and worry.'[101]

However, this 'community turn' was not only about reprivatisation in the sense of centring on households and families. Alongside the turn to privatisation and marketisation, it was also a turn to community organisations – charities, non-governmental and voluntary organisations – as service providers in the face of fiscal constraint. From Tony Blair's New Labourist 'third way' to David Cameron's 'compassionate conservatism', there has been a continuous interpellation of communities as partners, stakeholders and providers of public and social services and as a central pillar of improved provision and citizen empowerment at the local level.[102] Moreover, as the current label 'Voluntary, Community and Social Enterprise Sector' indicates, civil society organisations have been subject to professionalisation, entrepreneurism and commercialisation, making many of them almost indistinguishable from private companies.

Evidently, different social forces from across the political spectrum lay affirmative claims to the idea of friends, neighbours, religious communities, workers' organisations or other kinds of voluntary associations caring for one another in their local contexts. The late management consultant Peter Drucker placed great emphasis on community service to help the growing numbers of those in need such as people in poverty, people with disabilities, the elderly, or refugees in times of rapid social and economic change.[103] The economic theorist and political advisor Jeremy Rifkin insists on empathy and compassion as regulative ideals of a new post-scarcity economy.[104] Charity organisations, church groups and other volunteers help those in need. Political activists establish communities of mutual aid and care as a starting point for organising for change.

On the one hand, communities can provide care for the purposes of maintaining society and the economy in the face of (unquestioned) restraints on public funding for services, or the rise of new care needs in the face of social change.

Community caring can serve to maintain social cohesion without necessarily questioning existing relations of power or the systemic dynamics and structural inequalities producing rising care needs. Appeals to community caring can obfuscate welfare state retrenchment, masking both the dismantling of social entitlements and the deprofessionalisation of care, as sociologists Tine Haubner and Silke van Dyk have argued.[105]

On the other hand, appeals to collective care can also be a central rallying cry of grassroots social movements and a point of departure for resistance and radical change. Such movements build a sense of collectivity and confront the injustices of existing conditions for care while organising care for those who need it. Not only are self-help groups, in mental health for instance, often much better at providing certain kinds of care and support than professionalised top-down services;[106] but these grassroots social movements often create alternative structures through which people can sustain their livelihood without having to purchase increasingly expensive commodities. Silvia Federici calls these 'self-reproducing movements'.[107] Activist traditions of collective self-help and self-organisation are important terrains of transformation, where people come together to help one another out of need, but also to do things on their own terms and challenge exclusion, marginalisation and maltreatment, while seeking to generate possibilities for greater decommodification through collective mutual aid.[108] For minority groups, or in situations of scarcity, collective care is often less a matter of choice than of survival.[109]

In light of all this, we have to ask: what might a form of collective care look like that defied privatisation, eschewed financialisation, actively confronted the dismantling of social rights and questioned structural inequalities, as opposed to simply plugging gaps in social provision? As summarised by a trade union report from 1984, *Cashing in on Care*, real care in the community would mean 'choice about how and where to live, better and more flexible support services for those being cared for at home and for those undertaking the care ... using new and existing resources differently and more effectively with workers having more control over the range, quality and running of services ... [and] an end to people being hidden away forgotten in isolated institutions.'[110] The task remains ongoing.

Between Survival and Empowerment

When I was looking up figures on volunteering in Britain, I stumbled on a fact that I had not expected: after the Global Financial Crisis in 2008, there was a significant *drop* in volunteering in the UK overall (not just in contexts relevant to care). This drop evens out again somewhat after 2011.[111] Over the last years, researchers have tried to piece together the reasons for this dip. The picture that emerges seems somewhat counterintuitive at first. Rather than pitching in in times of need, it seems that the combined effects of economic hardship and austerity meant that people were more likely to concentrate on their own lives rather than the wider community or society.[112] Less affluent individuals and communities are especially unlikely to have the time and other resources to take on further commitments. People feel less secure, struggle to make ends meet and try to keep all the balls of commitment they are already juggling up in the air, without extra time to volunteer. Austerity measures after 2010 produced anxiety and fear of a precarious future, since most people grew acutely aware of their greater exposure to uncertainty and the prospect of not being cared for, while a minority have been able to immunise themselves. A YouGov poll in September 2018 showed that a mere 8 per cent of the population were 'very confident' they would be able to afford care in old age; nearly half of the respondents had no confidence in their ability to do so.[113] This anxious affect is undergirded by a rhetoric that preaches ad nauseam the virtues of competition and personal responsibility. Even a recent Budget Report from the UK Government recommends improvements in the British education system so that our pupils can succeed in the 'global race'.[114] Nobody should be surprised if such language and corresponding policies produce despondence and disaffection, with civic *dis*engagement one of the consequences.[115]

What would it mean to create the means, the time and the capacities for us all to care more for ourselves and each other in radical new ways, beyond the self-reliance of the individual household and without retreating into the exclusivity of local or activist networks? Actively caring for ourselves and for others in collective ways that afford us more control over our lives can be the basis for bringing about change. The question is how to do so in ways that are not exploitative or oppressive, or do not remain at the level of a mere administration of scarcity. Capitalism's care fixes never being total, the terrains of care and social reproduction are also conflicted and contested; they can be sites of resistance and creative rebellion in the struggle for change. This is a point I return to in the final chapter.

Thinking across the realms of production and reproduction, this chapter has looked at the care fix of austerity and the offloading of care work onto households and communities in ways that have exacerbated the existing neoliberal trend to reprivatise care and social reproduction. The focus has been on unpaid, informal (and semi-formal) care work in the home and beyond. Enclosed in the neoliberal notion of *private* responsibility is a double meaning of the term: private in the sense of personal responsibility, and private as in private property and private wealth accumulation facilitated through commodification, marketisation, outsourcing and shareholder investment. It is to the domain of the privatisation and marketisation of social care that we now turn.

4

A Perfect Storm

'A perfect storm' is the most widely used expression in the debate about the state of health and social care in Britain. In 2019, collating information from both service users and staff in health and social care, the Care Quality Commission (CQC) painted a dismal picture: difficulties getting appointments, referrals and follow-up services; long waiting times; people having to spend time in hospital due to lack of other options – that is, if beds are available. Often people have to reach a situation of extreme crisis before anything is done for them, and the uphill battle to access care leaves many feeling exhausted and frustrated. The struggle to access care, the CQC concluded, is a struggle that affects everyone.[1]

In social care the problems are even more acute than in healthcare, because of the lower professional status of social care in comparison to medicine. By placing adult social care under an analytical microscope, we can perceive the elements of the toxic mix of problems currently afflicting care: the unequal distribution of societal responsibility; the lack of value attributed to the work of caring; austerity and underfunding; the failures of privatisation and the consequences of marketisation and financialisation, and the promises as well as the illusions of assistive technologies and their role in helping meet societal care needs. Social care policy in Britain is devolved. This has led to minor differences in policy between England, Wales and Northern Ireland, for example with regard to eligibility. In addition, in Scotland and Northern Ireland health and social care are one system, making it possible to provide more integrated care across these services. However, it is only in Scotland that free personal care is provided for those who need it. This results in higher levels of support than elsewhere in the UK, especially for those receiving personal care in their own homes.[2] Bearing this in mind, along with the fact that cuts and marketisation are not everywhere exactly the same, the general trends explored in this chapter constitute challenges for social care across the UK.

Adult Social Care

The term 'adult social care' refers to the assistance provided to adults who require help with tasks such as washing, dressing, food preparation and eating, cleaning, shopping, administering medication and so forth. Many elderly people depend on social care: an estimated third of people aged eighty-five or older have difficulties with everyday tasks.[3] Adult social care also encompasses support for younger adults who may need it because of a physical or learning disability, or because they are struggling with a mental health condition. Social care covers residential care and nursing homes as well as homecare; it includes day care and supported living.

As an occupation, adult social care emerged as a part of the post-war welfare state, taking on tasks previously undertaken by women in the home or by charity organisations. As social care moved out of these spheres, it retained its image as work that does not require much professional skill and is mostly performed by women, due to persistent gendered expectations of societal roles. Today, local authorities provide social care on the basis of needs, with means testing for eligibility. Roughly a quarter of those in receipt of adult social care services are self-funded and pay privately for homecare, with about three-quarters funded by local councils.[4] In the case of residential care homes, the figure for self-funders is higher: here, 45 per cent were paying their own care home fees in 2019, marking a 5 per cent increase in ten years.[5] Noteworthy here is that the figures vary considerably across the country: the South East of England contains almost three times as many self-funders as the North East.[6]

In response to austerity, local authorities have tightened eligibility criteria and enforced such criteria more stringently in order to reduce the amount of claimants.[7] For example, the number of older people receiving community-based support (meals, daycare or homecare) decreased by over a quarter between 2009 and 2013.[8] Since 2010, the threshold at which people pay for their own social care has been frozen, which means in real terms that it has fallen, pushing more people into paying for social care privately, or going without if they cannot afford it.[9] In 2018, an estimated one in seven older people (1.4 million) in England were not receiving the care they needed.[10] Yet, as we know, the number of those needing care is increasing. Over the next twenty-five years, the population above the age of eighty-five will almost double.[11] Hence, considerably more people will require ongoing health and social care, even more so if they develop health conditions that mean they need to be cared for. A report for the House of Lords Select Committee on Public Service and Demographic Change has projected that by 2030 there will be 45 per cent more people living with diabetes, 50 per cent more with arthritis, coronary heart disease or stroke, and 80 per cent more living with dementia.[12]

As always, the economically disadvantaged suffer the most, being the ones least able to pay for their care privately. Private self-funders, on the other hand, can buy themselves out by paying a premium for better services. According to the CQC, we are moving towards a two-tier system in which some can afford health and social care and some cannot.[13] This is an understatement. In a care system that is not just fraying at the edges, but falling apart, it is only the extremely wealthy who can really afford luxury care, independently from a general societal care infrastructure. And yet it turns out that paying privately does not necessarily free someone from dependence on a collective care infrastructure: industry analyst Laing Buisson has reported that in care homes, fees for self-funders are set at a level that includes a subsidy for the shortfall in public funding for residents paid for by local authorities.[14]

And it is not simply those trying to access care who are struggling. Those who provide care are doing so under tremendously arduous conditions. All too often care workers face chaotic and inconsistent shift patterns, long hours, not enough breaks, shortages of staff, high staff turnovers and low pay, even below minimum wage standards. Increased resort to agency staff is a direct result of recruitment difficulties.[15] An agency worker will actually cost the business more, due to the cost of the service, but they may well be less skilled and unprepared to deal with complex needs.

Low pay, poor working conditions and lack of opportunities for career development characterise much of the social care sector, reinforced by the low status of care work in our society. Most social care jobs are not professionally regulated, which exacerbates the problem of low pay and leaves care workers with little political voice. Almost a quarter of staff across the social care workforce are on zero-hour contracts; in homecare the figure goes up to nearly 60 per cent.[16] According to studies by the Low Pay Commission and the Resolution Foundation, 11 per cent of the social care workforce may be receiving less than the legal minimum wage.[17] As a result the care sector suffers major workforce shortages and difficulties with staff retention. Vacancy rates currently lie at 7 per cent, and the social care sector has the highest turnover rate in the UK economy. Between 2012 and 2016 annual staff turnover rose by 5 per cent, growing from 28.4 to 33.8 per cent, even reaching 40 per cent in parts of the country.[18] In 2019, the UK

Homecare Association reported an overall staff turnover rate of 37.4 per cent in homecare.[19] Many people who work in frontline care work are also in receipt of welfare benefits, which, as social care expert Shereen Hussein explains, is evidence of low household income.[20] This tells us a lot about the economic background of those working in care. The direct link between low staff retention and working conditions is obvious when we consider how one study, surveying social care in the South West of England, found that the only organisation in their study not facing issues with staff retention was one that paid its care workers significantly above the minimum wage. It also paid everyone for hours worked, with extra pay for evening and weekend work, as opposed to payment on the basis of client visits.[21]

Quality of employment is the condition for good quality care. The two are inextricably linked. But the carer's very sense of commitment and responsibility for those they care for risks being exploited in order to keep a modicum of care in place, no matter the adverse conditions under which this care is to be provided.[22]

Working in a Care Home

Emem is a care worker in a residential care home for the elderly. When I spoke with him, I saw at once how much Emem loved his job. He told me he enjoyed working with elderly people and listening to their stories. When they were happy, he was happy. Then he knew he was doing a good job. For him, person-centred care was key to everything he did. Person-centred care meant recognising what the residents he cared for needed. One day he would be old, too, and he would need help, he told me. When Emem first came to the UK twenty years ago, most of the other staff were African or Jamaican, or from the Philippines. Today they are Eastern

European, many from Poland and Romania. Most managers, on the other hand, are British.

Emem explained that he helped residents with their day-to-day tasks, assisting them to wash, dress and eat. He also assisted them with activities, hospital appointments, keeping their rooms tidy and making their beds. He spent time either talking to them, reading them the newspaper, or making them tea or coffee. If the weather was nice, he took them for a walk in the sun. Some residents needed very little assistance; others needed full support. A personal care routine for one person usually took at least twenty-five minutes. It took ten or fifteen minutes just to wash someone, then they needed to be dressed. If someone stayed in bed all the time, it made them stiff. Most of the residents were bedbound and needed to be moved regularly by more than one care worker. Looking after an elderly person wasn't a job any one person could really do by themselves. And it took time and patience, lots of time and patience. You couldn't provide proper care in a rush, Emem assured me.

A number of residents had dementia. When someone had dementia, it could take about half an hour just to feed them one meal. Swallowing could be difficult; often a resident might not want to eat and needed encouragement just to open their mouths. When caring for them, Emem needed to take things slowly, speak to them, make eye contact and use body language to soothe them. When someone had dementia, they would come and go, come and go. Nothing could be done in a hurry. Most residents were over eighty-five, some were ninety. A few were even 100 years old. It took time to establish trust and to get to know someone well.

Once Emem looked after a resident called Cyril who had severe dementia. Cyril was also double-incontinent. Cyril's frustration and anger would often lead him to shout and lash out. So, Emem worked with Cyril. Day after day, he would speak to him and gradually found out what he needed. He inquired into Cyril's background and asked him what he had done for a living, took him out for walks in the local area and shopped with him, because he needed clothes. All this built trust. Slowly, Cyril came back. Now when Cyril needed to go to the toilet, he would call the staff and let them know. He just needed a little support to change and he needed someone to take the time to get to know him. But so often there was no time for building these kinds of trusting relationships. It was hard when you felt you needed to rush. It shouldn't matter if the job took half an hour longer, care needed to be done properly. If a care worker was under stress or overworked, they couldn't do their job properly. Sometimes Emem got stressed; often he got back pain and headaches.

The care home Emem worked at used to belong to the local council, but now a private company had taken over. As a result, his conditions and pay had changed considerably. He received less training and supervision, and his wages had been cut. Now he barely got more than the minimum wage, and had lost a lot of holiday. He also worked longer hours. When he was employed directly by the council, he worked an early shift one day and a late shift the next. The early shift was from 7 a.m. to 3 p.m. Now he worked twelve hours a day for three days a week. It was hard to keep standards up when you were working twelve-hour shifts. He only got half an hour's break on a twelve-hour shift and breaks were not paid, nor was food provided.

When he worked for the council, staff would take residents out in the minibus to ride around town for an hour or two. Now that they were privately run, that didn't happen. He could still be a member of the trade union, but the company didn't recognise the union. With the change to a private company, he had noticed that many of his colleagues were afraid to raise issues in case they lost their jobs. Most of the problems between staff had to do with the differences between agency and permanent staff. It was difficult to work together. Agency staff had less responsibility and came in on a day-to-day basis, so they didn't know what a resident really needed. And many agency workers were poorly trained. Some of them were new to the job, others didn't really want to work in a care home. Some of the night staff did their jobs very well and some of them just did their time. He wished there were more properly trained members of staff.

There were problems with staff shortages. If there weren't enough staff on the floor, Emem told me, residents were at risk. It was not only that someone might hurt themselves. When someone fell over, their confidence was shaken and it took some effort to get them back on track. Residents needed one-to-one care. They could get very frustrated. When this happened, they might start hitting the wall, or walking up and down the corridor shouting, rather like Cyril used to before Emem intervened. They might try to open the door or a window or something, because they wanted to go outside. In theory they were allowed out, but often there wasn't anyone to accompany them. So, they just walked around the corridors of the care home.

Emem had come to the conclusion that people thought those doing care work were stupid or couldn't find anything better to do; that they would rather do care work than clean the streets. He was quite dismayed that even his line manager seemed to think that. When he had raised an issue with her a while back, she had responded: 'If you're so clever, why are you working as a carer?'

Migrant Care Workers

Meeting a male care worker is not a frequent occurrence. Almost all of Emem's colleagues are women. As a rule, front-line care workers are working class, middle-aged and female. Over 80 per cent of adult social care workers are women.[23]

Men who work in adult social care are much less likely to be employed in frontline care; yet that changes when it comes to male migrant workers.[24] Ethnicity and migration background are factors that, aside from gender, account for employment in the adult social care sector. Black, Asian and Minority Ethnic workers comprise 21 per cent of the adult social care workforce, which is 7 per cent higher than the diversity of the overall population in Britain. There are also more migrant workers in this sector (17 per cent) than in the overall workforce in Britain (13 per cent). This figure breaks down to 8 per cent stemming from European Economic Area countries and slightly more – 9 per cent – from outside of the European Union.[25] In a survey carried out in 2009 on older-adult care, migrant nurses even accounted for 35 per cent of the workforce.[26]

The considerable contribution of migrant workers to health and social care in Britain has a history that reaches back to the post-war period and the establishment of the NHS. Commonwealth citizens from the Indian subcontinent and the Caribbean made up a substantial component of the NHS workforce at all levels from the 1950s onwards. A large number of Irish migrants have also historically been employed in the care sector. By the end of the 1960s, nearly half of the junior doctors working in hospitals in England and Wales were from overseas.[27] From the late 1980s to the late 1990s, foreign employment in the healthcare sector rose by 47 per cent.[28] While the 1990s saw active overseas recruitment abate somewhat, due to a shift in policy towards national training and recruitment, health and medical practitioners were still being fast-tracked under the Highly Skilled Migrants Programme. By 2003, nearly 30 per cent of all NHS doctors were foreign nationals, while 43.5 per cent of nurses entering the profession after 1999 were not born in the UK.[29] Many of these had come from countries such as the Philippines, South Africa and India with whom bilateral agreements existed, although such agreements pertained to recruitment into the public sector and did not encompass the private sector. Other countries of origin have historically included countries on the African continent such as Zimbabwe and Nigeria.

Nonetheless, direct recruitment is not the primary route for migrant workers to enter the care workforce in the UK. More commonly, the care sector is where people with a migration background find work. With the first round of EU enlargement in 2004, many EU citizens from the Eastern European accession states, especially Poland and Romania, came to the UK to work.[30] Their labour was less significant for the medical professions and more so for care work. Overall, between 1998 and 2008, the number of migrant workers in health and social care doubled.[31] In 2008 the UK government rolled out a new points-based system that restricted immigration further and added new penalties for the disregard of regulations. Together with a recruitment freeze in the NHS under reform of the Overseas Nurses Programme, this meant that direct recruitment from beyond the EU decreased significantly. Since 2008, new recruits to the migrant workforce in care have been from within the EU, especially from Eastern European countries.

There are stark regional variations in the composition of the labour force: in London in 2019, an estimate of 67 per cent of the total adult social care workforce had a BAME background, while in other parts of the country, this figure is significantly lower. In the North East and South West of England, for example, the estimate is 9 percent.[32] There are also differences with regard to the public and private sectors. Many more migrant workers are employed in the private sector than are working for local authorities or in the NHS, where wages and working conditions tend to be better. For example, hourly wages in the few care homes still operated by local authorities are on average higher than they are in the private sector.[33] Migrant care workers are disproportionately found in low-pay areas of the sector, and are at much greater risk of being paid below the minimum wage. As the International Labour Organisation confirmed in 2018: 'Public provision of care services tends to improve the working conditions and pay of care workers, whereas unregulated private provision tends to worsen them, irrespective of the income level of the country.'[34]

Research shows that many employers appreciate migrant care workers in particular, considering them to be hard-working and reliable. They are also seen as notably willing to help others and show a genuine interest in the people they care for. However, these qualities might not really be reducible to a laudable work ethic or caring attitude. The propensity of someone with a migration background to take a job that is badly paid, low-status, or for which they might be overqualified is summed up in a 2009 report on migrant labour and eldercare:

> What employers perceive as 'willingness' to work long hours or accept demanding working conditions is often the result of a lack of alternatives. Migrant workers may actually need to accept unfavourable working conditions because they do not have a strong family or social network to rely on; because they have a large family in the country of origin living on their support; or because their immigration status affects the opportunity to change employer and the eligibility for public benefits.[35]

Consequently, the very real experience of labour market vulnerability should not be allowed to disappear behind a 'smokescreen of culturalisation'.[36] However, this is not just an issue of recent migration, but also one of entrenched racialisation of labour markets. Black and Minority Ethnic people, including Brits, are disproportionately represented in the social care workforce.

With Britain's departure from the European Union, these structural conditions are likely to intensify as the availability

of EEA migrants for social care is diminished, thereby exposing the problems more starkly. However, while there is much
hand-wringing over workforce shortages in the face of Brexit
and limits on migration, the crux of the problem lies not with
too little or too much immigration, but with the structural
conditions of work in the care sector and the low value attributed to care work and hence care work*ers*. When care work
pays the same as a supermarket job, why endure the arduous
conditions for caring in the social sector?[37]

The Squeeze on Homecare

In recent years there has been an expansion of homecare, due
to both pressures on hospital beds (with the consequent earlier
discharge of patients) and to the increasing move away from
residential care towards at-home care in the endeavour to
save costs. A trade unionist I spoke to about homecare work
opined that the sector epitomised the problems with neoliberalism, especially in the treatment of women workers and of
the elderly and vulnerable, and the effects of cuts. Homecare
was never a high-status job in the first place, but at least it was
one that used to be publicly recognised, which it isn't now.
As with any care that people received, it rested on the degree
of training, the pay, the conditions and the treatment of the
workforce providing the care. In the UK, homecare workers
were almost exclusively female. They used to be employed by
local authorities. Now homecare was outsourced, with over
90 per cent of services in the voluntary and private sectors.
This entailed huge changes. Zero-hours contracts were rife,
and fast becoming the norm. In some cases where workers
had challenged zero-hours contracts, they had found themselves without any work. In the face of economic difficulties,
many care workers were desperate just to hang on to a job. As
travel time between visits was not paid for, a lot of homecare

workers were not even getting the national minimum wage. Call-cramming (the need to pack as many visits as possible in as short a time as possible) and the brevity of fifteen-minute visits meant that homecare workers were effectively working for nothing, because they could not possibly do what they were asked to do in the time that they were paid for.

When the job of homecare worker first emerged alongside the NHS with the post-war creation of the welfare state, tasks involved domestic jobs like cooking, cleaning and shopping, or collecting pensions for people who were too unwell or frail to leave the house. The district nurse, on the other hand, would administer medication, change catheters or provide stoma care. Homecare workers now did many of the tasks that district nurses used to do, the trade union rep told me. However, they did them without any training, or recognition in the form of qualifications. Furthermore, now they were earning less. Gone was basic stuff like cooking, cleaning and shopping, or the social contact of having someone to chat to and get to know. All of that was now done by relatives or by next-door neighbours, or else people had to pay for it themselves. Homecare now mostly meant getting people out of bed, washing and dressing them, getting their breakfast and sorting them out for the day. Often, homecare workers were required to do that in fifteen minutes. The whole situation was dependent on the goodwill and the unpaid work of women, either as employees or as family members or friends.

I was told that prior to the privatisation of homecare (which began to take off in the 1980s) and before the cuts following the 2008 financial crisis really bit, people knew that if they or their relatives needed a homecare worker, they would get one. This was not the case anymore. Homecare was no longer an automatic part of the welfare state. A local authority would not send you a homecare worker if you were just not very mobile, or you were lonely, or you needed a bit of help around the house. Homecare these days was an emergency service.

Now you only got a local authority–funded healthcare worker if you were in critical need. Who defined that, and by what criteria?

A local authority might want to ensure the quality of conditions and pay, but they couldn't with the money they had. Besides, once a service was no longer in their hands, what happened to wages was formally no longer their responsibility. Yet, even if you paid privately, you still got a homecare worker through the local authority who would have commissioned a private company or agency. That homecare worker would still be working under the same conditions, unless they were a personal assistant you employed directly. This was a reminder that care provision cannot be individualised, but requires the funding and maintenance of a care infrastructure.

Homecare workers with previous experience of working in factories thought that while factory work was dirtier, it was better because you have a team of workmates around you. In homecare, you could go for days without seeing anyone or talking to anyone except those you were caring for. You didn't interact with colleagues on a daily basis, you didn't see a supervisor. You were out there on your own, often in really difficult situations and doing very complex and demanding tasks. The emotional and sometimes physical demands of homecare were much tougher than some of what's seen as pretty hard factory work. All of this made it difficult to organise and campaign to improve the situation of homecare workers.

When I asked what needed to happen, the response was that funding was absolutely critical to achieve pay improvements, better conditions and staff retention. Plus, there needed to be a career structure within care, with a professional qualifications system and links and ladders into nursing or management. More than anything, the revaluation of care work was well overdue: is lifting bins or driving a lorry more of a skill than looking after elderly or vulnerable people?

Redrawing the Boundaries of Work

The picture painted above is one of a downward spiral of deskilling, in which tasks are taken out of the remit of the higher trained professional (such as a community nurse) and placed within the remit of the homecare worker, whose previous tasks may well be outsourced to family and friends in an unpaid capacity, or to no one at all. This is compounded by another factor, namely attempts to reduce the amount of paid labour time as the basis for reducing costs and maximising productivity, increasing care worker output per unit of time. On the one hand, savings are sought through cutting back paid labour time. On the other, there is a drive for care workers to tend to more people in ever less time.

On top of that, the practice of not paying for travel time between visits is widespread. According to the trade union UNISON, 63 per cent of homecare workers were not paid for travel time in 2018.[38] This is one of the main factors leading to homecare workers in effect being paid below the legal minimum wage.[39] The trend here corresponds to the current rise of the gig economy, where casualised workers are paid per individual task, or 'gig'.[40] The boundaries between what counts as work and what does not are thereby redrawn. Travel time is recast as non-work time on the pretext that it is time not directly spent caring – despite the obvious fact that being a homecare worker, that is, providing care to people in their homes, makes travelling between those individual homes part of the job, by definition.

Tracking Contact Time

Underscoring these regressive developments are digital technologies used to track homecare workers. Electronic monitoring can mean that care workers sign in and out by phone of a monitoring system when they arrive at and leave someone's home, scan a tag on the person's file with their smartphone or are tracked via smartphone using GPS technology.[41] Employment relations scholar Sian Moore and legal scholar Lydia Hayes have researched the widespread introduction of electronic monitoring by local authorities. They show how electronic monitoring facilitates a distinction between time spent working and time not spent working during a shift through the precise monitoring of 'contact time' – the duration of a visit in someone's home. In the context of what is known as 'time-and-task commissioning', 'contact time' becomes the metric for commissioning homecare services, as opposed to a set price for a visit.[42] Zero-hours contracts, rife in the homecare sector, add the finishing touch to this model: they function on the same principle of limiting what is considered to be the time that workers are productive, and hence paid. Furthermore, councils have moved to framework agreements designed to respond to need as it arises, rather than advance purchasing through which hours can be guaranteed.[43] All this syncs very well with the logic of cost-cutting, because it reduces what is understood to be time spent working while appealing to ideas of efficiency in the measurement of time spent on 'actual care', as Moore and Hayes explain.[44] For local authorities on tight budgets, these are ways to make money go further, with several councils publicly stating the benefits of electronic monitoring for saving money.[45] Yet, at what cost to care workers and the people they care for?

The consequences for homecare workers are a reduction in wages and a deterioration of working conditions, while service users also suffer the repercussions of care workers being pushed for time. However, something even more pernicious happens: the idea of what constitutes *actual* care is reconfigured in the process. Homecare workers find themselves having to cut out the relational, emotional and affective aspects of care work altogether in order to save time. Yet, as has been stated time and again in the research, it is impossible to care for people without the relational, emotional and affective dimensions, at least if one wants to retain a modicum of humanity while doing so.[46] In their study, Moore and Hayes describe how homecare workers may well take it on themselves to stay beyond allotted times if someone needs them, or something unexpected happens; or they may decide to pause for a chat with someone – who, don't forget, might otherwise be alone all day – but must first log out of the system, that is, forgo paid time.[47] As care work is redefined as the physical provision of support and assistance, the affective, relational and emotional dimensions of caring are increasingly relegated to unpaid realms. Thus, in addition to the stresses and strains of tighter time control on care workers, what we see again here is that even as the job of caring is made more difficult by the measures imposed, the system relies on the fact that care workers continue to care despite all this. In effect, homecare workers' compassion and sense of responsibility are enlisted in order to actually keep homecare services functioning.

Carebots and Technofixes

Musings over the impact of technology inform a lot of current debate about the future of care, including the purported scenarios of robots replacing care workers. Here, fears and hopes seem to be entangled. On the one hand there are concerns over job losses and unemployment due to automation. On the other, there is an expectation that technological developments could actually plug the growing gaps in the care workforce, thereby solving the care crisis. Moreover, electronic monitoring in homecare is an example of how digital technology is not necessarily deployed to replace workers as such. Instead, in the context of staff shortages and underfunding, it is used to squeeze more out of the existing workforce.[48] Of course, not all technological developments serve such problematic ends. Some assistive devices are plainly very helpful, for example when needing to lift someone with reduced mobility. No doubt it is a great help to care workers if some tasks are automated, freeing up their time for other tasks, even if one of the impediments to greater integration of technology remains its expense. The overarching point is that the relationship between care and technology is informed by politics and economics; we need to be attentive to the forces and actors driving certain kinds of mechanisation and the cultural contexts that shape (and are shaped by) the use of technology in care.

Technology does not develop in a vacuum. Instead, decisions are made about the problems technologies are meant to address, how these problems are to be addressed and, indeed, who foots the bill. It matters who makes those decisions, who deploys technology and to what end; it matters who the programmers and engineers are and what assumptions they hold; it matters what investment decisions, forms of ownership and business models inform the development and use of technology. Moreover, technology never merely replaces a task. Instead, the nature and even the meaning of tasks are transformed, while new tasks are also created in the process.[49]

We can divide care technologies into two categories: information and communication technologies (ICT) and assistive technologies. ICT can enable a variety of functions and interactions such as remote diagnosis, consultation and therapy. They also facilitate information-sharing among care workers and can better integrate the wishes and needs of care recipients, saving time and enabling communication when someone cannot travel. People in need of care can stay in touch with friends and family, while digital platforms and social networks allow care and support to be provided locally, by connecting those in need of care with formal and informal carers, including volunteers, community organisations and local services on- and offline.[50] Such digital infrastructures do not simply enable more or better communication; they also have a political economy. For example, Care.com is a platform that charges private households a subscription fee to connect with care workers offering childcare or eldercare services on an hourly basis.[51] Hired as independent contractors, the workers offering their services are part of a growing precarious workforce in the gig economy.[52] 'Be My Eyes' is a platform that enables volunteers to assist visually impaired people with a short online video call.[53] The platform is free to users and volunteers, but charges corporations to access its ecosystem and offer support to visually impaired users as a way of optimising its products and services. In the longer term, the company envisages using the data collected from each interaction between user and volunteer to help with machine learning for the development artificial intelligence (AI) products.[54] Casserole Club is a platform for neighbours to bring round a meal for someone who might in the past have been eligible for 'meals on wheels' – stepping in voluntarily where local councils have cut such services due to austerity, with the added benefit of conversation and social interaction as a way of combatting social isolation among elderly residents.[55] Local councils pay an annual fee to use the platform (currently between £30,000 and 50,000 depending on population size).[56] CoCare is an app aimed at improving homecare by moving away from time-and-task commissioning towards outcomes-based models.[57] Advocates celebrate this as a positive development.[58] Yet outcomes-based commissioning comes with new sets of problems when carried out in the context of tight budgets, because care outcomes are linked to priced performance indicators, the achievement of which is in turn linked to payment.

'Agetech', as the growing range of innovation for older people is known, includes assistive technologies like sensors to detect and alert in the case of a fall or accident, or sensors attached to household appliances that can sound an alarm or even alert someone remotely if necessary, for instance if water is left running.[59] Other developments include home automation packages that use sensing devices to construct a statistical model of a person's routine so that lights or household appliances can respond to their movements around the house, supported by 24/7 remote call-centre assistance.[60] GPS trackers can, of course, already be given to dementia suffers in case they are out on their own and get lost. In the realm of care, enabling those who need care to live independently through assistive technology is as much about enhancing human freedom as it is about reducing the need for human labour, whether in the form of a paid care worker or in the form of relatives, friends, neighbours or volunteers whose time is thereby freed up to do other things, not least to be available for the labour market. Agetech (for those who can afford it) may help with independent living, then; but it will not address the fact that too many people who need care – especially the elderly – spend long periods on their own, lonely and isolated.

There are also interactive, robotic devices. Paro the Seal is like an animated toy that uses insights from animal therapy to help dementia patients to relax.[61] The semi-humanoid robot Pepper is able to recognise faces and basic human emotions, can be equipped with fall detection software and can impart information and guide someone through a building. Pepper also has value as an edutainment-type device that can keep care home residents entertained and fit with physical and cognitive games, quizzes and exercises.[62]

Juva is a prototype modular robotic system developed with innovation funding from the UK government.[63] A spherical device mounted on a rail running around the ceiling of a room, it can be fitted with different assistive appliances depending on specific needs. Juva can fetch items like a pair of glasses or a cup of tea or help someone to stand up or sit down.[64] Its features can be modified as a person's care needs develop, using new insights from communication methods.

The aim would be to enable people to live independently for longer, postponing the need for care. Developers also envisage Juva to be of use in hospitals and care homes, arguing that it could significantly reduce the cost of care for local councils as well as individuals.[65] Of course, there is still an outlay for purchase, maintenance and energy consumption, and sites must be adapted to install it. Currently, Juva's future as an actual household appliance is uncertain. Substantial government funding would be required to develop it as a consumer product, because at this early stage financing its development is considered too high-risk for venture capital.[66] This is a reminder of how, as economist Marianna Mazzucato has stressed, it is usually public money that funds major innovations, as opposed to the private sector.[67]

Such technological developments throw up questions about the meaning of care. Although robots like Paro, Pepper or Juva could conceivably assist with everyday tasks that can be translated into repetitive, routinised and standardised procedures, they could never take on any of the more complex tasks of care work. When a machine takes on a task, it does not simply do the same thing a human being did beforehand. The task is transformed in the process. The idea that robots could *replace* care workers relies on a conception of care encapsulated in the reductionist notion of 'actual care' that surfaces in the context of homecare and electronic monitoring discussed above – as if 'actual care' were merely assistance with basic physical tasks. Indeed, attempts to rationalise care work and raise productivity give that exact impression: the activity of caring is broken down into repetitive and standardised tasks, which care workers perform at ever more breakneck speeds, leaving little time for the relational, affective and emotional dimensions of care.

Moreover, the low value attributed to social care entails its false characterisation as unskilled work, especially with regard to the interplay between physical and emotional dimensions.

It is a complex physical feat to help someone with the activities of personal care: getting up and going to bed, washing, eating and so forth; medical procedures such as catheter or stoma care. Moreover, helping someone with such tasks is not reducible to the physical motions, but involves the need to motivate the person, soothe them, direct them, reassure them and respond to social situations that are not predictable and not routinisable. This is especially relevant when someone has depression or dementia. In care work, physical and emotional tasks are intertwined and cannot be neatly separated, because care workers engage in in-depth ways with their charges: they listen, they observe, they interpret and make sense of someone's needs, they interact, assist, understand. Caring for others involves complex tasks that require sophisticated social and communicative skills as well as expertise, along with empathetic, interpretive and intuitive abilities – attributes that are more difficult to automate. However, it is those very skills and competencies that are either made invisible and seen as simply that which people bring to the job, or are externalised as that which is no longer considered part of care work's paid dimensions. Nobody should be under any illusions that the care crisis can be solved by technology alone. It could even be aggravated, especially if technology is used against care workers, or if technologies and the data that drive them are privately owned and used to boost profits. Instead, technology needs to 'help to produce better care with less stress', as Ai-Jen Poo, director of the US National Domestic Worker Alliance, has emphasised.[68]

Social Care Fix

By far the biggest expenditure in the care sector is on the work that goes into caring, precisely because care is so labour-intensive. This also means that it is in the area of labour that cost-cutting hits hardest. Where legal requirements to pay the minimum wage or regulations stipulating staffing requirements help prevent the worst in terms of the downward spiral of pay and conditions, reports on the predicament of many care workers in the UK show the extent to which the pressures of underfunding are offloaded onto care workers and the people they care for. This includes electronic monitoring and the widespread non-payment of travel time. There are frequent reports of homecare workers taking calls on their days off, due to staff shortages, or of uniforms, phone usage or petrol not being covered by employers, or of insufficient support for further training.[69] Add to this the circumvention of sick pay and holiday pay through zero-hour contracts. Care home workers face longer shifts and fewer breaks, declining pay and working conditions, less training and the limiting of supplies needed to carry out their work.[70] Against the backdrop of low societal recognition for care work, the fabric of social care has been repeatedly picked at to the point of rendering it completely threadbare.

Evidently, there is a care fix happening here, as the conditions of work are being steadily degraded while those working in the sector are expected to keep caring under adverse conditions. This care fix relies on two factors: the labour-market vulnerabilities of class, gender, ethnicity and migration status, and the commitment and sense of responsibility of those working in care to keep going against all odds. As one respondent to a 2016 UNISON survey into homecare summarised it: 'The service is run on emotional blackmail and goodwill.'[71]

Locating the Eye of the Storm

According to the Care Quality Commission, the perfect storm in adult social care is due to a combination of increases in demand, workforce shortages and access problems exacerbated by funding gaps.[72] However, developments in the corporate care home and homecare sectors suggest that this is not the whole story. Recent years have seen at least two high-profile cases of financial collapse among the large corporate chains.[73] In 2019, all four of Britain's biggest care home providers, each operating hundreds of care homes across the country, were up for sale and struggling to find buyers.[74] In 2011, the private for-profit provider Southern Cross collapsed because it could no longer keep up the payment of annually rising rents for the care home properties.[75] HC-One, founded from the collapse of Southern Cross and itself owned by a consortium of international investors, has more recently warned of financial troubles, despite having paid out £48.5 million in dividends in the preceding two years.[76] In 2019, Britain's biggest care home chain, Four Seasons, was one of those in severe difficulty. Falls in profits meant that Terra Firma, the private equity firm that owned the chain, was no longer able to service interest payments on company debts, although Terra Firma did post a 30 per cent rise in annual pre-tax profit in January of the same year.[77] According to reports, Terra Firma had been struggling since December 2017, when it failed to meet a £27 million interest payment.[78] Four Seasons was then placed in the hands of H2 Capital Partners, a US hedge fund that is the sector's biggest creditor.[79]

In homecare too in recent years, large providers have been leaving the sector.[80] In 2017 the outsourcing company MITIE, which had acquired the Enara Group homecare providers for £112 million in 2012, sold its homecare business to the private equity firm Apposite Capital after repeated profit warnings and a write-down of at least £150 million.[81] Another outsourcing company, Mears, originally specialising in the maintenance and repair of social housing, stated in the same year that its homecare business was making a £3 million loss.[82] Providers have been handing back contracts to local councils and even exiting the market altogether, because they cannot service contracts at the price local authorities are paying.[83]

Industry representatives blame local authority budget cuts and tightening of eligibility criteria for the problems in social care, along with increases in the minimum wage, the lack of new contracts and tighter immigration rules post-Brexit, and problems with staff retention.[84] There is broad agreement that more public funding is required: the *Competition and Markets Authority Report* identified an absolute minimum funding gap of £1 billion for social care in 2018.[85] Care England, the body that represents providers, has even suggested that four times that sum would be needed to stabilise the social care sector.[86] For all intents and purposes, it seems like not enough money is being made available for contracts to be serviced and that, hence, the problem is austerity.

A 2018 report by the business monitor Company Watch revealed that outsourcing and facilities management companies across the sector of public services – not just in adult social care – are shedding money, with profits having halved between 2012 and 2018. The report explained:

> The reduction in profit margins seems to support the view that, in their quest to win contracts, outsourcing companies often bid down their contract costs. With tiny profit margins made on contracts won and without enough cash to *fulfil debt obligation*, any glitch with one or more contractor or downturn in business is enough to turn the company on its head.[87]

There are three issues here. First, outsourcing companies have huge debts which they are unable to service. Why is that so? Second, some of them are facing a financial crisis while still having posted profit rises and paid out large dividends to shareholders. How can that be? Third, the care of some of the most frail and vulnerable in our society is in the hands of hedge funds and private equity companies whose sole purpose is to maximise profit. Who allowed that to happen and with what rationale? Such a situation indicates that the lack of public funding for care providers is by no means the only reason for the problems. While the situation is slightly different for care homes and for homecare, the perfect storm we are now seeing was precipitated by privatisation and the lack of financial regulation.

Care Homes as Real Estate Assets

Opus, a business advisory practice with expertise in social care, stated in 2019 that the four biggest care home chains operating in the UK have not been spending enough on maintaining facilities, instead racking up debts that swallow up local authority fees. Analyst Nick Hood argued that the 'debt-laden model, which demands an unsustainable level of return, is completely inappropriate for social care … hundreds of millions of pounds that could be going into improving facilities and care are being sucked out of the industry every year to fund the debt.' However, since company structures are so complex and include offshore entities, it is hard to find out where the money is going.[88]

Academics, journalists and independent think tanks have collated evidence to show how corporate chains extract wealth from the care home sector by charging high administration, consultation and management fees; taking advantage of tax legislation for the purposes of avoiding corporation tax; loading high debt obligations and interest payments onto providers as a consequence of leveraged buyouts; and paying dividends to shareholders. In the case of residential care home chains, the Centre for Health and the Public Interest has estimated that that around 10 per cent of funds 'leak' out as rent, dividend payments, net interest payments, directors' fees, and profits before tax, amounting to an annual total of about £1.5 billion.[89] This is roughly the same amount as the current estimated funding gap across the social care sector. When private equity firms entered the care home market, often preparing the business for outsourcing companies to take over in the long term, they engaged in 'leveraged buyouts'. This means buying a company using finance from multiple bonds issued to many creditors and secured against the assets of the company being acquired. Debt and interest repayments must then be paid out of the income the business generates. Debt financing is not just a way to reduce tax liability;[90] companies are also restructured to make them more profitable. This routinely involves reducing the wages and changing the working conditions of workers. Economic geographer Amy Horton's research on the financialisation of care homes found evidence that private equity companies sought to reduce staff costs by 30 per cent through wage reductions, changes to bank holiday pay or reductions in staffing levels.[91] Private equity firms usually sell acquired companies on again within three to five years, with the intention of making a quick profit. They are, in other words, less interested in the longer-term provision of care and more in the immediate financial gains to be made. Moreover, trading in securitised assets under favourable stock market conditions can mean that the financial value of companies is inflated when they are sold on. However, companies remain saddled with debts and interest payment obligations that cannot be serviced at a future date.[92] In an economic downturn, this problem becomes more acute. Financial interest in care homes has been particularly zealous given that the assets of care homes include real estate that is of considerable value. What has happened is that care home chains have been separated into two strands of ownership: property ownership (the care home buildings) and operative ownership (the care home business).[93] In the case of sale-and-leaseback models, companies can sell the care home premises but agree to rent them back. Ownership may be transferred to a related company, in which case only a nominal rent would be paid. However, properties can be sold to unrelated landlords. A danger here is that care home operators have to pay annually rising rents. If their income can no longer cover those costs, they risk having to raise fees or, even worse, face financial crisis.[94]

Government promotion of privatisation, coupled with a regulative environment permissive to financialisation, has exposed the social care sector to a pursuit of financial profit that relies on the guaranteed revenue streams of publicly funded contracts. Amy Horton shows that these developments are a result of three convergent features: first, a growing, captive (and vulnerable) population in need of care in an ageing society; second, in the case of care homes, the use of care home property assets to generate profits and secure loans for the purchase of further care homes, with a view to creating larger chains and thus economies of scale; third, an under-valued and disrespected workforce with little systemic power to resist the kinds of workplace restructurings that worsen their conditions and their pay.[95] What is this if not a care fix – one that enlists unpaid care to shore up profits? Processes of financialisation have caused considerable instability in the social care sector, while facilitating wealth extraction. And while the larger financialised corporate chains still make up less than a quarter of the sector, they exert considerable economic and political influence.

Corporatised Homecare

Homecare providers face challenges in a climate in which it is difficult to deliver care at the price that local authorities are able to pay under austere conditions. However, corporate facilities management companies and private equity firms have also entered the market for homecare. Investors regard this market as promising because of its growth potential, given that there is a growing ageing population and homecare is cheaper than residential care. Before 2010, the hope of investors was that homecare would be a profitable industry to invest in, as it would expand by buying up smaller providers and creating economies of scale.[96] Yet, the issue for profit-orientated businesses in the homecare sector is that economies of scale are hard to achieve without rapidly running into problems with service provision. There is not much that can be done to decrease costs while increasing the number of clients. Visiting people in their own homes and helping them with daily household tasks and personal care has limited potential for rationalisation. What is more, the larger the operation, the more managers and supervisors are needed, who in turn have to be paid, thereby merely increasing costs.[97] The real problem then lies in attempts to render homecare a profitable business with high returns.

Crisis of Privatisation

Underlying the problems in the care sector is not just the systematic underfunding that has been worsened by austerity, but the failures of privatisation and the kinds of business models that have been allowed to take hold in the sector. Today, only 7 per cent of social care services are directly in the hands of local authorities.[98] A series of legislative changes facilitated the establishment of a market for social care from the 1980s onwards. With the passing of the National Health Service and Community Care Act of 1990, local authorities were either to provide community care services directly, or arrange for the provision of such services while retaining the responsibility for eligibility and needs-assessment.[99] As discussed in the previous chapter, the impulse for this development came from mounting criticisms of an impersonal, institutionalised kind of care inconsiderate of the individual needs of users, amid accusations of inefficiency and concerns about rising costs. In its place, community care services were supposed to become decentralised, more responsive to the wishes of users and home-based where possible. The conviction took hold that a more effective system would be achieved through market mechanisms, with local authorities purchasing services from a growing private sector. Privatisation was actively promoted: 85 per cent of central government funding to local authorities was required to be spent on contracting out services, i.e. purchasing services from external providers.[100] The ambition to personalise care to suit the needs of individuals was intimately intertwined, from the outset, with the logic of markets and customers. Even if policymaking since then might have become more tailored to purported customer choice, there has been comparatively little concern for what care workers need to do their job well.

Privatisation has unfolded at different speeds in different areas of social care. The first to be privatised were residential care homes, with facilities being sold and privately run from the 1980s onwards. The outsourcing of homecare services followed in the 1990s. More recently, other social care services such as centres for people with learning disabilities have also been set up privately, with services purchased by local authorities. The kind of set-up in which private providers are commissioned by a public body to provide a service billed to the taxpayer is known as a 'quasi-market'. It's not an entirely 'free' market, where individual users of care services might engage in transactions in so far as they can pay for them; instead the state, via local authorities, carries the responsibility to 'shape' the market, which is to say, enable its functioning.[101] Local authorities currently do so in two ways. One way is through the widespread introduction of personalised budgets. The other is by purchasing services from private providers.

Cash for Care

With the rhetoric of empowerment, personalised budgets and direct payments for social care were introduced in Britain in the 1990s – first for disabled people, later for the elderly, too. Rather than accessing social care services directly, individuals receive direct cash payments on the basis of a needs and eligibility assessment performed by local authorities.[102] Personalised budgets were hailed as a way of increasing freedom and control for those who need care, but, as was perhaps to be expected, underfunding and a cost-saving agenda have not yielded much of the democratisation of needs assessments that their advocates within disability rights movements had hoped for.[103] Instead, personalised budgets have turned care recipients into care consumers. People can use the money to purchase homecare services, hire their own personal assistants or buy equipment. Not only do personal budgets reinforce market-orientated thinking and transactional logics, they also bring extra work with them. Personal budgets and direct payments have to be managed, which might not be so easy for those in need of social care, especially the elderly.[104] Hiring personal assistants turns care recipients into employers who must make sure to proceed in accordance with employment law, adding another burden. What's more, the hiring of personal assistants creates scope for the casualisation and informalisation of employment relations, where there are few checks or enforcements of employment law in place. Skills for Care found that 56 per cent of their survey respondents were a friend or family.[105] In other words, the policy facilitates the development of an informal labour market. The danger is that, once again, workers with little negotiating power within the labour market are exploited and/or that care workers are inadequately trained and qualified.[106]

Outsourcing Care Services

The other way that local councils 'shape the market' is by contracting out social care services to the private sector and selling off public infrastructure. Local authority contracts constitute guaranteed revenue streams for providers, the reason why quasi-markets are attractive to the private sector. With the introduction of a market logic came the introduction of competition. For providers this meant having to offer services at a commercially viable rate, enabling them to attract customers (whether private or local authority), cover the costs of running a business (including wages for workers and salaries for management), and generate enough surplus to invest in maintaining standards and improving facilities. In the early years of privatisation, many of the providers were small owner-manager businesses. However, since then corporations have entered the market, buying up public providers, the smaller owner-manager providers and non-profits, who normally operate with the expectation of smaller returns, have struggled to keep up under market conditions. Along the way, these corporations undertook restructurings to render businesses more profitable, not least in order to pay out dividends to shareholders.[107] In addition, the creation of a market for social care created investment opportunities for financial capital seeking high returns.

Privatisation was supposed to improve public services through competition and to generate savings through greater cost-efficiency and higher productivity.[108] Privatisation was also supposed to facilitate innovation by making available the capital needed for infrastructural improvements, creative experimentation, research and development. However, the realities of privatisation today look very different. In the case of care homes, industry representatives claim that the benefit of private investment is to develop and improve facilities. And yet, notwithstanding some reports of high-quality care provision, there are also too many incidents to the contrary. This suggests that privatisation per se does not automatically lead to improvements, while the imposition of competition and the need to generate profits places the kinds of pressures on services described in this chapter. Moreover, when things go wrong, investors protect themselves from exposure to risk through financial engineering, leaving care workers and care recipients to bear the brunt of crisis.[109]

Infinite Marginal Cost

Care work is a relational, affective kind of personal service requiring the intensive deployment of mind and body, for the most part in the presence of the person who is being cared for. Establishing and maintaining relationships, communicating with someone who may have impairments, making someone feel cared for and about – these are all activities that take time, in addition to the labour-intensive nature of helping someone with physical dysfunctionality. The time needed is not easily reduced, lest the quality of care be compromised. Care work cannot be easily rendered more productive through efficiency measures or the deployment of technology.

Any rationalisation in care work that does take place is mostly 'pseudo-rationalisation', like the redrawing of boundaries between productive and unproductive labour; the redefinition of what counts as a necessary task and what does not; the reduction of pay and conditions. In the 1970s, a homecare worker had three hours to light a fire, help someone up in the morning, get them dressed and make them breakfast; in the 1980s this was shrunk to one and a half hours.[110] Today having to light a fire is rare, because most people have central heating. In other words, there have been technological developments that have permitted the reduction of work. But other tasks have remained pretty similar, except that today's homecare worker will have ever less time to complete them. Think also of what else the care worker in 1984 may have done while lighting a fire; she probably had a conversation with the person she was visiting, not only providing an important aspect of care, but also getting a chance to evaluate how the person was doing.

Care work stands in contrast to industrial sectors that produce goods, where the routinisation of tasks, the deployment of technological innovations to tools and equipment, along with the moving of production to where labour costs are lower, have been constantly revolutionising productivity. This has led to celebrations of a coming society of abundance due to the phenomenon of zero marginal cost, the basis for a number of current predictions of the end of capitalism and the dawning of a post-capitalist society.[110] Today's technological advances, especially with regard to informational technologies, are supposedly catapulting us to a situation in which goods and services are no longer in rivalry (their consumption by one person not precluding their consumption by another), whereby an additional unit can be produced without increasing production costs. With care work, the opposite is true: the more people need to be cared for, the more costly it is. Some efficiency savings might be made, such as grouping people in one place (for example, in care homes), or developing assistive technologies that help with some of the physical or communicative tasks of caring. However, such efficiency gains are limited overall. This is not really a very lucrative industry, unless one is in the business of servicing a luxury market, which, given that everyone needs care, is not an option for society as a whole. Hence the provision of care is a deeply *political* question.

Calming the Storm

In a recent report, the Health Foundation and the King's Fund pointed out that the system of social care and the way it is publicly funded have been an ongoing cause for concern for at least twenty years, and the current situation is not safe.[112] Every so often, the social care crisis makes political waves and new fixes are proposed. In 2015, such care fixes included former chancellor George Osborne's extra £1.5 billion for the Better Care Fund, along with legislation allowing a 2 per cent council-tax increase to generate more funds for social care.[113] Neither of these came anywhere near stabilising social care and closing the rising funding gap, projected to increase to £6 billion by 2030.[114] In 2017, there was Theresa May's much-derided electioneering suggestion for what was dubbed the 'dementia tax'.[115] According to her proposal, the value of people's homes would not only be taken into consideration should they seek residential care, as is the case already, but also if they needed homecare. More recently, a debate has begun about the possibilities for the public provision of free personal care, as exists in Scotland, with various think tanks producing reports on how this could be funded through taxation.[116] In early 2020 a further £1.5 billion of local government funding for social care was announced, which councils argued was not enough to cover minimum wage increases.[117]

The systematic underfunding of social care is long-standing and entrenched, and it has been exacerbated by austerity. But to reduce the problems in social care to the lack of public funding is not just insufficient, it is dangerously deflecting. Underlying the problems in the care sector are the failures of privatisation and the kinds of financial model that have been allowed to take root. The logic of these business models means that any new money – assuming it were even made available – is likely to be procured in pursuit of profitability, as opposed to the satisfaction of need, and there will be no serious improvement of the situation for care workers or for those receiving care. Simply providing more money will not solve the problem when privatisation has been allowed to drain funding out of the public purse, making care conditions worse in order to generate profits. The evidence is clear: we need to change the way that care is provided, funded and regulated.

5

Banking on the Abandoned

One response to the care crisis that is gaining ground is prevention. For example, the 2019 NHS Long-Term Plan emphasises the prevention of avoidable illnesses such as those that stem from smoking, obesity, excessive alcohol consumption or other ramifications of unhealthy lifestyles. The impact of environmental factors such as air pollution is also acknowledged.[1] The thinking behind this is that a reduction of health and social care needs in the population saves money and reduces the burden on the public infrastructures for health and social care, as well as on welfare and social security spending: the fewer people needing care, the less costly it is.

Over the last ten years, Britain has been experimenting with new ways for private finance to address the social problems of our time, to which the care crisis of course belongs. It is in this context that the new focus on prevention has garnered interest from philanthropic and other financial investors looking to invest in projects that have a social impact. The founding blocks were laid under the auspices of New Labour in the early 2000s, when a taskforce for what is now known as 'social impact investing' was first set up. However, it was only after the Global Financial Crisis of 2008 that a window of opportunity for implementation opened.

Austerity Britain has offered a fertile ground for the development of social impact investing because of how cash-strapped government departments and local authorities seeking to reduce public spending could access financial assistance from the private sector. Where the UK government has been concerned with fiscal consolidation, achieving short- as well as long-term savings is a priority. The central organisation set up to help grow a market for social impact investing in the UK is called 'Big Society Capital', alluding to former Prime Minister David Cameron's idea of promoting voluntary social action and community empowerment while making huge budget cuts. The name underlines the proximity of the idea of the 'Big Society' to new forms of privatisation and financialisation.[2]

More recently, another social impact investing organisation, Social Finance, has responded to the NHS Long-Term Plan, arguing that at a time of stretched resources 'there may be a role for socially motivated investors in supporting innovation with primary care delivery and elements of preventive care [while] NHS grant programmes could also benefit from taking a more explicit "investment approach" to the management of such funding.'[3] The language here is cautious and tentative, yet these assertions are part of a movement to expand the influence of private finance in the areas of welfare, health and social care. Not only are cost savings to be generated for governments, but this model of care is also expected to yield financial returns for investors who provide the cash to develop new innovative models. The focus is on targeting individuals and shaping their conduct so that they live their lives in ways that are less of a cost burden to the health and social care system or to the welfare state.

Social Impact Bonds

One financial instrument developed for this purpose is called a Social Impact Bond (SIB). Social impact bonds can be used in a variety of community contexts to fund social innovation and are part of the broader social enterprise turn. This means that finance models can be quite different, ranging from community shares to more traditional forms of borrowing. With sharp relevance to the care crisis, a new kind of public–private partnership model of social impact investing is being rolled out in the context of government and local authority responsibilities for welfare, health, and social care.

Social impact investment differs from the kind of outsourcing of public services to private companies we reviewed in the previous chapter, where for-profit companies provide public services paid for by the local council. This new kind of public–private partnership is a way for private investors to finance interventions commissioned by governments or local councils. Unlike other types of bonds that pay a guaranteed interest, SIBs are performance-based: they pay by specific, priced results. A government body or local council commissions a service provider (charity organisation or social enterprise, or even a consortium of collaborating organisations) to produce a designated outcome within a certain time frame. A SIB is issued to generate private finance for the intervention. If – and only if – the intervention achieves its targets within the designated time frame, SIB investors get their money back, plus a premium. Depending on the way the SIB is constructed, investors can expect a financial 'return on investment' between 12 and 30 per cent.[4]

The very first SIB was launched in Britain in 2010 and was designed to reduce the reoffending rate of people with short-term sentences at Peterborough prison. Since then, another forty-odd SIB-funded projects have been rolled out in trials across the UK. With significant financial and infrastructural backing from philanthropic organisations and the UK government, SIB-funded projects are rapidly growing. Countries such as Britain, the United States, Australia and Canada have played a leading role in the expansion of social impact investing, lately followed by countries such as Germany, Belgium and Switzerland, along with some parts of South East Asia, while there is significant interest on the African continent. In developing countries, Development Impact Bonds, possibly with the involvement of large charities and non-governmental organisations, are the next step beyond development aid.[5] In 2019 there were 142 SIBs worldwide across the sectors of health, education, employment and social welfare in nearly thirty countries.[6] At the end of 2018, the global impact investing market (of which SIBs are one element) was worth $502 billion.[7]

In Britain, aside from tackling recidivism and homelessness, SIB financing has been used with the stated aims of preventing social isolation among elderly people, long-term chronic illness, young people from becoming NEET (not in education, employment or training) and children being taken into care. They are also being trialled in the context of end-of-life care, drug and alcohol dependency and mental health. The focus is overwhelmingly on the most disadvantaged in society and the most deprived areas of the country. The narrative is one of 'win-win': government departments and local councils gain access to much-needed finance, at a time when they are both strapped for cash and facing the fall-out from the deepening of social and economic inequality. At the same time, the deployment of market mechanisms is supposed to incentivise innovation and promote cost-efficiency, because service providers will have to make sure targets are met and investors receive financial returns. Prevention suits financialisation, because it allows for the costing of risk and the rendering productive of speculative futures.

Britain as Laboratory

The relative importance of financial services for the British economy helps explain why Britain has sought to lead in this particular financial innovation. Comprising 7 per cent of GDP in 2018, Britain's financial services sector was the seventh largest in the OECD in 2018 in terms of economic output (behind Luxembourg, USA, Australia and Canada, Switzerland and Ireland).[8] Encouraging the use of social impact investment in the UK and promoting London as a leading global hub connecting social enterprise to capital markets has been envisioned as a way for Britain to achieve a further competitive advantage in financial services.[9] This is not least because of the pivotal role that Britain has played as the home to many a seat of financial capital. The prevalence of this kind of financing in countries such as Britain is linked to the porousness of the state vis-à-vis finance, and a closer look shows that, in order to work, impact investing relies on state support in terms of funding, tax incentivisation and legislation.[10]

In the UK, two key legislative changes are the Localism Act (2011) and the Public Services (Social Value) Act (2012). The former grants greater powers to local councils and community groups to bid for and run services, while the latter requires organisations bidding for government or local council contracts to demonstrate the socially beneficial outcomes that they offer the community. With these developments comes a much more concerted focus on outcomes-based commissioning and payment by results as ways to monitor the achievement of social impact. The Care Act (2014) makes extensive reference to the plans for an increased focus on outcomes measurements under the auspices of the Public Services (Social Value) Act.

Reducing the Cost of Care

The narrative of social impact bonds is that they can help reduce the costs of welfare and care. As we have seen, most SIB projects to date focus on the socially disadvantaged and on particularly deprived areas of the country. This reveals a poignant link between austerity and the new type of private financing initiative: the very populations abandoned as a result of austerity measures are the potential targets of these interventions – disadvantaged families and young people, the homeless, people with mental health issues, the elderly. Except that now, these groups are recast as problems for society that cost the taxpayer money in terms of public spending on welfare and social security, health and social care. These are risks which must be reduced. As the UK Cabinet Office explains, 'the starting point for most existing SIBs is to estimate the cost savings (or avoided future costs) that will accrue as a result of improvements in outcomes.'[11] Such initiatives are premised on a different conception of the welfare state to that which sees a public infrastructure of care as part of a social provision. Here, the state and private finance work together in a public–private partnership intended as a vehicle for eliminating present and future social costs. After all, the homeless and people with drug and alcohol dependency issues are an expense for local authorities and health services. The elderly who feel lonely and isolated are more likely to fall ill and use costly GP and hospital services, or more likely to be taken into costly residential care. Children who are removed from their birth families or for whom foster or adoptive families cannot be found are a drain on local authorities. The NEETs are a cost to the social security system.

Getting the Measure of Society

The terms 'social value', 'social impact', 'added value' or also 'social return on investment' (SROI) refer to the non-financial impacts of programmes: the ways in which interventions contribute to a better functioning of society. Impact measures are readily quantifiable because the outcomes can be counted, for example the reduction of rough sleeping in a particular town. However, social impact can also include less tangible and more subjective factors that have an affective quality, such as feeling less lonely or isolated, having a sense of self-worth, having a voice, feeling sufficiently included in decision-making or feeling engaged in something meaningful.[12]

The ability to quantify and measure social outcomes is key for commissioning bodies wishing to determine the extent to which SIB-funded interventions achieve their aims. Clear metrics are also necessary to link them to capital markets. This is because investors must be able to ascertain the financial returns they can expect on their investments. As advocates suggest, the more effective measurements of social outcomes can be developed, the more financial investment will be attracted.[13] To this end, reliable measurements of social impact and financial return are absolutely crucial. Necessary are quantifiable, measurable targets that can be given a price tag, so that the economic value of outcomes can be determined, investors can compare the value of investing in one area compared with another, and commissioning bodies (such as a government department or a local council) can adjudicate between different tenders for the most cost-effective service provision. It must be possible to define outcomes that can be achieved relatively short-term, and the causal links have to be relatively simple (if x does y, then z happens).

There are several accounting models for setting prices and returns. The most widely adopted of these is the 'Social-Return-on-Investment' model (SROI).[14] This means that in tendering for contracts to provide services, the successful bid will be the one that credibly promises maximum social return for a given financial investment. One way of doing so is to quantify and ascribe monetary value to social outcomes calculated in cost-saving terms. This means quantifying how much money is saved for every £1 invested, in terms of social and community services which a local authority no longer has to provide.

Cost savings can be concrete savings such as a reduction in expenditure due to improved cost-effectiveness of an existing service – providing that service more cheaply. Or they can be projected savings, made because a SIB-funded intervention successfully resolves a social problem that would otherwise have lingered for governments and taxpayers: lonely and elderly people; people suffering from mental ill-health; people with type 2 diabetes; children taken into care because their families are struggling; people claiming benefits; rough sleepers.

Projected savings can be quite concrete, too: for example, reducing the amount of people using hospital beds, or the number of days a child spends in care services, or the rate of reoffending. Yet projected cost savings can also be more abstract. Examples here include the reduction of future costs to society by funding interventions aimed at transforming 'poorly adapted' individuals into 'well-adapted' ones who commit fewer crimes, find a job and are therefore less reliant on welfare. In such cases, counterfactuals are necessary to determine projected future savings or avoided future costs. This means proxies have to be invented that can quantify what costs *would have* been incurred had the intervention not been undertaken.[15]

Overall, metrics have to be set out such that they can be priced. In other words, such metrics become the basis on which the successes (or failures) of service providers are evaluated and the basis on which payments to investors are made. The following examples of current or recent projects undertaken in the UK are taken from the Impact Bond Global Database, maintained and published by the organisation Social Finance. These examples show just how central the cost-saving metric is:[16]

- Elderly in deprived areas experiencing social isolation are a cost to GP services and risk entry into residential care homes. Success is measured on the basis of reductions in feelings of loneliness using a predefined scale.

- Individuals with long-term chronic illness in deprived areas are a cost to the NHS. Success is measured on the basis of improvements in wellbeing using a predefined scale.
- Individuals at risk of developing type 2 diabetes are a cost to the NHS. Success is measured in terms of reduction in an individual's waist size, weight and blood sugar levels.
- Rough sleepers are a cost to the public purse in terms of crime, ill-health and claims to benefits. Success is measured in terms of overall rough sleeping in a particular area, entry into accommodation, employment and/or repatriation for EU migrants.
- Children at risk of being taken into care (and their families) are a cost to taxpayers when the children are in state care. Success is measured in terms of a reduction in days spent in care, improved school outcomes, improved wellbeing and reduced (re)offending.
- Young people at risk of becoming NEET are a cost to taxpayers in terms of unemployment benefit claims and crime. Success is measured by a rate card that prices payments in terms of improvements in school (attitudes, behaviour and attendance), qualification achievements, or sustained employment or volunteering.

With what justification are cost savings – actual or speculative – paid out from the public purse to private investors? The argument is that private investors must be incentivised and then rewarded for providing the financial resources to undertake these interventions. However, where cost savings constitute returns paid to investors, public funds are in fact transferred to private investors as profits. Even if cost savings are only paid out partially and not in their entirety, SIBs become an instrument that allows financial *investors* (the private sector) to pocket the very savings they claim to be helping *society* (the public) to make. Even more uncomfortably, economic inequality and social disadvantage become a source of revenue for private investors, a process which perpetuates further disadvantage.

In fact, researchers have found it difficult to access the information necessary to truly evaluate the financial dimensions of SIB-funded projects. The rates of return for investors and the ways in which SIB specialist organisations were reimbursed are seldom made public, because the data are considered commercially sensitive.[17] This belies the claim of the use of private finance enabling greater transparency and accountability, for instance because of the focus on outcomes as the basis for bond trade.[18]

Do SIBs Work?

One of the main arguments in favour of SIBs from the perspective of the public is that they provide a mechanism for shifting financial risk from the public to the private sector, precisely because financial investors only get paid if the designated outcomes are achieved within the given time frame *and* if savings are made. Despite SIBs being hailed as an all-round success by their advocates, so far there is little evidence that SIBs are actually delivering on their promises and solving the problems they claim to address, nor that they will save anyone any money. Film-maker Nadine Pequeneza, who spent more than three years researching SIB-funded projects in the US and Canada, concludes that:

> The theory that SIBs bring business rigor to solve social problems has not been demonstrated. Rather, the need to return profits in a timely fashion to investors has deterred the kind of comprehensive program evaluation that leads to possible program improvement ... Around the world governments have

bought into SIBs as a cost-saving measure; a way for private money to finance early interventions that help prevent expensive services downstream. In moving from theory to practice, many SIB pioneers have found this expectation can negatively impact program participants.[19]

Overall, SIBs seem to be offering simplistic solutions to complex social problems. The pressure to achieve targets may well result in outcomes being misrepresented to accord with stated aims and allow for payments to go ahead.[20] The danger is that easy targets are set and those individuals who are easy to work with are helped, while more challenging cases are overlooked. Indeed, in practice, evidence has been found that difficult cases have been set aside and only the ones likely to yield results focused on.[21] Furthermore, considerable costs are incurred with establishing, developing and scaling these kinds of projects. It is therefore highly questionable whether savings to the public purse are achievable at all once the costs of infrastructure and scalability are taken into account.[22]

This has led researchers evaluating SIB-financed cases to the conclusion that, all in all, SIBs do not actually reduce costs for commissioning bodies, who end up, in fact, compensating for the lack of savings. The exception might be the use of SIBs on a case-by-case basis where a very expensive service is spot-purchased, say in the case of children in care.[23] Such exceptional cases hardly provide enough grounds for a general implementation of SIBs. In cases where SIBs *were* helpful, it was because, rather than a strict focus on outcomes and savings, the finance was used to experiment and innovate. In other words, where service providers have disposed of ample sums to tend to the needs of the people they are trying to help, they have done some good work. But this has nothing to do with the structure of SIB-financed investment – it is simply a matter of providing the funds to enable difficult, resource-intensive interventions.[24] In fact, there is evidence so far that cashable cost savings are not being achieved in multiple cases.[25] For this reason, central government (the Cabinet Office) even created a 'Social Outcomes Fund' worth £20 million to 'top up' funding for projects that fail to meet their targets.[26] Currently, the greater proportion of payments to investors comes from central government and large national charities like the Big Lottery Fund.[27]

Targeting the Abandoned

Homelessness serves well to illustrate the problem, with rough sleeping being one of the first issues to be addressed by this new kind of public–private partnership. Homelessness is also an expression of the more general care crisis engulfing society. Homelessness in Britain today is the highest it has ever been on record,[28] and rough sleeping is one aspect of the broader phenomenon.[29] In England today, there are 165 per cent more rough sleepers than there were in 2010.[30] Thanks to government interventions in 2017–18, the figure has dipped slightly. Yet, especially in urban areas, homelessness continues to rise. Three-quarters of local councils consider rough sleeping a problem in their area; for nearly a quarter of them, rough sleeping is one of the major issues they are having to tackle.[31] Of significance too is the sharp rise in homelessness among migrants from Poland and Romania since 2017.[32]

According to the academic authors of the *Homelessness Monitor 2019* from which the above figures stem, there are three main structural causes of homelessness in Britain. First, the available housing stock quite simply does not match housing needs, and appropriate new housing is not being built.[33] Second, there is a lack of affordable housing for low-income households, due to the growth in the private rental sector, changes to housing association tenancy allocation policies and a reduction in social housing lettings; in addition, even social landlords are demanding more stringent checks on financial capability that make it hard for homeless households to access social tenancies.[34] Third, austerity measures have removed significant elements of the safety net for low-income households in ways that affect their ability to secure their housing.[35] The steady rise in housing costs is no longer covered by housing allowance and benefits, due to the freezes and caps put in place. Previously, Housing Benefit was supposed to protect household income from falling below basic benefit levels after having paid for housing. Changes to Housing Benefit mean this is no longer the case.[36] Moreover, delays for initial Universal Credit payments along with system errors are leading to rent arrears that are resulting in destitution.[37] Due to cuts to their funding as part of ongoing austerity measures, local councils have been forced to suspend any emergency assistance they were still able to provide for people facing destitution.

Poverty and structural disadvantage play a major role in homelessness, and being in financial straits leads to complex personal circumstances (including physical and mental health problems, or the loss of social relationships). The World Health Organisation has also acknowledged the link between material deprivation and mental health, notably in its 2017 study on the rise of depression and related conditions.[38] Importantly, however, while problems may appear as issues for the individuals concerned, it is the structural conditions of those problems that need to be addressed for any real alleviation to occur. As the authors of the *Homelessness Monitor 2019* stress, these structural conditions of homelessness – and especially the effects of austerity and the Global Financial Crisis – are not only being inadequately addressed, they are being positively denied by the UK Government.[39]

Given the alarming rise in rough sleeping, homelessness has been catapulted to the top of the list of growing social problems which the government and local councils are attempting to tackle. In the most recent rafts of measures, 'person-centred approaches' are favoured. On one level these are a welcome development, because they give case workers the opportunity to focus on the complex needs and specific situation of the individuals concerned (perhaps also explaining why these approaches have benefitted single people above all); but they are insufficient when they sideline or even obfuscate the structural conditions that produced the problem in the first place.

Judging by the metrics developed for SIB-funded projects addressing rough sleeping, there are no measures aimed at changing the structural conditions of homelessness, such as lack of housing, high rents, gentrification, or the effects of austerity. The most important goal is to get people off the streets, to the point where in one project EU migrants were even supposed to be repatriated (deported).[40] As the accounting experts who analysed the SIB-funded interventions in London confirm, the target was to get rid of the homeless, not solve the causes of homelessness. Moreover, their research shows that the metrics devised to calculate success, and thus payments to investors, 'were based on somewhat arbitrary forms of calculation, the purposes of which seems primarily to create an economic/profitable number to put in the SIB.'[41] This example shows the danger of shoehorning metrics into frameworks primarily geared towards facilitating the calculation of outcome payments, as opposed to addressing the problem at hand.

Personalising the Care Crisis

The overwhelming majority of SIB-funded projects are about giving personalised support (including therapeutic interventions) to individuals to help them to transform their personal situation, behaviour or attitudes. In other words, individuals are supposed to change themselves to become better adapted to the demands of the society they live in. For example, young people are to develop greater 'mental toughness', learn how to be more aspirational and ambitious, acquire a more positive attitude towards their education, achieve qualifications and gain employment; their families must learn to manage their conflicts and crises in better ways; the elderly must learn to be more community-orientated; and those with unhealthy lifestyles must learn how to be fit and healthy. In the various publications on social impact investing, a great deal is made of the endeavour of private finance to become more involved in tackling the challenging social problems of our time.

Yet, as the above examples show, SIB-funded interventions are not actually designed to alleviate *social* problems: they target *personal* problems that affect certain social groupings. Social and economic disadvantage is no longer the result of structural inequality, but the result of individual inadequacy. The social problem, then, becomes one of maladapted individuals. They need help to become good citizens, no longer a burden to the health- and social care or social security system. As the UK government pledged with its most recent Life Chances Fund, a new £80 million fund established in 2016 to develop more SIBs over a period of nine years: 'The aim is to help those people in society who face the most significant barriers to leading happy and productive lives.'[42] If we consider how many people's lives have been devastated by the austerity that was deemed necessary for the British economy to remain attractive to financial investors, it comes with a sour aftertaste that private finance is now invited in to improve those very people's chances.

The targeting of individuals for remedial intervention reinforces the idea that the remedy for the care crisis is to be found at the level of its symptom. The transformation of society is equated to individual change and personal responsibilisation. There is little concern with transforming the social, economic and political structures that create social disadvantage in the first place.[43] The fact that austerity measures and economic inequality have engendered the care crisis and made life hard for people is nowhere mentioned. The reality is that disadvantaged young people have lost state support (the EMA), seen cuts to youth and community services, and often face institutionalised racism, entrenched poverty and precarious labour markets; but none of these factors seem to feature in the approach taken. SIBs constitute a continuation of the neoliberal tendency towards a residualist welfare model and a narrow focus on labour market activation – except that now these efforts are becoming directly financialised, presenting opportunities for financial reward.

Only a cynic would decry the provision of personalised support to tackle the problems someone faces in life. However, the principle of personal responsibility for social disadvantage is hugely problematic, as is the invasiveness of disciplining and monitoring individual conduct, judging (and pricing!) the successes and failures of people who are already marginalised and disadvantaged. Poverty and economic inequality, environmental pollution and exposure to harmful products, work-related stress and precarious employment, loneliness and social isolation, lack of access to health and social care services: these are truly *social* problems, at the same time as their effects – of which ill-health is merely one well-documented example – take their toll on individuals.[44] These effects are linked to the way society is organised and to how the global economy functions. They have to do with how we produce and consume and with the ways that wealth is unequally distributed. They also have to do with the deregulation of labour markets and the retrenchment of publicly funded social security systems. The social challenges which SIBs address result from poverty and inequality. Why not concentrate our efforts on shaping an economy that does not produce poverty and insecurity, rather than turn those experiencing poverty and insecurity into opportunities for wealth accumulation?

Financialised Victorianism

An entrepreneurial concept of social change informs these developments, fusing the figure of the philanthropist with the figure of the entrepreneur. Those with wealth to invest decide what constitutes a 'social problem' and how it should be addressed. Moreover, the logics that govern financial markets and financial risk management come to exert an influence on the projects themselves. Investors (or their representatives) can sit on project management boards and thus shape the design of the project. Service providers can be periodically replaced if they do not deliver on outcomes, or indeed financing can be withheld if it looks like outcomes are not going to be met. Contracts can also be modified if subcontracted providers, such as a social enterprise or charity organisation, perform poorly.[45] For example, the investment bank Goldman Sachs (a pioneer of SIBs in the United States) pulled out of a project to reduce reoffending at Rikers Island prison in 2015. At the same time, since the investment was insured with Bloomberg Philanthropists to the sum of $6 million, there was no actual risk of losing any money.[46] The use of private finance to meet public policy goals means that these goals become subordinate to the demands of financial yield.[47] Advocates call this 'philanthrocapitalism', but a better term would be 'financialised Victorianism', given the recourse to wealthy private individuals for the alleviation of social problems.[48] Except now such ventures are not merely charitable endeavours, but opportunities for financial gain.

The overwhelming majority of social impact investment in Britain is financed by philanthropic foundations, trusts and charities, along with individual investors who invest via social investment funds. So far, this is not an attractive investment opportunity for those financial actors seeking commercial returns, not least because outcomes payments are often reinvested in the projects, as opposed to being paid out as actual returns.[49] Concessionary rates are supposed to be extended to investors who wish to support projects with a social purpose for ethical reasons. So far, this kind of social impact investing is not connected to global financial markets, which is why it can be beneficial as an investment opportunity.[50]

However, by the same token there is very little scope for financial risk management. A report by JP Morgan and the Global Impact Investing Network confirms that the lack of risk management strategies for investors is one of the main impediments to the growth of the market.[51] The City of London Corporation has also stressed the need for more 'complex financial instruments to shift risk reward requirements'.[52] Financial actors seek to mitigate financial risk. Investors need to securitise their investments such that if the projects are not successful, investors do not lose their money. As advocates clearly state, social investment is about 'financing the unbankable';[53] that is, it is about bringing into the realms of finance those organisations and initiatives that would normally not receive private finance because they would be considered too risky. In other words, social impact investing is supposed to turn the normal logic of financial investment – low risks and high returns – on its head, to enable high-risk, low-return investment. There is an obvious contradiction here. The logic of the enterprise dictates that to work on its own terms, investments must yield returns if they are to be of any real interest to financial actors.[54] The whole point is to harness the forces of the market and mobilise the financial incentive to achieve prescribed ends, portrayed as a perfect alignment of care with the goal of maximising financial returns. But this would mean that the high-risk/low-return guarantee cannot deliver. In order to really take off, SIBs would need to be exposed outright to financial risk management, perhaps through secondary markets, as opposed to being protected from them.

In fact, the UK government has explicitly stated it wishes to see a secondary market develop.[55] The aim is to 'create effective financial markets to trade and issue securities'.[56] In the long-term, social investment markets are to operate in the same way, that is, with the same kinds of risk and return characteristics as any other kind of financial market. Potential investors include governments, trusts and foundations, individual retail investors, wealthy individuals, and mainstream banks.[57] In the financial sector, discussions are ongoing with regard to how the cash flow of a SIB can be securitised and traded on the Social Stock Exchange (which has been trading securities and derivatives since 2013), so that impact investors can invest and raise capital.[58]

What is more, the originator of the ideas behind what have become SIBs, New Zealand economist Ronnie Horesch, maintains that tradability of the bonds is integral to their functioning. The problem with the present version of SIBs is that their focus is too short-term and that they do not allow for new entrants into the market for these 'problem-solving services', as he calls them.[59] Writing in the journal of the free-market think tank the Institute of Economic Affairs, Horesch explains that a secondary market would allow for the value of bonds to increase on the basis of increases in the probability of outcomes being achieved. This in turn would mean that bond-holders would do their utmost to make sure the outcomes are achieved in ways that save costs, so that the bonds increase in value.[60] Horesch argues that by its very logic, the market would 'favour the most cost-effective coalition of operators'.[61] What Horesch underplays here is the ways in which investors would seek to minimise their risk through on-selling or other forms of securitisation, thereby immunising themselves against losses – something a society confronted with rising problems of inequality, the people affected, and the social and care workers on their side, cannot do.[62]

It seems likely that secondary markets will develop for the purposes of securitisation, thus exposing this field of social policy – and with it the (often vulnerable) people and projects funded by SIB initiatives – to the vicissitudes of global financial markets and the negative effects of economic downturn.

Financial Care Fix

The promise of social impact investing is that it can help solve the care crisis by reducing the cost of welfare, health and social care to the public purse. Judging by the evidence so far, this is unlikely to happen. Some argue that it is nothing more than an attempt to upgrade the negative image of finance, without much scope to really gain ground. Yet, advocates in the world of finance have posited social impact investing as the new venture capital; they hope for the creation of a new market for financial investment and opportunities for profitable returns. As one of the most important initiators of social impact investing, Ronald Cohen, and his co-author, William Sahlman, explained in the *Harvard Business Review* in 2013:

> We live in a world awash with capital ... We also live in a world of remarkably low interest rates. If we can create instruments ... that can deliver a financial return of about 7 percent, a high social return and limited downside risk, then we can meet two needs. We can provide reasonable returns that are uncorrelated with equity markets and attract capital to entrepreneurs who can develop innovative and effective ways of improving the fabric of our society.[63]

Financial investors are not simply to be concerned with maximising their financial returns or managing their risk, they are to invest with a view to producing socially beneficial outcomes.

Caring Capitalism

The Global Financial Crisis of 2008 punctured the common sense of capitalism and plunged its financialised variant into an image crisis. In the face of the collapse of financial markets and the social consequences, a renewed conversation about the benefits versus the ills of the capitalist system erupted. Markets – specifically, in this context, unchecked financial markets – were seen to have created and exacerbated social ills and negative outcomes. While anti-austerity protestors gathered in the streets and politicians and economists debated the virtues or vices of financial regulation, business leaders, venture capitalists and other kinds of entrepreneurs gathered in places like the World Economic Forum in Davos to deliberate the need for a more socially minded capitalism, extolling the virtues of social enterprise.[64]

The buzzwords of this new, socially orientated capitalism are 'compassionate', 'ethical', 'caring', 'conscious', 'creative', 'inclusive' and 'responsible'. Yet, where hitherto forms of corporate social responsibility and philanthropy treated the ethical cause as *external* to the business model, now society is not a separate entity to take from or give back to. Instead, the social or environmental impact is *internal* to the ways in which business seeks to create and capture value. In other words, a profit motive does not necessarily stand in conflict with social concerns – businesses can indeed trade with an explicitly social purpose and produce social (and environmental) value. Consequently, a reinvigorated capitalism of this sort is about companies pursuing positive societal and environmental impacts while also making a profit, with attempts to stake out how finance can be put to good use and serve ostensibly better purposes than simply mitigating financial risk and maximising financial return, including addressing the care crisis. The slogan for this endeavour has been 'doing well by doing good'.[65] Financial investment with a social impact is a core aspect of the much-vaunted caring turn for capitalism, involving the financing of projects and enterprises that have an explicit social or environmental purpose. Impact investing seeks to show that, contrary to popular vilifications, finance *does* care.

Who would not want investors and entrepreneurs to put their money into good causes, rather than damaging ones? Yet the figure of the caring investor is problematic – but not because investors do not care. No doubt, there are people who would like to put their money to good use in the world. The figure of the caring investor is problematic in the same way as the figure of the 'greedy banker' identified as chief cause of the Global Financial Crisis. When such moral figures are created, the structural phenomena of political, social and economic inequality disappear from view. Especially during times of crisis, certain figures have been conjured up in the search for individuals or groups to blame for causing social problems or economic difficulties. When anger and frustration are directed at caricatures – whether 'corrupt politicians', 'benefit scroungers', 'illegal immigrants', 'feral youth' or any other convenient projection – they serve as the 'bad apples' to be taken out. Pointing the finger at scapegoats tends to provide simplistic explanations and misleading attributions of responsibility for social ills.

These emotive figures are vectors of what the late cultural theorist Stuart Hall and his co-authors called a 'displacement effect' in their book, *Policing the Crisis*, about the criminalisation of young black men in the early 1970s.[66] The designation of social problems as 'moral' shortcomings channels causes and solutions towards individual behaviour. Symptoms of structural crisis are recast as causes, and externalised. (In the case of Brexit and the EU Referendum, indeed, the externalisation was quite literal: Britain's problems came from outside – EU elites and migrants – and the solution was retreat and expulsion.) The deeper, more fundamental problems – and the structural relationships of power that they rest on – need not be addressed. This is a dangerous fallacy.

The same ideological logic can be applied to solutions. The figure of the caring investor represents the benign inverse of the bogeymen above. By the same token, the caring investor offers the possibility of remedy. I note a parallel here with the equally problematic argument that arose after the Global Financial Crisis – that having more women in the boardroom might have averted the crisis, because women are considered cautious, less reckless than men. But investors with 'good' intentions may exist just as much as investors with 'bad' intentions. The issue at stake is not the intentions of the investor or the moral quality of the object they invest in; the trouble is with the workings of these financial instruments and the logics of privatisation. Financialisation is not a simple process of allocating resources here or there. Financialisation imposes a set of disciplinary measures that shape the social processes it engages with, privatising gains and socialising risks and costs, as we saw in the last chapter.

Many people want a different, kinder society. Unfortunately, the praise of caring capitalism relies on a slippage in meaning. The celebration of a capitalist economy with an ethical orientation as a novel form of value creation, one that is socially just in ways it might not have been before, rests upon the construction of an antithesis between care and capitalism. 'Care' and 'capitalism' are portrayed as distinct and opposing entities that can be fused together to produce a better world. The contrast between care and capitalism also sits well with the criticism of individuals in the banking sector for their perceived personal greed and dishonesty, coupled with the short-term, profit-orientated thinking that is conventionally put forward as one of the causes of the crisis. Consequently, caring conduct must be the opposite of greed or dishonesty, or of thinking only of the short-term. Caring conduct must imply being mindful of the welfare of others and the wider community, being transparent, not just thinking about making a fast buck but planning for the longer term. These are all virtues attributed to the caring turn for capitalism.

There are false polarities being set up here. Caring relations are not alternative social and ethical practices that stand outside of capitalist social relations. Instead, they are subsumed and thus shaped by the needs of a capitalist economy. The subordination of care and social reproduction under the demands of capital mean that the two more often seem counterposed: care work is often carried out against the clock and with insufficient resources to meet needs fully. Care work cannot be infinitely rationalised, sped up and made more efficient on pain of compromising the quality of that care, and the relationships necessary to deliver it, in turn eroding its very provision. Meanwhile, capital is not something that can be imbued with moral agency per se. What matters to the capitalist system is economic value and its augmentation: profit, growth, dividends, returns on investment. In social terms, capital is a relationship founded on unequal power and unequal access to or control over the means of (social) (re)production. What is at stake, then, is the question of how the material relations of power and wealth that underpin the control over the reproduction of livelihood are organised, maintained and reinforced.

A Risky Experiment

Britain has been turned into a site of experimentation with new financial instruments for addressing the care crisis. While the government ploughs millions into making these instruments work, social entrepreneurs, financial investors and charity organisations are attempting to find out by trial and error what works and what does not. The very populations that have been abandoned by austerity or bear the destructive consequences of financialised capitalism are being recast as a cost to society and a risk to be managed using calculative instruments aimed at financial returns. This is nothing other than a variant of privatisation; SIBs are a way of transferring public funds to private hands under the guise of social and financial innovation. It is difficult to say whether these new public–private partnerships will be become generalised across society. It also seems doubtful that they even work on their own terms. All the while, the experimental attitude with which these financial instruments are being developed extends to those people most affected by the care crisis. In the process, what is established is a broader trend of financialised and entrepreneurial solutions to social problems in a climate of public service retrenchment and the expansion of market-orientated thinking, along with a more general culture of individualised prevention and better self-care as a method for overcoming the care crisis.

6

Take Care of You

Take Care of You! a smiling woman gestures from an advert on the tube. She is dressed in natural-looking clothes, white teeth gleaming, blond hair tied up in a ponytail, promoting what looks like a cookbook. As the care crisis intensifies, we are repeatedly urged to take care of ourselves. Ubiquitous, too, is the talk of 'wellbeing' to which, as we know, a whole industry of products, apps, advice and therapies is devoted, piling into the gap created by the dismantling of societal responsibility. There are two sides to this self-care fix that together articulate an outlook on the world that is congruent with the logic of financialised capitalism. First of all: take care of you, because you are your own most valuable asset – a form of human capital that will yield high economic returns if you look after it.[1] Second: take care of you, because nobody else will. Public services continue to be squeezed, collective solidarity undermined and labour markets deregulated. Since the Global Financial Crisis of 2008, the global economy has failed to really get back on track, that is, to return (as if it had ever been so stable) to steady accumulation and growth. The ensuing anxiety has engulfed society, as worries about economic growth impinge on everyday working environments and the people that inhabit them. As the process unfolds, we become more and more fearful of what might happen should we individually no longer be able to be productive or earn a living.

Clean Eating

In a bold pink font, the front cover of a magazine tells readers to 'eat clean' against the backdrop of a woman in a yellow, figure-hugging dress sunnily adorning the top right-hand corner of the page. A brief search on my smartphone quickly yields masses of material: clean eating blogs, clean eating cookbooks, clean eating diet plans, clean eating basic rules, clean eating magazines. To its proponents, clean eating is the very essence of care: it is all about caring for and about oneself. Ostensibly about what to put into or do to one's body, it is an entire way to engage with the world. If someone is a 'clean' eater, it doesn't mean that she is especially adept at eating a meal without spilling it down the front of her t-shirt. It means that the food she eats is exceptionally healthy and nutritious. 'Clean' food contains few to no chemicals, pesticides or refined substances.

Clean eating has taken the middle classes by storm. Scrolling down the feed of a #cleaneating Twitter hashtag gives a feel for what's at stake: 'Five mistakes you are making that are ruining your salad', 'Five surprising snacks that actually are making you hungrier', 'Six superfoods your grandmother ate – and you should eat too', 'Six foods your gut wants you to eat', 'Six dangerous food prep mistakes that make you sick'. Endless lists of pitfalls and top tips. The matter of what – and what not – to put in your body has spawned a host of services, produce and products that promise to help consumers be healthy, have the energy and clarity to perform well in their jobs, lead a happy life on every front and be a better person. The language of cleanliness signals a shift from a concern solely with *looking* attractive, that is, with appearance – the surface value of how we represent ourselves to the outside world. The shift is towards a concern with the condition of our very *being*. In other words, it is not about how you are on the 'outside', but how you are on the 'inside'. Moreover, being healthy does not replace looking attractive, for it is supposed to enhance your attractiveness from deeper within. Now, the aim is not to be the best there can be, as an external ideal to aspire to, but to be as good as *you* can be: to take care of yourself.

In Britain, like in so many countries of the Global North, some people have the privilege of worrying about toxins in their food while others struggle to put food on the table at all, dependent on charitable donations at food banks to survive.

The Malaise of the Orthorexic

There is something eerie about the new language of cleanliness. It has a kind of compulsive echo to it, redolent of a neurotic or even paranoid need to eliminate dirt and any kind of disorder from one's surroundings, fervently seeking protection from the dangers of contamination. The drive to *be* clean suggests wanting to purge the mess inside, while keeping the world's harmful dirt out. The quest for purity or purification interlocks with a tremendous fear of the toxic chemicals or heavy metals lurking in clothes, cookware, packaging or even tap water; the additives and pesticides in food, the dire consequences of eating anything processed or refined. Clean living becomes a form of protection against a terrible fate, one that syncs with attempts to take refuge in the sanctuary of ethical consumption and a sense of doing good. These are strategies to feel secure in an era of rapid social upheaval and technological innovation.[2] Of course there is heightened insecurity and loneliness, now that healthcare and care in old age are no longer a certainty. There is a search going on for control.

Clean eating even comes with its own disorder: orthorexia. 'Orthorexia nervosa' is a term coined by the US doctor Steven Bratman in 1997.[3] It defines a person's concern not with their body image, but with the quality of their food and the associated health benefits or drawbacks. The term acknowledges kinship to the eating disorder anorexia nervosa, while replacing 'ano' with 'ortho' – a root occurring in English-language compound words derived from the Greek (like 'orthodox') and meaning 'correct'. Orthorexic behaviours, Bratman writes, exhibit an

> emotionally disturbed, self-punishing relationship with food that involves a progressively shrinking universe of foods deemed acceptable. A gradual constriction of many other dimensions of life occurs so that thinking about healthy food becomes the central theme of almost every moment of the day, the sword and shield against every kind of anxiety and the primary source of self-esteem, value and meaning.[4]

Given that the orthorexic may find it difficult to observe the restrictions of their healthful regime, new forbidden items are, paradoxically, added to the list: the orthorexic feels bad when straying from the strict regime she has devised for herself, and may compensate for perceived failures with an even stricter one, running the risk of malnutrition. There is a busyness with self-care here, underscored by hyper-vigilance. At best, efforts to be healthy foster a kind of self-care that is counterproductive. At worst they constitute a form of self-harm.

Eating disorders, obsessive compulsive disorder and other forms of self-harm involve compulsive activities that provide temporary relief from some form of emotional chaos or mental distress that threatens to overwhelm and destabilise a person. However, the chosen activity does not deal with the internal conflict, that is, the underlying cause of the problem. In this sense, such activities are symptomatic and constitute a (short-term) fix. Moreover, the (displacement) actions themselves may well be harmful to the person engaging in them or at least cause distress to the person or others. Psychotherapists Miguel Benasayag and Gérard Schmidt also point to the ways in which feelings of disempowerment can yield a paranoid drive to gain a sense of safety.[5]

Orthorexia only affects a very small part of the population, if indeed it is recognised as a disorder at all. And not everyone who is concerned about the ills of industrial capitalism develops a neurotic condition. However, it is the extreme end of a trend. The psychoanalyst Susie Orbach charts the ways in which looking after oneself has become a moral issue. Orbach identifies the worrying rise of bodily discontent and diagnoses 'anxious embodiment' as a significant pathology of our time. She argues that escalating attempts to transform our bodies through consumption, surgery, diets and other kinds of regulatory and disciplining behaviours are an expression of how increasing numbers of people – often women – have come to regard themselves as deficient and seek to make themselves more acceptable to themselves and others. Her critique is of the capitalist industries and celebrity cultures that reinforce to us the idea that we are not good enough, offering idealised physiques for us to emulate and peddling false solutions and conflicting advice that only perpetuate insecurity and self-harm. At the same time these industries make fortunes by selling us products that rely for their appeal on the symbolic values of what has been deemed socially acceptable. Susie Orbach's notion of the search for a 'reliable body' is resonant: in a world that feels increasingly chaotic, we look for an anchoring point in ourselves and in the stability – real or perceived – of the materiality of our bodies.[6]

Following such paths of inquiry, it is illuminating to probe what the rise of clean eating tells us about the ways in which fear, insecurity and feelings of disempowerment are channelled into existential concerns about the demise of mind and body due to the dangers that loom in the outside world. Perhaps you have found yourself in the supermarket, peering at the ingredients of a jar of something or other, not quite understanding what it all means, unsure whether to buy the jar or not? You might not have resorted to looking up obscure chemical compounds on the internet, but maybe an uneasiness crossed your mind. Perhaps you wondered how food certifications work, who regulates them, who funds them, and whether what they say is really true.

Clean Beauty

Not long ago, in the cosmetics section of a department store I picked up a tube of face cream. I was told by the assistant that this brand sold the 'cleanest' products on the market, meaning they were free of synthetic preservatives, petrochemicals, colourings or other ingredients considered 'unsafe' for humans and the natural environment. Similarly to clean eating, clean beauty promises purity as a bulwark against the multifarious toxicities of industrialised capitalism: harmful substances and environmental pollution, as well as the stress of the modern world with its physiological ramifications: care for your skin by protecting it from careless cosmetics. The emphasis in the clean cosmetics market is high performance and safety, as opposed to natural origins.[7] 'Natural' products are reputed to be a bit messy, not least when trying to mix your own face cream from the contents of your fridge; or they turn out to be ineffective. The clean aesthetic is one of functionality, no frills, less is more. However, this only applies when it comes to ingredients. When it comes to pricing such products, then more is still more. Market share is expected to expand rapidly, currently growing about 200 per cent each year.[8] One global beauty industry analyst is convinced: 'I don't think this is something that will disappear. It's a way of life.'[9]

In the era of social media marketing and ethically minded millennials, proponents of clean living applaud that 'any ingredients list can now be dissected and debated before you hand over the cash, making the world of beauty more democratic.'[10]

Democracy here is synonymous with the market: it is steered by a proliferating network of 'conscious consumers' who seek to educate themselves, assisted by companies that offer apps to check what might be hiding in that shampoo you're hovering over in the supermarket aisle. Industry experts suggest that the clean beauty 'movement' results in part from a lack of regulation of the cosmetics industry, especially in the US. Regulation in the EU is much better.[11] Still, some products contain ingredients which, albeit not banned, may be considered controversial in terms of their effects on human health or the environment.[12] This can fuel anxiety over whom to trust. What we see in the trends of clean living and self-care is what happens when a sense of powerlessness is so widespread, and faith in political solutions so weak, that taking matters into one's own hands, shopping smart and coming up with a clever business idea often seems like the best solution.

Cleaning Up Capitalism

Who does not want to be able to flourish in life? Who does not want to be able to eat nutritious food? Who does not want to be able to use safe products? The calamities of corporate, profit-driven, industrialised mass production are wreaking havoc with our lives and with the planet. Our air is polluted, our oceans full of plastic and anthropogenic climate change threatens the survival of humans and the other species with whom we share the earth. Clean care is a response to the excesses of capitalist industrial production and to an overwhelming sense of peril and precariousness. However, it is a response that inserts itself into the common sense of financialised capitalism and funnels solutions to the very real problems we face through individual consumption or conduct.

The new clean living renders criticism of industrial production productive by channelling it into personalised, entrepreneurial solutions centred on the development of consumer products and services. It is part and parcel of a movement with an entrepreneurial conception of social change. Repeated ideological attacks on the very idea of regulation have merged with a belief in its futility in this age of corporate power. Instead of fighting for better regulation or even a transformation of capitalist production, instead of joining forces with other social and political movements seeking systemic change, what is on offer are personalised, market remedies that do not call consumption itself into question. The responsibility for change lies, once again, with individuals, while the ability to strategise and implement that change lies with people with money to invest, or who can attract investors and start-up capital. Power resides in the strategic alliance between consumer demand and entrepreneurial drive. However, congruent consumption is not the same thing as acting together. Endless commodification, where problems and their solutions pop up on an ever-accelerating conveyor belt of lotions and potions, does little to tackle the underlying problems of dirty production, exploitation and alienation. The structural conditions of capitalism that led to these problems in the first place are virtually ignored. Continued commodification serves simply as a *perpetuum mobile* of a socially and environmentally unsustainable economic system. The price mechanism in and of itself cannot tell us what is good and what is bad, right or wrong: it is not an ethical barometer.[13]

As an endless proliferation of more and more products and services compete for attention, those who do not have money are excluded. The profit logic still reigns supreme, and the crisis management strategies and critiques end up pushing capitalist logics deeper into the social fabric. There is an attempt to fuse self-care with asset management – 'take care of you; you are your own best asset!' – and with solicitude for the world – 'if you care about the planet, buy "cruelty-free" cosmetics!' While there are many positive impulses to live healthy lives, an obsessive absolutism seems to threaten to take over at any point. People drink too much alcohol, so a teetotal movement develops.[14] Eating too much fat is unhealthy, so people try to banish all fat from their diets. Little thought is given to the question of *why* people drink too much or eat unhealthily. What are the causes of loneliness? Why are people burned out and stressed? There's always a symptom and a solution, but never a cause. The horizon of change is limited and so the turn is inward, while the consumption of products and lifestyles promise a care fix.

Labours of Self-Care

What is on offer is democracy through the market and social and environmental justice through prosumption (the idea that consumers take part in shaping the products they buy).[15] Product optimisation through consumer participation is good business – hoodwinking us into thinking that the market and democracy are the same thing. An incredible amount of work is being done here, care for the self that is orientated towards being a good, economically productive citizen able to practice restraint and maintain self-discipline. Prosumer democracy is actually the unpaid labour of self-care that is shared with companies so they may improve their products. Twitter, Facebook and Instagram become the new way of 'clocking-in' or, perhaps better, 'checking-in'. Documenting one's habits, accomplishments and maybe even failures becomes evidence of the labours of self-care offered up to peers or to companies who confirm and validate the work done. Huge swathes of unpaid marketing and advertising labour feed the *perpetuum mobile* of prosumption. It is care work gone into overdrive, with the hope of getting a handle on the external world by changing oneself and becoming better at self-management.

In a world of competing knowledges, you have to become

your own expert in order to make sense of so much conflicting and confusing information. Who can you trust? If you do not know who to trust, you trust in yourself. Indeed your 'self' – body, mind and spirit – becomes the bulwark against multiple dangers, so you desperately try to fashion this self accordingly. You become your own scientist, doctor, nutritionist, and the body and its symptoms become your monitoring device. Nevertheless, it is hard to find peace of mind amidst the endless array of products, services and advice that keep you busy forever researching things, comparing them, finding out what the best or cheapest products are or who might be taking you for a ride.

The body becomes both the container of anxiety and the tool for providing certainty. Fitbits, calorie counting, body-mass index measures, blood tests: all of these quantify how we should or should not be caring for our bodies. Being able to measure and count things is supposed to generate certainty. Our constant ratings and measurable outcomes can in turn be routed through financial markets for the purposes of extracting surplus value. The obsession with measurement and anticipatory (preventive) futures is at the heart of a kind of care regime that is tailored to an asset-self that not only seeks to put in so as to draw out, but also has to manage and avert risk – a generalised feature of politics and the economy in financialised capitalism.

The imposition of measurement is not a post-hoc form of accounting for what has already been produced. Metrics are a form of power that have social effects as a form of control that shape our conduct and thinking.[16] The body becomes its own truth system and performance data speak our truth for us. With the proliferation of measurement and the intensification of control, there is also a sense in which a feeling of control becomes ever more elusive. Hence we allow ourselves to be drawn deeper into a world which promises to help us (re)gain it. This is especially so when fuelled by lifestyle reporting that suggests eating or not eating certain foods, behaving in particular ways, or having a particular mindset will cause personal harm: one day it was fine to put a spoonful of sugar in your tea, the next day sugar is destroying your gut from the inside. Sugar, fat, carbohydrates, coffee and even negative thinking have all had their moment as affective containers for anxieties over health.[17] While not everything that is reported is wrong, it is certainly not all right either. Often medical evidence that is cited is based on experiments that make statistical inferences, such as the calculation of probabilities or the establishment of correlations. These are all too quickly elevated to the status of truth by headline-grabbing styles of media reporting. Here is yet another way we become governed by metrics as well as by statistics.

Clean Loving

It is not only clean eating and clean skincare (or more recently even clean sleeping) that are marketised as an intimate form of self-care.[18] Sifting through Twitter, I stumbled across a link: an interview with someone who opened the very first cuddling agency in the UK. Intrigued, I skim-read the article and immediately typed in the address. *BeSnuggled* offered different kinds of cuddle packages and the website explained that to be accepted as a client for a thirty-minute-long, or even evening-long cuddle, one had to send in a copy of one's passport and a brief explanation of motivation. Considerable efforts were made to distance the cuddling business from sex work. This was presumably to protect cuddle workers from unsolicited moves by clients, while also warding off stereotypical gendered assumptions associated with sex work about who might be buying intimate services from whom. The descriptions suggested a friendly half-hour with a friend, someone you trust, someone you feel comfortable with. A photo showed a female cuddler smiling with open arms and wearing pyjamas. According to the website, people of all genders and all walks of life book professional cuddlers, from stressed, worn-out mothers to people going through divorces or recovering from illness, to young and middle-aged men, single and married.[19]

It is possible to complete a professional diploma to become a Certified Professional Cuddler. This entails acquiring technical skills, such as mastering different cuddling positions.[20] However, not all skills can be learned: a prospective cuddler needs to possess the appropriate *disposition* in order to be hired. This caring disposition involves being non-judgmental, LGTBQ-friendly and having a capacity for empathy.[21] At the same time the cuddling service is inserted into a medicalised discourse about the human requirement for touch and bodily contact. Touch is said to be routinely lacking in many people's lives due to the high degree of alienation and atomisation in contemporary society, where we spend a lot of time staring at computer screens. As the Cuddle Professionals International website explains: 'While digital technology may provide connection, it doesn't provide physical touch and it can't replace real-life friendships.'[22] The service of cuddling someone is thus shifted to the register of health and medical needs: a problem can be diagnosed and the remedy prescribed. Scientific evidence is invoked, with references to the positive psychological effects of a drop in stress hormones as an example of the biochemical processes triggered in the body by being touched.[23] The website explains that lack of touch leads to health problems such as stress and depression which can therefore be prevented – so the website implies – by buying professional cuddles.[24] The appeal to the normative values of professionalism – especially the authority of expertise – serves as a marketing tool to create the conditions for the acceptable commodification of cuddling.[25]

Cuddle therapy throws up questions about the boundaries of marketised services. Cuddle therapy might seem strange in so far as we consider bodily touch something to be exchanged in unpaid, intimate relationships. However, getting a massage, a manicure or a haircut, seeing a therapist, relationship counsellor or life coach are quite normalised. Where is the difference between these personal services and cuddling services? Where do we draw the line between the transactional relationships we conduct through the market and our assumably 'unaffected' lives beyond it? Maybe a professional cuddler is actually much better at cuddling than a layperson? Then again, maybe it is impossible to receive the same quality of touch from someone who is paid to do so as from someone with whom we share a personal relationship?

Despite the efforts of pioneering entrepreneurs to drag cuddling services into the realms of professional respectability, there is a reason why the idea of contracting a cuddle therapist feels strange. We do not want all of our social relationships to be colonised and determined by market transactions. Commodifying touch in this way suggests we can siphon off particular elements of intimate care relations to the market. The suggestion is that we can access human touch at our convenience without having to engage in the time-consuming complexities of personal relationships, or be beholden to the intricacies of commitment.

For those who can afford it, the market allows for a clean break from having to genuinely relate to others, negotiate needs, desires and difficulties. Buying into this idea of autonomous agents means erasing the emotional labour that goes into forging, enriching and maintaining relationships. We erase the fact that relationships happen *between* people, they are mutual, they are a being-in-relation. That caring is something shared; I care for you, you care for me. We do not just work stuff out with and for ourselves, we work through and on each other in complex relationships of caring, both given *and* received. And while we're not all scouring our calendars to see where we can fit in a quick cuddling fix to make sure our corporeal and psychic needs are met in the face of the alienation and virtualisation of our lives, the example of cuddle therapy serves to heighten our sense of what the marketisation of social life does to our social relations and our sense of self.

Platform Care

New kinds of self-care platforms accompany these developments. If there are apps to measure and monitor our physical performances, there are also apps to help us manage depressive episodes, keep anxiety in check, maintain mindfulness, and seek out online counselling or medical support.[26] One such platform is Babylon Health, currently operating in the UK, Rwanda, Singapore, Canada and the United States and providing users with data-driven tools for the self-management of conditions that include health, mood and activity monitoring as well as symptom checking. Artificial intelligence and machine learning are deployed to constantly refine the interpretation of symptom descriptions by users, with a view to better diagnostics and advice.[27] Aside from these tools, users are able to consult a GP online or by telephone twenty-four hours a day, seven days a week. If a user needs to see a doctor in person, they visit a Babylon Health clinic. The aim is to increase user self-management of healthcare needs and decrease the need for interaction with medical professionals.[28] Users who sign up privately pay a subscription fee.[29]

A version of the service is also available via the NHS under the name GP at Hand, which was first trialled in London before being rolled out in other cities. Users who register with the service are automatically de-registered from their existing GP practice and must use a Babylon GP at Hand (BGPaH) clinic. GP at Hand purports to provide a solution to the ongoing crisis in primary healthcare for two reasons. First, because patients can avoid long waiting lists and waiting times and have a video consultation with a doctor within two hours. Second, because the app saves the NHS money, by increasing the occasions when users can self-manage their health without needing to be seen by a doctor. Clearly, financial returns are expected: this private start-up is valued at $2 billion, after raising $550 million from international investors in 2019.[30]

The service is particularly popular with a population that is young, affluent and relatively fit. Older people, those with more complex health needs, or those with caring responsibilities are less likely to use it.[31] Patients with fewer healthcare needs are less costly to treat. Medical professionals have repeatedly raised concerns that by taking the younger, healthier patients away from NHS GP practices and leaving those with more complex health needs behind, the company takes away the resources GP practices need to treat these patients.[32] Meanwhile, NHS GPs operate as a de facto safety net, for Babylon users have the right to switch back whenever they want or need to do so.[33] Currently, GP practices are funded through weighted payments for each patient. This weighting takes into consideration the healthcare needs of the particular population a practice serves, including factors such as age, sex, and socio-economic situation. Risk is pooled, because those who are younger and fitter require less attention and therefore fewer resources. The basic principle of risk-pooling is that our health needs vary over the course of a lifetime. Emphasising individual freedom and the right to choice, Babylon's business model actively undermines both the principle and the material base of the collective solidarity and risk-pooling that are fundamental to a public healthcare system.

Advocates may argue that this is merely a teething problem of organisational change that will be solved if and when everyone is moved to GP at Hand. However, moving everyone to GP at Hand is no solution either, for then GP services will have been effectively privatised. GP at Hand is nothing more than a digital reloading of public–private partnerships that serve as the basis for financial wealth extraction. Self-care in this model is the basis for a tech-driven mode of accumulation fuelled by the privatisation of public cost savings. More and better self-care aided by digital technology is supposed to save the NHS money through reduced GP visits. A private company is making money out of charging the public purse a fee to manage its crisis of primary healthcare funding. In other words, money is *taken out* of public healthcare and placed into private hands. Moreover, as is well known from other similar platforms, placing the data that users produce while using the platform in private hands raises serious questions about privacy and security, while aiding private companies to further develop technologies as services which they then sell back to us.

The Crisis of Self-Optimisation

Take care of yourself, and the world will be taken care of. In *The Wellness Syndrome*, organisation scholars Carl Cederström and André Spicer unpack what they identify as an ideology of wellness that pushes us towards the consumption of products as part of our work on ourselves. They argue that what is ostensibly a quest for happiness and wellbeing often only thinly disguises an anxious pursuit of perfection and optimal functionality. Moreover, this wellness ideology reinforces personal responsibility, as well as suggesting that you can exercise, supplement, or even mindfully navigate your way out of every problem.[34]

An imperative to optimise and maximise your value for the labour market has long been part of a neoliberal regime oriented towards self-actualisation wedded to productivity and growth, in turn reliant on a veneration of the work ethic and a consumer culture that offers correspondent products, services, lifestyles, mindsets.[35] Motivation is couched in a positive affect that seeks to enlist joy and desire: you should do in life the things you love, and if you're not doing what you love, then it is down to you to change your attitude and your situation so that you can. Critical management scholar Stefano Harney points out that the dominant form of capitalist production in the era of neoliberal globalisation has been what he calls 'logistical capitalism', based on the idea that constant improvement is necessary and possible (stemming from the Japanese business practice of *Kaizen*, the continuous improvement of processes).[36]

For all the positive rhetoric of betterment, the imperative of always having to improve is premised on ontological inadequacy. This manifests as anxiety precisely because it cannot be directly grasped, while being relentlessly pervasive.[37] Most of the time, you're not told outright that you're no good. Yet, in competition with others, it's a constant struggle to get what you need. By placing unmanageable expectations on themselves, many give themselves and others a hard time for not being up to scratch and needing to work harder, to be better. Life-long learning ceases to be a joy and becomes a duty; growth becomes an obsession, rather than an expansion of capacity. Self-improvement is an anxious defence against increasing precarity – the spectre of un- or intermittent employment and falling wages on the one hand, and retrenching welfare states on the other. You might not always be able to make a living, and there's no guarantee of care if you cannot. You must be flexible and self-reliant. This is reinforced by negative images of collective solidarity, for example in the persistent shaming of welfare recipients. Ontological inadequacy, essentially a lack of self-esteem, makes you more compliant and more exploitable.

Debates over the sharp rise in burnout, stress and depression remain omnipresent. More and more people are feeling overwhelmed by the demands placed on them in their work and their everyday lives, especially as they look to an uncertain future. Besides having to deal with increased precarity and insecurity, the demands of work to be more, give more and do more are ruthlessly eroding the boundaries between our working lives and personal lives, a process facilitated by technology and underscored by ideas of 'doing what we love' and 'giving our souls to the factory'.[38] In the face of exhaustion and a sense of loss of control, we are learning that we need to take care of our bodies, even in today's digitally enhanced and virtualised world.

Financialised capitalism, demanding ever more access to us in order to valorise our every move, seeks at the same time to remunerate this ever less – not least by uncoding labouring activities in the endeavour to abolish work and hence justify non-remuneration, evident in the discourses of a 'sharing economy' that were laid over the gig economy when it first emerged. That is one explanation for why the work of social reproduction, the collective practices of care of self and others, are transformed into moral questions and judgments about appropriate individual behaviour. That way, social reproduction as a sphere of unpaid work is rendered invisible as it is collapsed into questions of the right and wrong ways to live. So, we are quite literally picking up the tab by having to maintain more and more of our social reproduction in commodified forms. And if you cannot afford to do so, then you should do the work on yourself to make sure you replenish your capacity for toil and maximise your economic productivity.

Self-Care Fix

Self-care gained considerable ground after the Global Financial Crisis. Even a simple analysis of mentions on the internet shows a dramatic uptick in the use of the term since around 2010.[39] There is a new edge to the clamour about self-conduct.

The idea of caring for oneself takes on an urgency in response to economic, social, environmental and political crisis. We are see(k)ing a break with some of the hitherto neoliberal narrative of optimisation, competition and achievement-at-all-costs. This is evident in the discourses of self-care. They often explore how to create more time and more balance, how to be more mindful, caring and compassionate towards ourselves and others. The imperative to take care of oneself is a response to the experience of a growing care deficit in society.

There are a number of understandable and interlocking social and economic reasons for the turn to self-care in attempts to find coping mechanisms for the present predicament. First – and most simply – people cannot keep going for ever without the chance to replenish their physical and mental resources. Second, the very caring resources required to replenish are being constantly drained. Third, the neoliberal promise that hard work and investment in the project will yield fruit has been dramatically undermined for large swathes of the population, if indeed it ever held. Nonetheless, we are currently witnessing the integration of self-care into a crisis management strategy addressing the consequences of an overdrive of those aspiring or compelled to be good neoliberal subjects. Self-care is now supposed to act as a bulwark against the burnout and exhaustion that result from the endless imperatives to achieve more, better, faster, amid the erosion of work–life boundaries. Women who care too much are also supposed to develop better strategies to protect themselves from 'overgiving' as a result of consistently carrying the burden of care for others, in a society predicated on self-improvement and self-actualisation. Even in the healthcare system, suggestions for better self-care have become part of standard advice.[40]

Self-care obfuscates the structural causes of societal problems: if you're not coping, it's your fault. You try to change your attitudes, routines, habits and outlooks on life in order to be better adapted, thereby losing sight of the social, economic and political forces that shape the conditions under which you broach the challenges you feel you face. Self-care casts problems as just another opportunity for personal growth. Self-care suggests that if you help yourself, then everyone will be helped.

The promotion of this kind of sense of self puts personal responsibility centre-stage and is a kind of care fix that privatises the responsibility for care. Self-care thereby becomes a way of trying to take back control and continue to cope. In the face of experiences of stress and burnout there is an encouragement to engage in what sociologist Stefanie Graefe calls a

> retroactive coping with or proactive prevention of exhaustion [leaving] no sphere of life untouched: be a competent manager of your own resources, anticipate your breaking points, engage in regular exercising, take in fresh and wholesome food, nurture relationships, engage in civic life, but moderately and in line with your own values.[41]

In the face of a crumbling public and collective healthcare system and growing care inequalities; in a world that feels complex and complicated at a time when structural change seems beyond reach, self-care becomes a way to manage that inserts itself into the entrainments of financialised capitalism.

Against Self-Care Solutionism

It is evident that the rise of self-care has created a huge consumer market, another facet of the wellness syndrome and the prerogative of privilege, thereby easily delinked from the social relations individuals exist within. Nonetheless, the idea of self-care really stems from progressive and radical impulses. Within professions that involve care for others, such as nursing, therapy or social work, self-care practices are crucial to avoiding compassion fatigue, burnout and exhaustion. Self-care practices redirect care away from the sole focus on others and towards protecting oneself so as not to be used up in the attempts to help others – whether one wants to help, has an obligation to help or is paid to help. Providing care under duress or in particularly difficult or precarious working conditions necessarily impacts on a person's ability to care, but also on their ability to maintain positive perceptions of self-worth.[42] For example, someone experiencing compassion fatigue will start to feel overwhelmed and overexposed, like they are running on empty. This intensifies when they have been working under conditions that do not provide them with support and respite in order to replenish their caring capacities. They start to feel drained, are tired all the time and the smallest of tasks feels overwhelming. They feel they cannot cope and they start to blame themselves. The more someone blames themselves and the more it feels like there's no change in sight, the more despair they feel. When the situation seems hopeless, insomnia and depression can result.[43] Care workers need stable and nurturing conditions from within which to provide care. This means maintaining physical health, having stability in one's life and the social support of companionship, encouragement, advice, and aid within a safe and secure working environment. Clearly, self-care has to be embedded in adequate structural conditions for caring and not be instrumentalised as a substitute for them.

Self-care practices don't have to be reduced to detached or marketised self-orientated practices; they can involve setting up supportive networks that are not separate from the endeavour of making sense of the social structures and unequal power relations that we exist within. Linking our personal situations to the broader context, we can make connections between our experiences that are located within the political and economic structures that produce the problems as *social* problems. This was the foundation of the feminist affirmation that 'the personal is political'.[44] Indeed, those engaged in social and environmental justice movements know that caring too much about the cause without being attentive to one's own wellbeing, especially when struggling against the odds, can be detrimental not only to health, but to the ability to stay involved in political activism in the longer term and not burn out.[45]

When, in 1988, Black feminist Audre Lorde penned the much-quoted line 'caring for myself is not self-indulgence, it is self-preservation and that is an act of political warfare', she was insisting that self-care was profoundly political in the struggle for both survival and to bring about real social change.[46] With this, Audre Lorde positioned the need to take care of oneself and value oneself against the ways in the livelihoods of people considered unwanted or unneeded are made impossible. When you regularly experience violence and degradation, attacks on your self-esteem and your sense of self-worth, taking care of yourself is an act of resistance. It is about valuing yourself in the face of repeated societal messages that who you are, what you do or how you wish to live, has no value. It is a way of pushing the internalised oppression back out, and it is a way of supporting yourself and others facing similar injustices when there is very little outside support. At a time when precarious employment seeks to demand more and more flexibility and the logic of profit and competition demands our permanent strive to improve, accepting ourselves as who we are, just as we are, is an act of political resistance, as disability rights activist and comedienne Francesca Martinez has insisted.[47] Thus, self-care is not simply privilege and self-indulgence, especially to those who have less social privilege and whose self-esteem is constantly undermined by society.[48] Self-care actually has more radical roots in approaches that seek to protect the welfare of those on whom a disproportionate burden of care is placed, have to care for others or for whom society does not care adequately.

At the same time, the utility of self-care has been inserted into a consumer culture as the political impetus of self-care travels across hierarchies of privilege, including ethnicity and migration status, able-bodiedness or class. The language of self-care exudes a kind of tactical polyvalence (a term used by philosopher Michel Foucault to explain how words have different meanings and can be used for quite contrary objectives in different social contexts) that in turn risks making invisible the claim that Audre Lorde intended to stake out: that some lives matter more than others and that for those whose lives have less value, survival is in itself an act of resistance against the destruction of that life and the forms in which it is lived.[49] While self-care has been posited as a possible path of resistance against capitalism – and in particular a way for those carers who spend a disproportionate amount of their time concerned with the care of others – self-care becomes an exceptionally privileged advantage of having the time and means to be concerned with oneself in such an extensive way. Who gets to have a self, fashion a self, assert a self? Indeed, who does the work of helping others to have a self?

The point is not to play self-care off against caring about others. Indeed, our lives are a constant negotiation between the need for connection and the need for autonomy. Being caught up in self-referentiality and lacking empathy is problematic; as is being overly concerned with serving the needs and wishes of others. Yet, the emphasis on personal responsibility that underpins many current conceptions of self-care calls on us each to take good care of ourselves by strengthening our personal capacities to cope with what life throws at us. This disregards both the interdependence of social relationships and the reality of structural inequalities that determine societal access to care as well as the distribution of care work. Caring is an important component of social life. Practices of self-care are not always already co-opted or neurotic. They don't always simply reproduce the existing order, nor are they always exploited by capitalism. However, the ability to care for ourselves and one another *is* dependent on adequate social, economic and political conditions. The question is how to create the conditions for better care for all.

Conclusion

Escaping the Care Fix

The care crisis is everywhere. In the wake of austerity and against the backdrop of the failures of privatisation, overstretched and underfunded public services have left people in the lurch. Expensive childcare exposes the limits of a dual earner model for households, and it is still women who are doing much of this care work. Care workers are overburdened and underpaid. Demographic changes affect care, too. An ageing population means more people live longer and with complex care needs. Many elderly people are already not receiving the care they need. Mobility and migration mean we want care infrastructures to be adaptable to change. Vulnerable populations such as single mothers, people with disabilities, refugees or the long-term unemployed are affected most when benefits and services are cut. But vulnerability is not an inherent or inevitable characteristic of any of these populations: it is a function of the disadvantages of structural inequality and neglect that need not be that way. Stress, burnout and a rise in mental health issues, including among children, are definite causes for concern. The flipside is a burgeoning wellbeing industry, ready to diagnose an infinite range of conditions while offering the concomitant solutions at a hefty price. The care crisis does not affect everyone in the same way, whether locally or globally. But societies that systematically erode their care infrastructures cannot thrive in the long term. The coronavirus crisis has been a painful lesson in this regard.

Charting a Way Out

As the world becomes seemingly more uncaring, the calls for people to be more compassionate and empathetic towards one another – in short, to care more – grow louder. But the work of caring never stopped, even as it is done under increasingly difficult conditions. What is more, compassion is all too quickly mobilised to plaster over an enduring crisis of care. The deep and multi-faceted crises of our time will not be addressed by simply (re)instilling the virtues of empathy. We are stuck in a *perpetuum mobile* of care fixes that cannot solve the underlying care crisis in any sustainable way, instead merely displacing it. From the frantic caring of the new clean living to the abandonment of those who are of no interest to financial services or conspicuous consumption, except where the abandoned can be financialised; from the overburdening of some people with care duties while others go carefree, to the exploitation of care workers whose already tenuous situations are made worse as care is further marketised and more jobs are casualised; from the instrumentalisation of compassion in the interests of keeping everything going; to the many general appeals for more empathy and compassion as a solution to society's woes: our present is a system that emphasises personal responsibility while expanding the opportunities for marketisation and financialisation that are premised on precariousness and the perpetuation of unequal burdens of care work and unequal access to care. How do we escape the toxic mix of problems that characterise the current care crisis and the short-term fixes that entrench division and need?

Yes, we need to care better for each other. The central question is how to do so in more sustained and sustainable ways. However, this is not a goal that can be achieved by trying to harmonise compassion with markets, nor will simple earnest calls for everyone to care more and be considerate of others be enough to effect real change. Instead there must be a transformation of the structural conditions for care. This will only happen if care has a different status and is organised differently, not just as a feeling or a way of behaving, but rather as a social and material practice – at the level of institutions and the everyday.

One response to the growing care crisis is to expand the care economy. There is an expectation that the rise in the demand for care, whether arising from demographic changes, such as an ageing population, or social changes, such as a larger female labour force, will result in the market for care getting bigger. The dynamic of growth and expansion that characterises capitalist economies drives a process of ever-increasing commodification. In the search for new investment opportunities, new areas of social life are brought into markets, including financial markets. The realm of care is no exception. However, turning care into a commodity soon comes up against limits, because care is not infinitely rationalisable and productivity gains are few. Thus, care can only be mass-marketed in limited ways. If these dynamics are left to their own devices, there is a deterioration of standards of care, of wages and of working conditions for carers. If anything, care becomes a luxury commodity for those willing and able to pay lots of money; alternatively, profits for care providers have to be subsidised by the state. In other words, valorising care in this way actually involves a systematic devaluation of care in order to extract surplus value. Moreover, the idea of cost saving – whether to facilitate wealth extraction or whether to operate under conditions of austerity – means that reserve capacities are depleted. This makes the care infrastructure fragile and vulnerable to unexpected events like the coronavirus pandemic.[1]

Public investment in the care economy can further economic growth by enabling greater female participation in the labour market. In this more progressive model, tax receipts generated by economic growth pay for expanded social infrastructure.[2] In countries such as Britain and the US the conventional wisdom of the post-war era has been that economic growth benefits all:[3] we contribute our labour to the overall 'pie' of gross domestic product and in return receive the dividend of wages or access to publicly funded infrastructures. But the doctrine of economic growth rests on several untenable premises. It has never been true that economies can keep growing endlessly and that everyone will thereby be cared for. When we consider how women's unpaid and invisibile caring and reproductive labour in homes and communities underwrote the productive capacities of workers, this is unambiguous. As more women have entered the labour force without a significant transformation of the sexual division of labour, this reproductive resource has been depleted.[4] Further, economic growth does not automatically lead to its equitable distribution, as the stark increases in economic inequality and wealth concentration show. According to a recent Oxfam report, between 2011 and 2017 average wages rose by 3 per cent while dividends to wealthy shareholders rose by 31 per cent in advanced economies.[5] Colonial and neocolonial initiatives have spurred the exploitation of land, labour and resources from countries in the Global South and severely decreased sustainable livelihoods for their populations. The planet's ecological limits urgently demand a different economic model; climate change and environmental destruction can no longer be ignored. But if care cannot solve the problems of capitalism, capitalism is indeed preventing us from solving the problems of care. Ending the care crisis means transforming the conditions for caring. To do so requires fundamentally rethinking how to value care.

Valuing Care

Following the Global Financial Crisis of 2008, governments bailed out many banks and businesses that were deemed systemically indispensable. The COVID-19 pandemic has challenged the criteria of just who or what the system needs, and the workers who keep life going have received much more attention. Many people went out on their doorsteps to 'clap for our carers' every week.[6] This ignited a debate over whether or how such symbolic appreciation could evolve into the greater valuing of healthcare workers, and of *all* carers.[7]

Feminist scholars, activists and practitioners have long demanded the transformation of societal responsibilities for caring. Truly valuing care will mean allocating more time, money and societal capacities to it. It will also mean elevating care's undervalued political and ethical status in our everyday attitudes and practices and in their underlying objectives. Because care is not regulated by one domain but is influenced by state and market policies and public and private motives, and because it entails paid and unpaid labour, creating change will require rethinking care in the household, the workplace and beyond – in relation to one another and as mediated by the state. Truly valuing care means having time for unpaid caring in our everyday lives and publicly funding a care infrastructure with well-paid care work. Taken together, the two strategies could form the basis for ending the care crisis.

Care for All

Care is not a luxury good. Everyone needs to be cared for and everyone needs access to care, although not everyone has the same needs. An effective care infrastructure cannot be built on personal responsibility – not everyone is able to care for themselves. No one should be left without care because they have no one to care for them; nor should access to care be based solely on whether someone happens to like someone else, acts out of charity, or acquires a sense of responsibility through kinship. So, there need to be universal guarantees in place that all people will be entitled to care. This calls for a capacious understanding of care that recognises diversity and is sensitive to different needs in enabling and empowering ways.

Effective and inclusive care requires a collective social infrastructure based on risk-pooling. We must expand publicly funded childcare, mental healthcare, adult social care and eldercare through a progressive reform of the tax system – which should include regulating against offshoring and tax evasion. For example, a number of proposals (including costings) exist already that call for the establishment of a National Care Service. They include suggestions for local authorities to design and deliver free services directly, instead of issuing personal budgets for the individual purchase of marketised services, or the commissioning of services from private providers. This can involve bringing services back in-house, as well as publicly funding new and innovative models for care.[8]

Definancialise Care

Valuing care means allocating resources, not taking them away. There is an urgent need to dismantle the apparatus that allows private wealth extraction from society's care structures, so that any new funds made available for the public care infrastructures do not simply prop up profits. Care needs to be shielded from the volatilities of financial markets, not be drawn deeper into them. Therefore, the realms of care should not be available to high-risk forms of financial investment, including private equity and debt-based forms of financial engineering, where expectations of high returns on capital are upheld at the expense of quality of employment and quality of care. Nor should public services and the care sector be exposed to free trade agreements that undermine labour, consumer and environmental protections.[9] This is a pressing issue in the wake of Britain's departure from the European Union.

With the rise of entrepreneurial approaches to social change coupled with the social turn of finance, local community attempts to organise care in new kinds of collectives, networks and cooperatives also risk serving as fields of experimentation for the development of new kinds of financial business models. Such developments merely deepen our dependency on finance as a mode of accumulation and as a form of social organisation, and our exposure to the volatility of global financial markets that comes with it. We should proceed with caution when encouraging micro-lending, crowdfunding or community shares, time banks or alternative currencies that become training grounds for the investor self and follow in the steps of asset-based community development, which is premised on the deeper penetration of free-market principles into the social fabric of communities.[10] We must conceive and practise different modes of valuing care than those that serve financial wealth extraction.

Care for Carers

Quality and safety of employment is a condition of the quality of care. Care work must be better paid, with better working conditions, better training, more resources and improved technological support that enables better caring. *All* care workers need secure employment conditions and adequate salaries that include sick pay, holiday pay and pay for overtime; provision for the materials and resources required; training and opportunities for further qualification and the time and means for exchange with co-workers.[11] This means an immediate end to zero-hour contracts and to the time pressures that many care workers face, so that the needs of care workers and those cared for are centre-stage. For example, the Ethical Charter developed by the trade union UNISON proposes standards for homecare to which commissioning bodies can sign up, thereby committing to ensuring better pay and working conditions for care workers, as opposed to the race to the bottom in the competitive service economy.[12]

Care workers are experts. Their experience, knowledge and skill are crucial to designing and developing better care infrastructures that give care workers more control over their work. This requires a real democratisation of workplaces and a voice for care workers. There should be more equal consideration of the needs of those who care and those who are cared for through the establishment of a common ground between everyone involved in the process of caring, from professional and informal carers, the cared-for and their friends and relatives. Collaboration between professional care workers, care recipients and informal carers should be encouraged, recognising that care is not merely a service that is provided and consumed, but something that is necessarily collaborative and co-produced.[13]

Worker-owned cooperatives or other self-managed organisations affiliated to trade unions that collaborate with local authorities could also be part of this model.[14] *Buurtzorg* (Dutch for 'neighbourhood care') in the Netherlands is one example of an effective organisation that has garnered international attention. *Buurtzorg* is a non-profit homecare organisation whose self-managed teams of nurses cooperate with their patients to enable them to live as independently as possible. Self-management puts the knowledge and expertise of care workers centre-stage, eliminating costly tiers of administrators. Nurses routinely carry out simple and more complex tasks, intentionally subverting hierarchies of expertise.[15] *Buurtzorg* is one example of bottom-up innovation making care more effective and resource-efficient without cutting corners or lowering standards.

Time to Care

The existing care infrastructure must be expanded so that all people have access to the expertise and skill of professional care workers, and so that those workers are better supported. However, not all care work can or should be undertaken by professionals. Caring for ourselves and for each other remains a crucial aspect of social life and an important element of what gives our lives meaning and purpose. But caring for ourselves and each other and redistributing care requires having more time to do so, which means reclaiming time from waged work.

There is a long-standing debate in feminist movements as to whether this time for caring should be compensated for in some way.[16] These debates have produced at least three demands: the demand for unpaid reproductive labour to be acknowledged as 'productive' and thus factored in measures of GDP; the demand for the cost of care and social reproduction to be met by public investment in infrastructures such as childcare, education, healthcare, eldercare and community services;[17] and the demand for remuneration to support the undertaking of this work in an unpaid capacity. Remuneration can be indirect, as entitlements to a pension, sick pay and other kinds of welfare and social security payments. Remuneration can also be direct in the form of income subsidies; the Carer's Allowance in the UK, paid leave for care, or even something much more radical, like a Universal Basic Income, or a reduction in hours spent in employment at the same level of pay. These are all ways of collectively making time for the unpaid work of caring.

The international Wages for Housework campaign began in the early 1970s in countries that included Italy, the UK, Germany and the US, and was particularly active until the mid 1980s (with some groups existing to this day).[18] Campaigners demanded wages for the work women were doing and fought to render the home and community visible as sites of labour and unpaid sources of wealth production. The demand for wages for housework – not wages for house*workers* – was not a bid to reiterate that a woman's place was in the home. Rather it sought to challenge the roles assigned to women and thus to *de-gender* the social division of labour, not simply for the sake of greater equality between the sexes, but as a crucial step in bringing about an altogether different kind of society. The demand for a wage for all the unpaid reproductive and care work undertaken in the home was only partly about the money: it was to show that women's reproductive labour was not remunerated by capital because it was a key source of its surplus. The point was to liberate reproductive activities from their orientation towards capital's needs and demands and highlight that capitalism *cannot*, in fact, fully pay for all this work. Drawing attention to the capitalist exploitation of social reproduction demonstrates that unpaid reproductive and care workers are *already* working and staking a claim to the social wealth already produced. In the same way that the demand for 'wages for housework' was not simply about paying women to be housewives and mothers, so too today's demands for a Universal Basic Income cannot simply be about enduring the status quo while receiving an income for doing so.

The more we can collectively address and satisfy our care needs, the less we have to earn to pay for care or other compensatory goods and services – goods and services that promise freedom from reliance on other people but which require more and more money to buy them. Completing the vicious circle, these are often aimed at optimising our waged work productivity. Care has been conceptualised and organised to enable us all to do more waged work; once we relinquish that idea, we can explore other possibilities. From this perspective, caring for each other is a resource that builds our capacities to live well and reduce precariousness. Instead of producing ever more for the market, can we envisage radically different ways of distributing time and resources?

Care in Common

I used to visit my grandmother in a care home. I did so even though her dementia meant that she did not know it was me, her granddaughter. I was just a nice person who sat with her, if her comprehension even went that far. My nan had no concept of a granddaughter who loved her. Yet, she still had sensation in her body. She could still see (although I didn't know how clearly). She could still feel someone caressing her. She could still hear someone speaking soothing words. Even if she could not conceptualise such sensations in the abstract, she could experience them in their immediate effects – a hand, a touch, a smile, a kiss, a reassurance. She could still perceive presence. In this case, our family ties were the condition of my visit, but they were not what really mattered. What mattered was my *presence*. And if I could be a caring presence for my nan, there was no reason why I could not be that for others, too. This prompts the question: what commitments to one another can we have beyond those based on familiarity or familial ties? How do we forge new commitments? Caring for people who cannot care for themselves should not be a personal, familial responsibility, but the responsibility of everyone in proximity.

With or without a welfare state and public services, modern economies have hitherto relied heavily on the family for their functioning. Even with some dilution (and queering) of this model, it is still the case that the family remains the basic unit of informal care in society. Nonetheless, this reliance on the family is fraying. Not only women are overburdened – dual-earner partners are equally exhausted, even when the care work is shared. Moreover, increased mobility has meant that family members often live apart and at a distance and cannot easily care for one another. What could our commitments to caring for one another look like beyond the heteronormative nuclear family and the imperatives of kinship? Broadening the responsibility for care beyond the family and extending our care networks means involving more people and being creative about caring arrangements – not as the kinds of fleeting transactions promoted by financialised capitalism and digital platforms, where we put each other to work to satisfy what we think it is that we need, outsourcing the satisfaction of fragments of need to different people, who become interchangeable or connective nodes in an endless network of immanent experiences. Rather, as efforts premised on inventing and sustaining new ways of 'commoning' care where we live and work, as the Care Collective has advocated.[19]

A 'commons' is a resource that is open-access and can be shared by all, unlike both private property and public ownership or management. Open-source software is an often-cited example of a contemporary commons. Something that is held in common means that access to it is universal, not organised on the basis of hierarchies, and decision-making over its governance is participatory. Common*ing* refers to the practice of doing something in common with others in which the production, consumption and distribution of a social good (such as care) is based on the real and sustained social interaction through which commitments are forged.[20] This also means recognising – giving space and time to – the affective and emotional labour that is needed to maintain relationships.

As the care crisis has intensified, including during the COVID-19 pandemic, people have pooled their capacities and resources in local networks of mutual aid, care cooperatives or collectives and found ways to share informal caring for children, the elderly, those with disabilities or those who are unwell in their local communities or shared networks.[21] Some of them draw on practices of self-help and self-organisation developed in radical and progressive social movements. Others get together in their neighbourhoods or in online communities and simply find ways to help each other. Further examples include projects aimed at building housing that allows for intergenerational living and caring for one another, or initiatives to integrate care homes and nurseries. There is much potential to build on and develop here. At the same time, such efforts to collectivise and prefigure care in more generative, inclusive and meaningful ways can be turned against the commons – instrumentalised to plug gaps in public provision, maintain exclusion or privilege and thereby reproduce inequalities. Therefore, developing collective forms of care and reproduction means challenging and transforming existing social and cultural divisions and hierarchies – whether class, ethnicity, gender, age or geographical location – and the relationships of power and inequality that shape them. This is, of course, easily written in the abstract. In practice it involves efforts to engage across difference, which will not always be without conflict.

Democratise Care

A collective infrastructure for care requires institutions that can organise and allocate the necessary resources. One such institution is the welfare state. Anyone seeking progressive change will be ambivalent about the welfare state. Is it the culmination of hard-won social rights fought for by successive social movements? Or is it the material manifestation of co-option, a tool to both discipline and deter struggles for a better world? Can a welfare system so intricately bound up with the developments of industrialised capitalism be anything but the latter? What might an emancipatory version look like? Service user and disability rights movements give us a cautionary perspective on the welfare state, immunising against nostalgia and rose-tinted views forgetful of the realities of exclusion, punishment and abandonment that have been all too pervasive. Scholar-activist Peter Beresford notes that a lack of political participation has been a feature of the welfare state since its inception. This placed the general population in a passive role as recipients of assistance, precluding a real sense of ownership and active involvement in a direct democratic process.[22] Also excluded were the voices of the caring and the cared for.

In her book, *Caring Democracy*, the political theorist Joan Tronto argues that 'democratic politics should centre upon assigning responsibilities for care and for ensuring that democratic citizens are as capable as possible of participating in the assignment of responsibilities.'[23] A caring democracy would thus not simply be about changing forms of political representation or who represents us, but rather about changing the very way that we conduct politics and what themes we foreground.[24] The question of democracy is not merely one of the negotiation of interests, nor is it simply about participation; rather it pertains equally to the *scope* and *processes* of, as well as *access* to, democratic decision-making, hand in hand with the ethical values that underpin it.

How can we avoid an overly bureaucratic, unwieldly and top-down state? A principle of subsidiarity makes more sense. Much of social and community care in Britain is already administered at the level of local authorities. Here there is scope for greater democratisation, for example through an assembly format that enables the political participation of everyone who lives in a municipality (whether permanently or temporarily) and is involved with providing or receiving care and tailoring this to the needs and wishes of the local population, as put forward by the Foundational Economy Collective.[25]

A complementary consideration is that of the necessary

transformation of public institutions towards alternative models of ownership based on alternative modes of valuing care. Remunicipalisation movements in Europe and elsewhere have sought to reverse privatisation and bring services back into the public hands of municipalities and local authorities. Key to these initiatives has been the elimination of the profit motive and the rollback of corporate control over key utilities, especially where this has had detrimental effects on universal access, quality of service provision and costs. Remunicipalisation seeks to devise alternative ownership, access and decision-making models that are not orientated towards financial profit.[26] Utilities are placed under the democratic control of the municipality, allowing residents to develop socially and ecologically sustainable models that foster equity and solidarity, while guaranteeing workers' rights and access for all.[27] Remunicipalisation movements assert control over resources such as water and energy, and engage in a range of care-related services, from nursery schools, childcare, and school catering, to cleaning, public parks and sports.[28] There is scope for the principles of municipalism to be extrapolated from physical infrastructures to social infrastructures, without abandoning local authorities under the premise of decentralisation and empowerment, as has been the case with the extensive cuts to local government funding over the last decade of austerity in Britain. Scholar-activists Keir Milburn and Bertie Russell have sought to think about the combination of alternative ownership models and democratisation under the banner of 'public–commons partnerships,' a tool with which to imagine an alternative to hitherto public–private partnerships.[29] A form of 'care municipalism' based on public funds and non-profit ownership models could offer a democratic locale for the negotiation of participation, ownership and the allocation of resources, without the dangers of exclusivity that are hazards of small, self-selecting collectives.

Putting Care in Its Place

Ending the care crisis will require a profound shift in mentalities. It will require an agreement to allocate far more societal resources – means, time and capacities – to care. Considerable political will is needed to put the issue of care at the forefront of what we do, whether in our relationships, communities, neighbourhoods, workplaces or politics. This does not mean making caring the guiding principle of all conduct, or positing caring as the solution to all woes. But it does mean giving care a prominent place as a structural condition of our lives. I know that invoking an all-inclusive 'we' is perilous: it is easy to fall into the trap of seeking to produce the most general agreement possible among disparate forces whose interests may well be counterposed. Moreover, to speak from the position of 'we' is often to suggest a bird's-eye view where the perspective may well be much narrower. The question of who this 'we' may include is inseparable from the social and political conflicts of our present that ensue from deepening inequalities, racism and rising nationalisms. However, some kind of 'we' built on inclusive solidarity is necessary to achieve change. There is no stand-alone answer, no neat policy proposal, no technocratic solution to the crisis of care, and what I have sketched out here is intended as a contribution to the developing conversation. A growing movement to end the care crisis is currently demanding that care work and the labour of social reproduction be 'recognised, reduced and redistributed', while ensuring decent pay and working conditions in the care sector.[30] These are key demands. However, to escape incessant care fixes and end the care crisis, we must reclaim the means to care from the prerogatives of profitability and put better ways of valuing care into practice.

Acknowledgements

This book would not exist without my editor Rosie Warren who accompanied the process from the beginning with patience and brilliance. Leo Hollis and everyone at Verso made the book possible. I am especially indebted to a number of people who either helped with aspects of the interviews, pointed me to important texts, provided background information or commented on work-in-progress: Donatella Alessandrini, Maria Backhouse, Ulrich Brand, Maaike Engelen, Dawn Foster, Stefanie Graefe, Carly Guest, Tine Haubner, Amy Horton, Susan Kelly, Vivian Latinwo-Olajide, Ed Lewis, Jo Littler, Marianne Maeckelbergh, Mike Rafferty, Malcolm Richardson, Greg Ryan, Johan Siebers and Dexter Whitfield. Tammy Mayr-Segal and Domi Mayr let me use their apartment to write and were always so enthusiastic, as were Anando, Pia and my sister. Tilman Reitz provided intellectual insight and unwavering support with infinite generosity.

My sincerest gratitude to you all.

Finally, a heartfelt thank you to everyone who shared their stories with me. The responsibility for my argument and for any errors remains entirely my own.

Notes

Introduction

1 P. Beresford, 'From "Vulnerable" to Vanguard: Challenging the Coalition', *Soundings* (2012), pp. 46–57.

2 J. Elias et al., 'Towards a New Deal for Care and Carers', Report of the PSA Commission on Care (2016), commissiononcare.org.

3 R. Loopstra and D. Lalor, *Financial Insecurity, Food Insecurity, and Disability: The Profile of People Receiving Emergency Food Assistance from The Trussell Trust Foodbank Network in Britain*, The Trussell Trust, June 2017.

4 UK Government Office for Science: *Foresight Future*, Final Project Report, London: The Government Office for Science (2013), p. 2.

5 Care Quality Commission: *The State of Healthcare and Adult Social Care in England 2018/2019*, Crown Copyright (2019), p. 7.

6 Ibid., p. 14, citing the Local Government Association.

7 Ibid.

8 S. Clarke (ed.), *Brexit Britain: Reshaping the Nation's Labour Market*, London: Resolution Foundation (2017), p. 10.

9 Bessa et al., 'The National Minimum Wage, Earnings and Hours in the Domiciliary Care Sector', University of Leeds/UK Government Low Pay Commission Research (2013), pp. 21, 31.

10 Chartered Institute for Personnel Development, *Zero Hours and Short Hours Contracts in the UK: Employer and Employee Perspectives*, Policy Report, London: CIPD (2015), p. 40.

11 A. Sparrow, 'Junior Doctors' Strike: BMA "Totally Irresponsible", Says Jeremy Hunt', *Guardian*, 7 February 2016.

12 G. Plimmer, 'Britain's Biggest Care Homes Rack Up Debts of £40,000 a Bed', *Financial Times*, 14 July 2019.

13 See also D. Whitfield, *Public Alternative to the Privatisation of Life*, Nottingham: Spokesman Books (2020), esp. pp. 30, 48–51, 152.

14 L. Bernaria, G. Berik, M. Floro, *Gender, Development and Globalisation: Economics as if all People Mattered*, London: Routledge (2015), 2nd edition, p. 104.

15 International Labour Organisation, *Care Work and Care Jobs for the Future of Decent Work*, Geneva: ILO (2018), p. xxix.

16 F. Williams, 'Towards a Transnational Analysis of the Political Economy of Care', in R. Mahon and F. Williamson (eds), *Feminist Ethics and Social Policy: Towards a New Global Political Economy of Care*, Vancouver: University of British Columbia Press (2012), pp. 21–38, 30.

17 UN Refugee Agency: *Global Trends: Forced Displacement in 2016*, Geneva: United Nations High Commissioner for Refugees (2017), unhcr.org.

18 A. Travis, 'Migrant Rescue Operations Must Be Stopped at Earliest Opportunity – Minister', *Guardian*, 30 October 2014.

19 L. Povlika, 'Women and the Crisis of Care in the United States', *Generations* 41(4) (2018): 29–35.

20 M. Benasayag and G. Schmit, *Les Passions Tristes. Souffrance Psychique et Crise Sociale* [*Sad Passions: Psychic Suffering and Social Crisis*], Paris: La Découverte (2006).

21 M. Wieviorka, 'Financial Crisis or Societal Meltdown?' in M. Castells, J. Caraça and G. Cardoso (eds), *Aftermath: The Cultures of the Economic Crisis*, Oxford: Oxford University Press (2012), pp. 82–103, 95 f.

22 G. Plimmer and P. Clark, 'Inside UK Care Homes: Why the System Is Failing Its Coronavirus Test', *Financial Times*, 24 April 2020.

23 L. Platt and R. Warwick, 'Are Some Ethnic Groups More Vulnerable to COVID-19 than Others?' Institute for Fiscal Studies, 1 May 2020.

24 S. Long, 'Coronavirus Pandemic Exposes Fatal Flaws of the "Just-In-Time" Economy', ABC News, 1 May 2020.

25 P. Mirowksi, *Never Let a Serious Crisis Go to Waste: How Neoliberalism Survived the Financial Meltdown*, London/New York: Verso (2013).

26 J. Coleman, 'Greek Bailout Talks: Are Stereotypes of Lazy Greeks True?' BBC News online, 10 March 2015, bbc.com.

27 Interview with journalist Douglas Keay published in the magazine *Woman's Own*, 23 September 1987, archived online by the Margaret Thatcher Foundation; available at margaretthatcher. org.

28 G. Becker, *Human Capital: A Theoretical and Empirical Analysis, With Special Reference to Education*, Chicago: University of Chicago Press (1993).

29 In the US: N. Folbre, 'Demanding Quality: Worker/Consumer Coalitions and "High-Road" Strategies in the Care Sector', *Politics and Society* 34(1) (2006): 11–31; in the UK: S. Rai, C. Hoskyns

and D. Thomas, 'Depletion: The Cost of Social Reproduction', *International Feminist Journal of Politics* 16(1) (2013): 86–105.

30 Office for National Statistics, *Population Estimates by Output Areas, Electoral, Health and Other Geographies, England and Wales: mid-2018* (2019), ons.gov.uk.

31 OECD, *Labour Force Participation by Sex and Age*, stats.oecd.org [accessed 12 May 2020].

32 C. Morini, 'The Feminisation of Labour in Cognitive Capitalism', *Feminist Review* 87(1) (2007): 40–59.

33 A. Hochschild and A. Machung, *The Second Shift*, London/New York: Penguin (1983/2003), and N. Gerstel, 'The Third Shift: Gender and Care Work Outside the Home', *Qualitative Sociology* 23(4) (2000): 467–83.

34 N. Fraser, 'Contradictions of Capital and Care', *New Left Review* 100 (2016): 99–117, p. 103.

35 M. O'Hara, *Austerity Bites: A Journey to the Sharp End of the Cuts in the UK*, Bristol: Policy Press (2015), p. 265.

36 A. Chakraborty, 'How Far Does Cameron Want to Shrink the State? Ask Barnet's Binmen', *Guardian*, 1 June 2015.

37 Migration Advisory Committee, *EEA Migration in the UK: Final Report*, London: Migration Advisory Committee (2018), p. 71.

38 B. Silver, *Forces of Labour: Workers' Movements and Globalization Since 1870*, Cambridge: Cambridge University Press (2012), p. 120.

39 A. Hochschild, 'Global Care Chains and Emotional Surplus Value', in A. Giddens and W. Hutton (eds), *On the Edge: Living with Global Capitalism*, London: Jonathan Cape (2000), pp. 130–46.

40 C. Rottenberg, *The Rise of Neoliberal Feminism*, Oxford: Oxford University Press (2018).

41 Hochschild, 'Global Care Chains and Emotional Surplus Value'.

42 C. Wichterich, *Care Extractivism and the Reconfiguration of Social Reproduction in Post-Fordist Economies*, ICDD Working Papers, Kassel: International Center for Development and Decent Work (2019).

43 D. Harvey, 'The Geography of Capitalist Accumulation: A Reconstruction of the Marxian Theory', *Antipode Journal of Radical Geography* 2 (1975): 9–21 and D. Harvey, *The Limits to Capital*, Oxford: Oxford University Press (1982); Silver, *Forces of Labour*.

44 Fraser, 'Contradictions of Capital and Care', 112.

45 Association of Directors of Adult Social Services, *Budget Survey 2019*, adass.org.uk, p. 31.

1. What Is Care?

1 B. Fisher and J. Tronto, 'Toward a Feminist Theory of Caring', in E. Abel and M. Nelson (eds), *Circles of Care: Work, Identity and Women's Lives*, New York: New York State University Press (1990), pp. 35–62, 40; cf. P. England and N. Folbre, 'Emerging Theories of Care Work', *Annual Review of Sociology* 31 (2005): 381–99; cf. C. Wichterich, 'Reincarnation or Death of Neoliberalism? The Rise of Market Authoritarianism and its Challenges for Labour', XII GLU-Conference 2017, JNU, New Delhi.

2 E. Sammam et al., 'Women's Work: Mothers, Women and the Global Childcare Crisis', London: Overseas Development Institute (2016), p. 19.

3 Office for National Statistics, *Household Satellite Accounts 2005 to 2014* (2016), ons.gov.uk.

4 International Labour Organisation, *Care Work and Care Jobs for the Future of Decent Work*, Geneva: International Labour Office, ILO (2018), p. xxix.

5 Ibid.

6 Ibid.

7 Overseas Development Institute, 'Women's Work', pp. 23–5.

8 Eurofound European Quality of Life Survey (2016) cited in A. Manoudi et al., *An Analysis of Personal Household Services to Support Work-Life Balance for Working Parents and Carers (Synthesis Report, ECE Thematic Review 2018)*, European Commission Directorate Employment Social Affairs and Inclusion, April 2018, p. 14.

9 N. Folbre, 'The Care Penalty and Gender Inequality', in S. Averett, L. Argys and S. Hoffmann (eds), *The Oxford Handbook of Women and the Economy*, Oxford: Oxford University Press (2017), pp. 749–66.

10 International Labour Organisation, *Care Work and Care Jobs*, p. xxxv.

11 Ibid., p. xxxviii ff.

12 N. Folbre, '"Holding Hands at Midnight": The Paradox of Caring Labor', *Feminist Economics* 1(1) (1995): 73–92.

13 International Labour Organisation, *Care Work and Care Jobs*, p. xxxviii ff.

14 For further discussion, see S. Himmelweit, 'The Prospects for Caring: Economic Theory and Policy Analysis', *Cambridge Journal of Economics* 31(4) (2007): 581–99, 582.

15 D. Graeber, 'Caring Too Much: That's the Curse of the Working Classes', *Guardian*, 26 March 2014.

16 R. McGreevery, 'Charging for Toilets PR Stunt, Says Ryanair Boss', *Irish Times*, 7 March 2009.

17 V. Elmer, 'Inside the World of the Modern-Day Butler', *Fortune*, 4 March 2013.

18 Cf. D. Winnicott, *Playing and Reality*, London: Tavistock Books (1971).

19 On the phenomenon of 'mother-blaming' in relation to mental illness and learning difficulties, cf. I. Courcy and C. des Rivières, '"From Cause to Cure": A Qualitative Study on Contemporary Forms of Mother Blaming Experienced by Mothers of Young Children with Autism Spectrum Disorder', *Journal of Family Social Work*, 20(3) (2017): 233–50.

20 Care Quality Commission, *The State of Healthcare and Adult Social Care in England 2018/2019*, Crown Copyright (2019), p. 17.

21 See C. R. Figley, *Compassion Fatigue: Secondary Traumatic Stress from Treating the Traumatized*, New York: Bruner/Mazel (1995).

22 L. Raw, *Striking a Light: The Bryant and May Matchwomen and Their Place in History*, London: Bloomsbury Press (2011), p. 28.

23 E. Hobsbawm, *The Age of Extremes 1914–1991*, London: Abacus/ Time Warner Books UK (1994), pp. 257–87.

24 OECD, *Labour Force Participation by Sex and Age*, stats.oecd.org [accessed 12 May 2020].

25 A. Davis, *Women, Race and Class*, London/New York: Penguin (1982).

26 S. Federici, *Caliban and the Witch: Women, the Body and Primitive Accumulation*, Brooklyn, NY: Autonomedia (2001), p. 97.

27 Cf. C. Robinson, *Black Marxism: The Making of the Black Radical Tradition*, Chapel Hill, NC: UNC Press (1983).

28 S. Federici, *Revolution at Point Zero: Housework, Reproduction and Feminist Struggle*, Brooklyn, NY: Common Notions/PM Press (2012), p. 29.

29 Cf. P. Hill-Collins, *Black Feminist Thought*, London: Routledge (2008).

30 The term 'externalisation' is widely used within feminist theory to describe this process of offloading of costs, but also the effects of environmental pollution and damage to Global South countries. Federici, *Revolution at Point Zero*, p. 104. More recently, sociologist Stephan Lessenich has used the concept of 'externalisation' to designate the ways in which capitalist societies offload the social and environmental consequences of consumption, thereby perpetuating global inequalities. S. Lessenich, *Living Well at Others' Expense: The Hidden Costs of Western Prosperity*, Cambridge: Polity Press (2019).

31 K. Weeks, *The Problem with Work: Feminism, Marxism, Antiwork Politics and Postwork Imaginaries*, Durham, NC: Duke University Press (2011), p. 27.

32 Cf. J. Finch and D. Groves, *A Labour of Love: Women, Work and Caring*, London: Routledge and Kegan Paul Books (1983), p. 15.

33 A. Hochschild, *The Managed Heart – Commercialization of Human Feeling*, Berkeley: University of California Press (1983).

34 See also I. Bakker and S. Gill, 'Global Political Economy and Social Reproduction', in Bakker and Gill (eds), *Power, Production and Social Reproduction*, Basingstoke/New York: Palgrave MacMillan (2003), pp. 3–16.

35 P. Beresford, *All Our Welfare: Towards Participatory Social Policy*, Cambridge: Policy Press (2016), pp. 48 ff.

36 For an analysis of the male breadwinner model of welfare, see J. Lewis, 'Gender and the Development of Welfare Regimes', *Journal of European Social Policies* 2(3) (1992): 159–73.

37 N. Fraser and L. Gordon, 'A Genealogy of Dependency: Tracing a Keyword of the US Welfare State', *Signs* 19(2) (1994): 309–36.

38 M. Cooper, *Family Values: Between Neoliberalism and Social Conservatism*, Brooklyn, NY: Zone Books (2017).

39 P. Dunleavey and C. Hood, 'From Old Public Administration to New Public Management', *Public Money and Management* 14(3) (1994): 9–16, p. 9.

40 A. Batnitzky and L. McDowell, 'Migration, Nursing, Institutional Discrimination and Emotional/Affective Labour: Ethnicity and Labour Stratification in the UK National Health Service', *Social and Cultural Geography* 12(2) (2011): 181–201.

41 C. Kyriakedes and S. Virdee, 'Migrant Labour, Racism and the British National Health Service', *Ethnicity and Health* 8(4) (2010): 283–305; see also S. Beishon, S. Virdee and A. Hagell, *Nursing in a Multi-Ethnic NHS*, London: Policy Studies Institute (1995).

42 G. Bhambra, 'Colonial Global Economy: Towards a Theoretical Reorientation of Political Economy' (forthcoming).

43 Federici, *Caliban and the Witch*, p. 75; Finch and Groves, *A Labour of Love*; G. F. Dalla Costa, *The Work of Love: Unpaid Housework and Sexual Violence at the Dawn of the 21st Century*, New York/Brooklyn: Autonomedia (2008).

44 C. Wichterich, *Care Extractivism and the Reconfiguration of Social Reproduction in Post-Fordist Economies*, ICDD Working Papers, Kassel: International Center for Development and Decent Work (2019), p. 12.

45 P. Butler, 'Big Society Undermined by Cuts and Distrust, Says Study', *Guardian*, 7 May 2012.

46 Cf. P. Beresford, 'From "Vulnerable" to Vanguard: Challenging the

Coalition', in S. Davison and J. Rutherford (eds), *Welfare Reform: The Dread of Things to Come (Soundings)*, London: Lawrence Wishart (2012), pp. 66–77.

47 P. Beresford, *What Future for Care? Viewpoint Informing Debate*, York: Joseph Rowntree Foundation (2008), p. 9.

48 Ibid.

49 L. Piepzna-Samarasinha, *Care Work: Dreaming Disability Justice*, Vancouver: Arsenal Pulp Press (2018), p. 41.

50 M. Blyth, *Austerity: The History of a Dangerous Idea*, Oxford: Oxford University Press (2013), p. 2.

51 Oxfam, *The True Cost of Austerity and Inequality: UK Case Study* (2013), oxfam.org.

2. Paying for the Crisis

1 R. Martin, *Financialization of Daily Life*, Philadelphia: Temple University Press (2002), p. 105.

2 B. Jessop, 'The Heartlands of Neoliberalism and the Rise of the Austerity State', in S. Springer, K. Birch and J. MacLeavey (eds), *The Handbook of Neoliberalism*, London: Routledge (2017), pp. 410–21.

3 Ibid. For historical context, see T. Piketty, *Capital in the 21st Century*, Cambridge, MA: Harvard University Press (2013).

4 M. Blyth, *Austerity: The History of a Dangerous Idea*, Oxford: Oxford University Press (2013), p. 5.

5 T. Herndon, M. Ash and R. Pollin, 'Does High Public Debt Consistently Stifle Economic Growth? A Critique of Reinhart and Rogoff', *Cambridge Journal of Economics*, 38(2) (2014): 257–79; G. Osborne, 'A New Economic Model (Mais Lecture)', Cass Business School, 24 February 2010, archived at: conservative-speeches.sayit.mysociety.org.

6 J. Ostry, P. Loungani and D. Furceri, 'Neoliberalism: Oversold?' *Finance and Development* 53(2) (2016): 38–41.

7 P. Mirowski, *Never Let a Serious Crisis Go to Waste: How Neoliberalism Survived the Financial Meltdown*, London/New York: Verso Books (2013).

8 UK Government, *Spring Statement 2019: What You Need to Know*, 13 March 2019, archived at: gov.uk.

9 Institute for Fiscal Studies, *The September 2019 Spending Review: Austerity Ended, Or Perhaps Just Paused?* London: Institute for Fiscal Studies (2019), archived at: ifs.org.uk.

10 R. Crawford and B. Zaranko, *Tax Revenues and Spending on*

Social Security Benefits and Public Services Since the Crisis, London: Institute for Fiscal Studies (2019), pp. 6, 8.

11   S. Duffy, *Counting the Cuts*, London: Centre for Welfare Reform (2014), p. 5.

12   P. Butler, 'Welfare Spending for UK's Poorest Shrinks by £37bn', *Guardian*, 23 September 2018.

13   Local Government Association, *Local Government Spending: Moving the Conversation On*, London: Local Government Association (2018), p. 3.

14   B. Roantree and J. Shaw, 'What a Difference a Day Makes: Inequality and the Tax and Benefit System from a Long-Run Perspective', *Journal of Inequality* 6 (2018): 23–40, 38.

15   L. Antonucci, L. Horvath, Y. Kutiyski and A. Krouwel, 'The Malaise of the "Squeezed Middle" – Challenging the Narrative of the "Left-Behind Brexiter"', *Competition and Change* 21(3) (2017): 211–29.

16   S. Duffy and C. Gilberg, *Extreme Poverty in a Time of Austerity: Submission to UN Special Rapporteur on Extreme Poverty and Human Rights by the Centre for Welfare Reform*, Centre for Welfare Reform, 11 September 2018, p. 6.

17   Equality and Human Rights Commission, *The Cumulative Impact of Tax and Welfare Reforms* (2018), p. 23; for projections on child poverty, see Resolution Foundation, *Living Standards Outlook*, London: Resolution Foundation (2019), p. 4.

18   J. Ginn, 'Austerity and Inequality. Exploring the Impact of Cuts in the UK by Gender and Age', *Research on Ageing and Social Policy* 1(1) (2013): 28–53.

19   Runnymede Trust, *Intersecting Inequalities: The Impact of Austerity on Black and Minority Ethnic Women in the UK*, report by the Women's Budget Group, RECLAIM, Coventry Women's Voices and the Runnymede Trust, London: Runnymede Trust (2017), p. 4.

20   Joseph Rowntree Foundation, *UK Poverty 2019/2020*, York: Joseph Rowntree Foundation (2020), p. 25.

21   Ibid., p. 12; House of Commons Library, *Poverty in the UK: Statistics*, Briefing 7096, London: House of Commons, 5 September 2019. Figures are after housing costs.

22   House of Commons Library, *Poverty in the UK: Statistics*, p. 26.

23   Social Metrics Commission, *Measuring Poverty 2019*, London: Social Metrics Commission (2019), p. 32.

24   Equality and Human Rights Commission, *Cumulative Impact of Tax and Welfare Reforms*, p. 75.

25   Disability Benefits Consortium, quoted in F. Ryan, *Crippled: Austerity and the Demonisation of Disabled People*, London: Verso (2019), p. 18.

26 Institute for Fiscal Studies, *Living Standards, Poverty and Inequality in the UK: 2019*, London: Institute for Fiscal Studies (19 June 2019).

27 M. Oakley, *Independent Review of the Operation of Jobseeker's Allowance Sanctions Validated by the Jobseekers Act 2013*, London: Department for Work and Pensions (2014), cited in P. Taylor-Gooby, 'The Divisive Welfare State', *Social Policy and Administration* 50(6) (2016): 712–33, 722.

28 Equality and Human Rights Commission, *The Cumulative Impact of Tax and Welfare Reforms [Executive Summary]* (2018), p. 21.

29 Ibid., p. 22, emphasis added. The report also points out that 2018 and 2019 saw some increases to welfare, e.g. the Best Start Grant replacing Sure Start and an increase in Carers' Allowances, cf. p. 128.

30 J. Green and S. Lavery, 'The Regressive Recovery: Distribution, Inequality and State Power in Britain's Post-crisis Political Economy', *New Political Economy* 20(6) (2015): 894–923.

31 Taylor-Gooby, 'The Divisive Welfare State', 718. See also Office for National Statistics, *Poorest Households Spending More on VATable Items than in 1986* (2011), archived at webarchive.national archives.gov.uk, ons.gov.uk.

32 Ibid.

33 H. Miller, *What's Been Happening to Corporation Tax?* Briefing Note, 10 May 2017, Institute for Development Studies, archived at ifs.org.uk.

34 Ibid.

35 Ibid.

36 Runnymede Trust, *Intersecting Inequalities*.

37 Taylor-Gooby, 'The Divisive Welfare State', p. 719.

38 K. Farnsworth and Z. Irving, 'Austerity: More Than the Sum of Its Parts', in Farnsworth and Irving (eds), *Social Policy in Times of Austerity: Global Economic Crisis and the New Politics of Welfare*, Bristol: Policy Press (2015), p. 16.

39 Local Government Association, *Local Government Spending*, p. 3. This is a conservative figure. The Centre for Welfare Reform adjusts the figures for inflation and economic growth to propose that, in real terms, local government cuts amount to nearly 80 per cent of funding in total. S. Duffy, *Counting the Cuts*, London: Centre for Welfare Reform (2014), p. 5.

40 This occurred in 2013. Local Government Association, *Local Government Spending*, p. 4.

41 D. Paine, 'Revealed: The "Staggering" £4bn Cost of a Decade of Job Losses', *Local Government Chronicle*, 12 September 2018.

42 Duffy and Gilberg, *Extreme Poverty in a Time of Austerity*, p. 5.

43 Ibid.

44 R. Pearson, 'A Feminist Analysis of Neoliberalism and Austerity Policies in the UK', *Soundings* 71 (2019): 28–39, 35.

45 H. Wakefield, *Triple Whammy: The Impact of Local Government Cuts on Women*, Women's Budget Group (2019), p. 8.

46 Ryan, *Crippled*, p. 34. A. Williams, P. Cloke, J. May and M. Goodwin, 'Contested Spaces: The Contradictory Political Dynamics of Food Banking in the UK', *Environment and Planning* 48 (2016): 2291–316, 2294.

47 Local Government Association, *Local Government Spending*, p. 4.

48 Ibid.

49 S. Bushe, P. Kenway and H. Aldridge, *The Impact of Localising Council Tax Benefit*, York: Joseph Rowntree Foundation (2013).

50 Centre for Late Life Learning, *The End of Formal Adult Social Care*, London: ILC-UK (2015), p. 3.

51 Institute for Fiscal Studies, *English Council Funding: What's Happened and What's Next?* IFS Briefing Note BN250, London: Institute for Fiscal Studies (May 2019).

52 M. Gray and A. Barford, 'The Depths of the Cuts: The Uneven Geography of Local Government Austerity', *Cambridge Journal of Regions, Economy and Society* 11 (2018): 541–63, 546; on the unequal geography of local council cuts, see also A. Tinson, C. Ayrton and I. Petrie, *A Quiet Crisis: Local Government Spending on Disadvantage* (Executive Summary), New Policy Institute (2018), p. 1.

53 HM Treasury, *Spending Review 2010 (Cm7492)*, Crown Copyright (2010), p. 50.

54 D. Cameron, 'The Big Society', Hugo Young Lecture, 10 November 2009; transcript available at conservative-speeches.sayit. mysociety.org.

55 P. Blond, *Red Tory: How the Left and Right Have Broken Britain and How We Can Fix It*, London: Faber and Faber (2010); J. Norman, *The Big Society: The Anatomy of the New Politics*, Buckingham: University of Buckingham Press (2010).

56 A. Swerksy and J. Plunkett, *What If We Ran It Ourselves? Getting the Measure of Britain's Community Business Sector*, London: Social Finance UK (2015).

57 Local Government Association, *Local Government Spending*, p. 7.

58 The 2019 clip can be watched here: camden.gov.uk/camdens-financial-challenge; the 2014 clip can be watched on YouTube, 'Camden Council's financial challenge', September 5, 2014; the older billboard posters are archived at islingtongazette.co.uk.

59 United Nations Office of the High Commissioner, *Statement on Visit to the United Kingdom, by Professor Philip Alston, United Nations Special Rapporteur on Extreme Poverty and Human Rights*, 16 November 2018.

60 W. Davies, 'The New Neoliberalism', *New Left Review* 101 (2016): 121–34.

61 Taylor-Gooby, 'The Divisive Welfare State', p. 729.

62 These are the figures for 2017–18. Cf. Department for Work and Pensions, *Fraud and Error in the Benefit System: 2017/2018 Estimate* (2019), assets.publishing.service.gov.uk.

63 HMRC, *Measuring Tax Gaps 2019 Edition: Tax Gaps Estimates for 2017–2018* (2019), assets.publishing.service.gov.uk, p. 17.

64 T. Jensen and I. Tyler, 'Benefit Broods: The Cultural and Political Crafting of Anti-Welfare Common Sense', *Critical Social Policy* 35(4) (2015): 1–22, 5 and 9.

65 See D. Etherington and A. Daguerre, *Welfare Reform, Work First Policies and Benefit Conditionality: Reinforcing Poverty and Social Exclusion?* London: Centre for Enterprise and Economic Development Research, Middlesex University (2015).

66 J. Hills, *Good Times, Bad Times: The Welfare Myth of Them and Us*, Bristol: Policy Press (2015).

67 UK Office for National Statistics, *How Is the Welfare Budget Being Spent?* (2016), ons.gov.uk.

68 Jensen and Tyler, 'Benefit Broods', pp. 5 and 9.

69 UK Government, 'Health and Work Service Supplier Announced', press release, July 2014.

70 A. Gentleman, 'After Hated Atos Quits, Will Maximus Make Work Assessments Less Arduous?' *Guardian*, 18 January 2015.

71 Taylor-Gooby, 'The Divisive Welfare State', p. 722.

72 G. Plimmer, 'Fostering Sector Ripe for Consolidation', *Financial Times*, 20 January 2013.

73 Cabinet Office, *Government Digital Strategy*, November 2012, archived at assets.publishing.service.gov.uk. See also Cabinet Office and Government Digital Service, *Government Transformation Strategy*, Policy Paper, February 2017.

74 P. Alston and C. van Veen, 'How Britain's Welfare State Has Been Taken Over by Shadowy Tech Consultants', *Guardian*, 27 June 2019; see also Child Poverty Action Group, 'Computer Says No – Stage One: Information Provision', London: Child Poverty Action Group (2019).

75 V. Lowndes and K. McCaughie, 'Weathering the Perfect Storm? Austerity and Institutional Resilience in Local Government', *Policy and Politics* 41(4) (2013): 533–49, 541.

76 J. Clayton, C. Donovan and J. Merchant, 'Emotions of Austerity:

Care and Commitment in Public Service Delivery in the North-East of England,' *Emotion, Space and Society* 14 (2015): 24–32.

77 Ibid., p. 30.

78 R. Crawford, G. Stoye and B. Zaranko, *The Impact of Cuts to Social Care Spending on the Use of Accident and Emergency Departments in England*, IFS Working Papers, No. W18/15, London: Institute for Fiscal Studies (2018), p. 8.

79 Ibid., p. 15.

80 Care Quality Commission, *The State of Healthcare and Adult Social Care in England 2018/2019*, Crown Copyright (2019), p. 41.

81 Ibid., p. 7.

82 S. Ghafur, 'Seven-Day NHS: A Frontline Perspective', Nuffield Trust Blog, 14 December 2016, nuffieldtrust.org.uk; I. Torjeson, 'Government Should Think Again About Prioritising Seven-Day NHS Services, King's Fund Says', *British Medical Journal*, BMJ (2016): 354: i3860.

83 N. Merrifield, 'Student Nurses and Midwives Stop Getting Bursaries from Today', *Nursing Times*, 1 August 2017, nursingtimes.net.

84 L. Stanley, 'Governing Austerity in the United Kingdom: Anticipatory Fiscal Consolidation as a Variety of Austerity Governance', *Economy and Society* 45 (2016): 3–4, 303–24; 308.

85 L. Summers, 'The Age of Secular Stagnation and What to Do About It', *Foreign Affairs*, 15 February 2016.

86 Crawford and Zaranko, *Tax Revenues and Spending*, p. 2.

87 Ibid., p. 10.

88 Farnsworth and Irving, 'Austerity: More Than the Sum of Its Parts', pp. 25, 37.

89 Crawford and Zaranko, *Tax Revenues and Spending*, p. 10.

3. Who Cares?

1 A. Rimmer, 'The Impact of the Junior Doctor Contract: One Year On', *British Medical Journal*, BMJ 358: j4125 (2017), p. 2. Since then, there has been a review of the contract and a new, updated deal agreed that includes increases to weekend and night shifts and some extra funds for less than full-time trainees. Cf. British Medical Association, 'Agreed New Contract Deal for Junior Doctors in England', 17 January 2020, bma.org.uk.

2 See nhsemployers.org/pay-pensions-and-reward.

3 S. Farris, *In the Name of Women's Rights: The Rise of Femonationalism*, Durham, NC: Duke University Press (2017), esp. chapter 5.

4   I. Seu and S. Orgad, *Caring in Crisis? Humanitarianism, the Public and NGOs*, Cham, Switzerland: Palgrave Pivot (2017).

5   R. Solnit, *A Paradise Built in Hell: The Extraordinary Communities That Arise in Disaster*, London: Penguin Books (2009).

6   A. Biesecker, C. Braunmühl, C. Wichterich and U. Winterfeld, 'Die Privatisierung des Politischen: Zu den Auswirkungen der doppelten Privatisierung' ['The Privatisation of the Political: On the Effects of Double Privatisation'], *Femina Politica* 16(2) (2007): 28– 41, 30.

7   Office for National Statistics, *Changes in the Value and Division of Unpaid Care Work in the UK: 2000 to 2015*, London: Office for National Statistics (2016), p. 3.

8   R. Pearson, 'A Feminist Analysis of Neoliberalism and Austerity Policies in the UK', *Soundings* 71 (2019): 28–39, 35.

9   I. Bakker, 'Neoliberal Governance and the Reprivatisation of Social Reproduction', in Bakker and S. Gill (eds), *Power, Production and Social Reproduction*, New York: Palgrave Macmillan (2003), pp. 66–82. See also D. Tepe-Belfrage and S. Wallin (eds), 'Austerity and the hidden costs of recovery: Inequality and insecurity in the UK households', special issue of the journal *British Politics* 11 (2016).

10 S. Rai, C. Hoskyns and D. Thomas, 'Depletion: The Cost of Social Reproduction', *International Feminist Journal of Politics* 16(1) (2013): 86–105.

11 See O. Sullivan, 'Gender Inequality in Work-Family Balance', *Nature Human Behaviour* 3 (2019): 201–3, 201.

12 A. Evers and H. Winterberger, *Shifts in the Welfare Mix: Their Impact on Work, Social Services and Welfare Policies*, Abingdon: Taylor and Francis (1990).

13 International Labour Organisation, *Care Work and Care Jobs for the Future of Decent Work*, Geneva: International Labour Office (2018), p. xxxviii.

14 L. Gordolan and M. Lalani, *Care and Migration: Migrant Care Workers in Private Households*, London: Kalayaan and Oxford: COMPAS, Oxford University (2009).

15 See: kalayaan.org.uk and thevoiceofdomesticworkers.com.

16 For details, see: gov.uk/domestic-workers-in-a-private-household-visa; see also J. Ewins, *Independent Review of the Domestic Worker Visa, Final Report*, UK Government, 6 November 2015, assets.publishing.service.gov.uk.

17 International Labour Organisation, *Care Work and Care Jobs*, p. xl.

18 A. Decker and J. Lebrun, *PHS Industry Monitor – Statistical Overview of the Personal and Household Services Sector in the EU*, European Federation for Services to Individuals (2018), p. 13.

19 International Monetary Fund, 'Household Debt, Loans and Debt Securities – Percent of GDP', IMF Data Mapper (2019), imf.org.

20 S. Himmelweit, 'Changing Norms of Social Reproduction in an Age of Austerity' (2017), iippe.org, p. 1; see also D. Harvey, *Seventeen Contradictions and the End of Capitalism*, London: Profile Books (2014), p. 194.

21 C. Berry, 'Austerity, Ageing and the Financialisation of Pensions Policy in the UK', *British Politics* 11(1) (2016): 2–25.

22 For an in-depth discussion of household debt, see J. Montgomerie, *Should We Abolish Household Debts?* Cambridge: Polity (2019).

23 D. Bryan and M. Rafferty, *Risking Together: How Finance Is Dominating Life in Australia*, Sydney: Sydney University Press (2018), pp. 192–6.

24 H. Penn, 'Childcare Market Management: How the United Kingdom Government Has Reshaped Its Role in Developing Early Childhood Education and Care', *Contemporary Issues in Early Childhood*, 8 (3): 192–207, cited in S. Farris and S. Marchetti, 'From the Commodification to the Corporatization of Care: European Perspectives and Debates', *Social Politics* 24(2) (2017): 109–31, 118.

25 Pearson, 'A Feminist Analysis', p. 35.

26 Office for National Statistics, *Changes in the Value and Division of Unpaid Care Work*.

27 Ibid.

28 Trades Union Congress, *Nearly Seven Million Grandparents Provide Regular Childcare*, TUC Press Release, 17 December 2013.

29 J. Mortimer and M. Green, *Briefing: The Health and Care of Older People in England 2015*, London: Age UK (2015), p. 32. Cited in J. Elias et al., *Towards a New Deal for Care and Carers*, Report of the PSA Commission on Care (2016).

30 Office for National Statistics, 'Home Produced "Adultcare" Services', *Household Satellite Accounts 2005 to 2014*, Chapter 3 (2016), ons.gov.uk.

31 Ibid.

32 Carers UK, *Missing Out: The Identification Challenge*, London: Carers UK (2016), p. 3.

33 Carers UK, *Juggling Work and Unpaid Care: A Growing Issue*, London: Carers UK (2019), p. 10.

34 Ibid.

35 Ibid.

36 Office for National Statistics, *Unpaid Carers Provide Social Care Worth £57 billion*, 10 July 2017, ons.gov.uk.

37 Carers UK, *State of Caring: A Snapshot of Unpaid Care in the UK*, London: Carers UK (2019), p. 4.

38 L. Buckner and S. Yeandle, *Valuing Carers 2015: The Rising Value of Carers' Support*, London: Carers UK (2015), p. 4.

39 Ibid.

40 L. Clements, 'Why Care Act Risks Shunting NHS Responsibilities on to Councils and Vulnerable Adults', *Community Care* (July 2014), archived at: communitycare.co.uk.

41 Carers UK, *State of Caring*, p. 14.

42 Ibid.

43 Ibid., p. 5.

44 NHS Digital, *Personal Social Services Survey of Adult Carers in England 2014–15* (2015), archived at: nhs.uk.

45 See also C. Guest, O. Corrigan and O. Koffman, '*You Really Do Give Up Your Own Life, Once You Become a Full-Time Carer': Exploring the Lived Experience of Carers in South Essex*, Project Report, Healthwatch Essex (2015).

46 Carers UK, cited in Care Quality Commission, *The State of Health Care and Adult Social Care in England 2018/19*, Crown Copyright (2019), p. 16.

47 Carers UK, *State of Caring*, p. 6.

48 H. King, 'Care Act 2014: A Step in the Wrong Direction', *Nursing Times Blog*, 27 November 2014.

49 Department for Health and Social Care, *Carers Action Plan 2018–2020: Supporting Carers Today*, London Department for Health and Social Care (2018).

50 M. Bulman, 'Number of Young Carers in UK Soars by 10,000 in Four Years, Figures Show', *Independent*, 28 January 2018.

51 Ibid., and childrenssociety.org.uk.

52 D. Hounsell, *Hidden from View: The Experiences of Young Carers in England*, London: The Children's Society (2013), p. 8.

53 C. Dearden and S. Becker, *Young Carers in the UK: The 2004 Report*, London: Carers UK and The Children's Society (2004), cited in ibid., p. 9.

54 Hounsell, *Hidden from View*, p. 18.

55 Ibid., p. 5.

56 S. Becker and J. Sempik, 'Young Adult Carers: The Impact of Caring on Health and Education', *Children and Society* 33(4) (2019): 377–86, 385.

57 Ibid., 377.

58 Ibid., 388.

59 C. Leyshon, M. Leyshon and J. Jeffries, 'The Complex Spaces of Co-Production, Volunteering, Ageing and Care', *Area* 51(3) (2018): 433–42.

60 C. Naylor, C. Mundle, L. Weaks and D. Buck, *Volunteering in Health and Care: Securing a Sustainable Future*, London: The King's Fund (2013), p. 2.

61 National Health Service, *NHS Long-Term Plan* (2019), p. 90, available at: longtermplan.nhs.uk.

62 The Behavioural Insights Team, 'Does Social Action Help Develop the Skills Young People Need to Succeed in Adult Life?' 15 January 2016, archived at: behaviouralinsights.co.uk/education-and-skills.

63 R. Perlin, *Intern Nation: How to Earn Nothing and Learn Little in the Brave New Economy*, London/New York: Verso (2011).

64 K. Allan, 'Volunteering as Hope Labour: The Potential Value of Unpaid Work Experience for the Un- and Under-Employed', *Culture, Theory and Critique* 60(1) (2019): 66–83.

65 National Health Service, *NHS Long-Term Plan*, p. 90.

66 Volunteering Matters, 'Volunteering Matters for Social Prescribing', 3 September 2019, archived at: volunteeringmatters.org.uk; see also england.nhs.uk/personalisedcare/social-prescribing.

67 V. Lowndes and K. McCaughie, 'Weathering the Perfect Storm? Austerity and Institutional Resilience in Local Government', *Policy and Politics* 41(4) (2013): 533–49, 540.

68 Care Quality Commission, *State of Health Care*, p. 20.

69 Lowndes and McCaughie, 'Weathering the Perfect Storm?', 541; R. Scott and S. Howlett, *The Changing Face of Volunteering in Hospice and Palliative Care*, Oxford: Oxford University Press (2018), p. 32.

70 K. Southby and J. South, *Volunteering, Inequalities and Barriers to Volunteering: A Rapid Evidence Review*, Leeds Beckett University (commissioned by Volunteering Matters) (2016), p. 7.

71 Ibid.

72 UK Government Department for Environment, Food and Rural Affairs, 'UK Retail Price Changes by Food Group, 2007 to 2018', *Food Statistics in Your Pocket: Prices and Expenditure*, 26 June 2019, archived at: gov.uk/government/publications/food-statistics-pocketbook.

73 As researched by Sabine Goodwin of the Independent Food Aid Network, foodaidnetwork.org.uk.

74 Trussell Trust and Independent Food Aid Network, 'Volunteers Across the UK Giving at Least £30 Million a Year in Unpaid Work to Support Foodbanks', press release, 17 October 2017, trusselltrust.org.

75 R. Loopstra and D. Lalor, *Financial Insecurity, Food Insecurity, and Disability: The Profile of People Receiving Emergency Food Assistance from The Trussell Trust Foodbank Network in Britain*, The Trussell Trust (June 2017), trusselltrust.org.

76 Trussell Trust, 'Primary Reasons for Referral to Trussell Trust Food Banks in 2018–19' (2020), trusselltrust.org.

77 M. Holehouse, 'Poor Going Hungry Because They Can't Cook, Says Tory Peer', *Daily Telegraph*, 8 December 2014 and J. Kirkup, 'Some People Using Foodbanks Buy Cigarettes Instead of Food', *Daily Telegraph*, 8 December 2014. These newspaper reports both refer to the All-Party Parliamentary Inquiry into Hunger in the United Kingdom that emphasised the alleged flaws of people experiencing food poverty. A. Forsey, *An Evidence Review for the All-Party Parliamentary Inquiry into Hunger in the United Kingdom*, London: The Children's Society (2014).

78 BBC News, 'Jacob Rees-Mogg: Food Banks "Rather Uplifting"', 14 September 2017, bbc.com/news.

79 Trussell Trust and Independent Food Aid Network, 'Volunteers Across the UK'.

80 P. Caplan, 'Big Society or Broken Society? Food Banks in the UK', *Anthropology Today* 32(1) (2016): 5–9.

81 S. Volpe, '"There Is Still that Stigma": Healthwatch Camden Launch Food Poverty Campaign', *Ham and High*, 8 May 2019. On stigma and foodbank use: K. Garthwaite, 'Stigma, Shame and "People Like Us": An Ethnographic Study of Foodbank Use in the UK', *Journal of Poverty and Social Justice* 24(3) (2016): 277–89.

82 A. Williams, P. Cloke, J. May and M. Goodwin, 'Contested spaces: The Contradictory Political Dynamics of Food Banking in the UK', *Environment and Planning* 48 (2016): 2291–316.

83 K. Garthwaite, 'It Is Not the Hungry Who Gain Most from Food-banks, It Is Big Business', *Guardian*, 25 March 2019.

84 P. Monfort, 'From Compassion to Critical Resilience: Volunteering in the Context of Austerity', *Sociological Review* 68(1) (2020): 110–26.

85 S. Ross, D. Fenney, D. Ward and D. Buck, *The Role of Volunteers in the NHS: Views from the Front Line*, London: King's Fund (report commissioned by the Royal Voluntary Trust and Helpforce) (2018), p. 33.

86 Ibid., p. 5.

87 Ibid., p. 27.

88 Ibid., p. 6.

89 Ibid.

90 Ibid., p. 97.

91 Naylor et al., *Volunteering in Health and Care*, p. 15.

92 Ibid., p. 40.

93 Ross et al., *The Role of Volunteers in the NHS*, p. 12.

94 For evidence of excessive use of force by police against migrants in the Calais camp, see Human Rights Watch, '"Like Living in Hell":

NOTES FOR PAGES 97 TO 102

Police Abuses Against Child and Adult Migrants in Calais', 26 July 2017, hrw.org.

95 'False generosity' is a term coined by the Brazilian pedagogue Paolo Freire. See P. Freire, *Pedagogy of the Oppressed*, New York/London: Continuum (2000 [1970]), p. 54.

96 For a recent book that tells refugees' stories, see D. Trilling, *Lights in the Distance: Exile and Refuge at the Borders of Europe*, New York: Picador (2018).

97 Volunteering Matters/Local Government Association, 'Volunteering and Social Action and the Care Act: An Opportunity for Local Government' (2016), archived at: volunteeringmatters. org.uk, p. 3.

98 A. Power and E. Hall, 'Placing Care in Times of Austerity', *Social and Cultural Geography* 19(3) (2018): 303–13, 309.

99 S. M. Hall, *Everyday Life Austerity: Family, Friends and Intimate Relations*, Cham, Switzerland: Palgrave McMillan (2019), esp. chapter 3.

100 National Union of Public Workers/Services to Community and Trade Unions, *Cashing in on Care*, London and East Midland Divisions (1984), pp. 1, 4.

101 London Weekend Return Group, *In and Against the State*, London: Pluto Press (1979), p. 125.

102 R. Macmillan and A. Townsend, 'A New Institutional Fix? The "Community Turn" and the Changing Role of the Voluntary Sector', in C. Milligan and D. Conradson (eds), *Landscapes of Voluntarism: New Spaces of Health, Welfare and Governance*, Bristol: Bristol University Press (2006), pp. 15–32.

103 P. Drucker, *Postcapitalist Society*, New York: Harper Collins (1993), p. 167 ff.

104 J. Rifkin, *The Zero Marginal Cost Society*, New York: St Martin's Press (2015), p. 340 ff.

105 S. van Dyk, 'Post-Wage Politics and the Rise of Community Capitalism', *Work, Employment and Society* 32(3) (2018): 528–45 and T. Haubner, *Die Ausbeutung der sorgenden Gemeinschaft: Laienpflege in Deutschland* [*The Exploitation of the Caring Community: Informal Care in Germany*], Frankfurt/New York: Campus (2017).

106 C. Naylor et al., *Volunteering in Health and Care*, p. 10.

107 S. Federici, *Revolution at Point Zero: Housework, Reproduction and Feminist Struggle*, Brooklyn, NY: Common Notions (Imprint of PM Press) (2012), pp. 44–5.

108 See, for example, H. Hobart and T. Kneese, *Radical Care* (special issue), *Social Text* 38(1) (2020).

109 A. Emejulu and L. Bassel, *Minority Women and Austerity:*

Survival and Resistance in France and Britain, Bristol: Policy Press (2018).

110 National Union of Public Workers/Services to Community and Trade Unions, *Cashing in On Care*, p. 4.

111 C. Lim and J. Laurence, 'Doing Good When Times Are Bad: Volunteering Behaviour in Economic Bad Times', *BJOS* 66(2) (2015): 319–44.

112 Ibid.

113 YouGov Survey, 'How confident are you that you would be able to cover the cost of care for yourself in old age, if you needed it?' (2018), yougov.co.uk.

114 HM Treasury, *2014 Budget Report* (HC 1104), Crown Copyright (2014).

115 Lowndes and McCaughie, 'Weathering the Perfect Storm?', 541.

4. A Perfect Storm

1 Care Quality Commission, *The State of Health Care and Adult Social Care in England*, Crown Copyright (2019); see also: G. Cory, C. Roberts and C. Thorley, *Care in a Post-Brexit Climate*, London: Institute for Public Policy Research (2017), pp. 7–9.

2 D. Bell, 'Free Personal Care: What the Scottish Approach to Social Care Would Cost in England', Health Foundation, 30 May 2018, health.org.uk.

3 Age UK, 'Briefing: Health and Care of Older People in England in 2019', ageuk.org.uk, p. 5.

4 UK Homecare Association, *An Overview of the UK Homecare Market*, Wallington: UK Homecare Association (2019), p. 9.

5 Laing Buisson, *Care Homes for Older People Market Report*, London: Laing Buisson (2019), p. 36.

6 National Audit Office, *Adult Social Care at a Glance*, London: National Audit Office (2018), p. 16.

7 Nuffield Trust, The Health Foundation and the King's Fund, *The Autumn Budget: Joint Statement on Health and Social Care*, November 2017, p. 20, nuffieldtrust.org.uk.

8 S. Ismail, R. Thorlby and H. Holder, *Focus On: Social Care for Older People*, London: The Health Foundation and Nuffield Trust (2014), p. 27.

9 M. Samuels, 'More Care Home Residents Will Have to Self-Fund as Means-Test Threshold Frozen for 10th Year', Community Care (2020), communitycare.co.uk.

10 Care Quality Commission, *State of Health Care*, p. 7.

11 Office for National Statistics, *National Population Projections* (2019), ons.gov.uk.

12 House of Lords Select Committee on Public Service and Demographic Change (2013) cited in S. Bottery, M. Varrow, R. Thorlby and D. Wellings, *A Fork in the Road: Next Steps for Social Care Funding Reform*, London: The Health Foundation and the King's Fund (2018), p. 8.

13 Care Quality Commission, *State of Health Care*, p. 40.

14 Laing Buisson, 'Care Home Funding Shortfall Leaves Self-Funders Filling £1.3 Billion Funding Gap', press release, 27 January 2017.

15 A. Cangiano, I. Shutes, S. Spencer and G. Leeson, *Migrant Care Workers in Ageing Societies: Research Findings in the United Kingdom*, Oxford: COMPAS, University of Oxford (2019), p. 101.

16 Skills for Care, *The State of the Adult Social Care Sector and Workforce in England*, Leeds: Skills for Care (2019), p. 36.

17 Cited in Department for Business, Innovation and Skills and HM Revenue and Customs, *Ensuring Employers Comply with National Minimum Wage Regulations*, London: National Audit Office (2016), p.20.

18 R. Read and L. Fenge, 'What Does Brexit Mean for the UK Social Care Workforce? Perspectives from the Recruitment and Retention Frontline', Health and Social Care in the Community 27 (2019): 676–82, 679.

19 UK Homecare Association, *Overview of the UK Homecare Market*, p. 21.

20 S. Hussein, '"We Don't Do It for the Money" … The Scale and Reasons of Poverty-Pay Among Frontline Long-Term Care Workers in England', *Health and Social Care in the Community* 25(6) (2017): 1817–26, 1824.

21 Read and Fenge, 'What Does Brexit Mean for the UK Social Care Workforce?', p. 679.

22 Hussein, '"We Don't Do It for the Money"'.

23 Skills for Care, *State of the Adult Social Care Sector*, p. 66.

24 S. Hussein and K. Christensen, 'Migration, Gender and Low-Paid Work: On Migrant Men's Entry Dynamics into the Feminised Social Care Work in the UK', *Journal of Ethnic and Migration Studies*, 43(5) (2016): 749–65, esp. 754–5.

25 Skills for Care, *State of the Adult Social Care Sector*, p. 66.

26 Cangiano et al., *Migrant Care Workers in Ageing Societies*, p. 58.

27 E. J. B. Rose et al., cited in ibid., p. 37.

28 Ibid.

29 M. R. D. Johnson and P. McGee, cited in J. Simpson, A. Esmail, K. Virinder and S. Snow, 'Writing Migrants Back into NHS History: Addressing a "Collective Amnesia" and Its Policy Implications',

Journal of the Royal Society of Medicine 103(10) (2010): 392–6, 392.

30 S. Hussein, 'The Dynamic Role of Migrants Employed in Social Care in the UK: Reflections and Policy Implications' (2017), kcl.ac.uk.

31 Cangiano et al., *Migrant Care Workers in Ageing Societies*.

32 Skills for Care, *State of the Adult Social Care Sector*, p. 72.

33 Bowman (2015) cited in D. Burns, L. Cowie, J. Earle, P. Folkman, J. Froud, P. Hyde, S. Johal, I. Rees Jones, A. Killett and K. Williams, *Where Does the Money Go? Financialised Chains and the Crisis in Residential Care*, Centre for Socio-Cultural Change Public Interest Report (March 2016), p. 21.

34 International Labour Organisation, *Care Work and Care Jobs for the Future of Decent Work*, Geneva: International Labour Office, ILO (2018), p. xli.

35 Cangiano et al., *Migrant Care Workers in Ageing Societies*, p. 108.

36 C. Wichterich, *Care Extractivism and the Reconfiguration of Social Reproduction in Post-Fordist Economies*, ICDD Working Papers No. 25, International Centre for Decent Work and Development, University of Kassel (April 2019), p. 12.

37 Cangiano et al., *Migrant Care Workers in Ageing Societies*, p. 92.

38 UNISON, 'Homecare Workers Paid Less than the Minimum Wage', press release, 30 January 2019, unison.org.uk.

39 Hussein, '"We Don't Do It for the Money"'.

40 U. Huws, N. Spencer, D. Syrdal and K. Holts, *Work in the European Gig Economy*, Foundation for European Progressive Studies, in cooperation with UNI Europa and the University of Hertfordshire (2017).

41 S. Moore and L. J. B. Hayes, 'Taking Worker Productivity to a New Level? Electronic Monitoring in Homecare: The (Re)production of Unpaid Labour', *New Technology, Work and Employment* 32(2) (2017): 101–14, 102.

42 Ibid., p. 112.

43 D. Burns, J. Earle, P. Folkman, J. Froud, P. Hyde, S. Johal, I. Rees Jones, A. Killet and K. William, 'Why We Need Social Innovation in Homecare for Older People', CRESC Public Interest Report, Centre for Research on Economic and Socio-Cultural Change (2016), p. 8.

44 Moore and Hayes, 'Taking Worker Productivity to a New Level?', 108.

45 L. J. B. Hayes and S. Moore, 'Care in a Time of Austerity: The Electronic Monitoring of Homecare Workers' Time', *Gender, Work and Organisation* 24(4) (2016): 329–44, 334.

46 See for example N. Folbre, 'Should Women Care Less? Intrinsic

Motivation and Gender Inequality', *British Journal of Industrial Relations* 50(4) (2012): 597–619.

47 Moore and Hayes, 'Taking Worker Productivity to a New Level?', 111.

48 Cf. N. Folbre, 'Nursebots to the Rescue? Immigration, Automation, and Care', *Globalizations* 3(3) (2006): 349–60.

49 J. Wacjman, 'New Connections: Social Studies of Science and Technology and Studies of Work', *Work, Employment and Society* 20(4) (2006): 773–86.

50 S. Bottery et al., *Home Care in England: Views from Commissioners and Providers*, London: The King's Fund (2018), pp. 32–5.

51 See: care.com.

52 N. Srnicek, *Platform Capitalism*, Cambridge: Polity Press (2017), p. 76.

53 See: bemyeyes.com.

54 Singularity University, 'Be My Eyes Case Study – Startup Customer Stories' (2018), su.org.

55 D. Brindle, 'Meals on wheels under threat as more councils drop service due to cuts', *Guardian*, 8 November 2016.

56 Futuregov, *Casserole Club – Software as a Service Pricing Document* (undated), digitalmarketplace.service.gov.uk.

57 See: thisiscocare.com.

58 LGiU, 'CoCare: Measuring What Matters' (2020), lgiu.org.

59 J. Margolis, 'Agetech Could Transform the Care Industry', *Financial Times*, 17 July 2019.

60 S. Carretero, *Mapping of Effective Technology-Based Services for Independent Living for Older People at Home*, JRC91622, European Union Joint Research Centre website (2015).

61 See: parorobots.com.

62 See: softbankrobotics.com/us/pepper.

63 Department for Business, Energy and Industrial Strategy (2019): *Care Robots Could Revolutionise UK Care System and Provide Staff Extra Support*, press release (November 2019), gov.uk/government/news.

64 For details, see: youtube.com/watch?v=aAvq98K5zfk

65 See: chiron.org.uk.

66 N. Harris, *Chiron – Final Report (Executive Summary)*, Designability (2018). Available at: chironrobotics.files.wordpress.com, p. 4.

67 M. Mazzucato, *The Entrepreneurial State*, Cambridge: Anthem Press (2013).

68 A.-J. Poo, *The Age of Dignity: Preparing for the Elder Boom in a Changing America*, New York: The New Press (2009), p. 145.

69 I. Koehler, *Key to Care: Report of the Burstow Commission on the*

Future of the Homecare Workforce, London: LGiU/Mears (2014), p. 6.

70 A. Horton, 'Financialization and Non-Disposable Women: Real estate, debt and labour in UK care homes', *Environment and Planning A: Economy and Space* (July 2019), sagepub.com.

71 Unison, *Suffering Alone at Home: A Unison Report on the Lack of Time in Our Homecare System*, London: Unison (2016), p. 3.

72 Care Quality Commission, *State of Health Care*.

73 G. Plimmer, 'Care Home Operator Four Seasons Appoints Administrators', *Financial Times*, 30 April 2014.

74 G. Plimmer, 'Britain's Biggest Care Homes Rack Up Debts of £40 000 a Bed', *Financial Times*, 14 July 2019.

75 BBC News, 'Southern Cross Set to Shut Down and Stop Running Homes', 11 July 2011, bbc.com.

76 Plimmer, 'Britain's Biggest Care Homes Rack Up Debts'.

77 Ibid.

78 G. Plimmer, 'Four Seasons to be Taken Over by H2 Capital Partners', *Financial Times*, 11 September 2019.

79 Ibid.

80 G. Plimmer, 'British Homecare Group Saved by Last-Ditch Sale', *Financial Times*, 30 November 2018.

81 G. Plimmer, 'Outsourcer Mitie Sells Homecare Business for Just £2', *Financial Times*, 1 March 2017; G. Plimmer, 'UK Homecare on Brink of Collapse', Says Report', *Financial Times*, 20 March 2017.

82 Plimmer, 'British Homecare Group Saved'.

83 Association of Directors of Adult Social Services, *Budget Survey 2019*, adass.org.uk, p. 31.

84 G. Plimmer, 'Britain's Biggest Care Home Business for Sale', *Financial Times*, 21 May 2018.

85 Competition and Markets Authority, *Competition and Markets Authority Report, 2017/2018*, gov.uk/government/publications.

86 Plimmer, 'Britain's Biggest Care Homes Rack up Debts'.

87 Emphasis added. Company Watch, *Industry Watch – Outsourcing*, Company Watch Financial Analytics, London: Company Watch (2018), p. 2.

88 Plimmer, 'Britain's Biggest Care Homes Rack up Debts'.

89 V. Kotecha, *Plugging the Leaks in the UK Care Home Industry: Strategies for Resolving the Financial Crisis in the Residential and Nursing Home Sector*, London: Centre for Health and Public Interest (2019), p. 4.

90 Burns et al., *Where Does the Money Go?* p. 23.

91 Horton, 'Financialization and Non-Disposable Women'.

92 Ibid., p. 3.

93 V. Kotecha, *Plugging the Leaks in the UK Care Home Industry: Strategies for Resolving the Financial Crisis in the Residential and Nursing Home Sector*, London: Centre for Health and Public Interest (2019), p. 10.

94 J. Ford, 'Private Equity Is the Wrong Prescription for Social Care', *Financial Times*, 17 December 2017.

95 Horton, 'Financialization and Non-Disposable Women'.

96 P. Temple, 'Profiting with a Clear Conscience' (Opinion: My Portfolio), *Financial Times*, 13 April 2007.

97 Burns et al., 'Why We Need Social Innovation in Homecare'.

98 Skills for Care, *State of the Adult Social Care Sector*, p. 7.

99 National Health Service and Community Care Act 1990, Part III (Preamble), legislation.gov.uk.

100 B. Hudson, *The Failure of Privatised Adult Social Care in England: What Is to Be Done?* London: Centre for Health and the Public Interest (2016), p. 7.; cf. G. Wistow, M. Knapp, B. Hardy, J. Forder, J. Kendall and R. Manning, *Social Care Markets: Progress and Prospects*, Bristol PA; Buckingham, England: Open University Press (1996), p. 5.

101 The role of local authorities in 'shaping' the market is highly explicit in the most recent legislation pertaining to social care, the Care Act 2014.

102 Department of Health and Social Care, *Social Care – Charging for Care and Support*, Local Authority Circular LAC(DHSC)(2018)1, Crown Copyright (January 2018).

103 See for example C. Slasberg, P. Beresford and P. Schofield, 'Further Lessons from the Continuing Failure of the National Strategy to Deliver Personal Budgets and Personalisation', *Research, Policy and Planning* 31(1) (2014): 43–53.

104 J. Woolham, G. Daly, S. Sparks and K. Ritters, 'Do Direct Payments Improve Outcomes for Older People Who Receive Social Care? Differences in Outcome Between People Aged 75+ Who Have a Managed Personal Budget or a Direct Payment', *Ageing and Society* 37(5) (2017): 961–84.

105 Skills for Care, *Individual Employers and the Personal Assistant Workforce*, London: Skills for Care (2019), p. 4.

106 C. Ungerson, 'Whose Empowerment and Independence? A Cross-National Perspective On "Cash for Care" Schemes', *Ageing and Society*, 24(02) (2004): 189–212.

107 Unison and European Services Strategy Unit, *Does Excelcare Really? An Investigation into the Transfer of 10 Residential Care Homes by Essex County Council to Excelcare Holdings PLC*, Newcastle/Chelmsford (2007).

108 D. Whitfield, *Public Alternative to Private Finance*, Nottingham:

Spokesman Books (2020), p. 1.

109 Burns et al., 'Why We Need Social Innovation in Homecare', p. 8.

110 National Union of Public Workers/Services to Community and Trade Unions, *Cashing in on Care*, London and East Midland Divisions (1984), p. 20.

111 J. Rifkin, *The Zero Marginal Cost Society*, New York: St Martin's Press (2015); P. Mason, *PostCapitalism: A Guide to Our Future*, London: Penguin (2016).

112 Bottery et al., *A Fork in the Road*, p. 2.

113 HM Treasury, 'Chancellor George Osborne's Spending Review and Autumn Statement 2015 Speech', 25 November 2015, gov.uk.

114 Bottery et al., *A Fork in the Road*, p. 2.

115 P. Beresford, C. Slasberg and L. Clements, 'From Dementia Tax to a Solution for Social Care: Radical Thinking on Social Care is Crucial for the Well-being of All of Us', *Soundings Journal of Politics and Culture* 68 (2018): 78–93.

116 H. Quilter-Pinner and D. Hochlaf, *Social Care: Free at the Point of Delivery*, London: Institute for Public Policy (2019), and Bottery et al., *A Fork in the Road*.

117 M. Samuel, 'Government Confirms Extra Social Care Cash but Council Leaders Bemoan Failure to Fund Wage Rise', *Community Care* (2020), communitycare.co.uk.

5. Banking on the Abandoned

1 *The NHS Long-Term Plan*, London: NHS (2019), esp. Chapter 2: 'More NHS Action on Prevention and Health Inequalities' (pp. 33–9).

2 E. Dowling and D. Harvie, 'Harnessing the Social: State, Crisis and (Big) Society', *Sociology* 48(5) (2014): 869–86.

3 Social Finance UK, *Investing in the Enablers of Integrated Care*, London: Social Finance (2019), p. 4.

4 D. Whitfield, *Alternative to Private Finance of the Welfare State: A Global Analysis of Social Impact Bond, Pay-for-Success and Development Impact Bond Projects*, ESSU and the Australian Workplace Innovation and Social Research Centre, University of Adelaide (2015), p. 17.

5 Centre for Global Development and Social Finance, *Investing in Social Outcomes: Development Impact Bonds*, Report of the Development Impact Working Group (2013).

6 Brookings Institution, *Global Impact Bond Database* (May 2019), brookings.edu.

7 H. Mudaliar and H. Dithrich, *Sizing the Impact Investment Market*, New York: Global Impact Investing Network (2018).

8 C. Rhodes, *Financial Services: Contribution to the UK Economy*, House of Commons Briefing Paper 6193, 31 July 2019, pp. 5, 8.

9 City of London Corporation, *Developing a Global Financial Centre for Social Impact Investment* (authored by Price Waterhouse Cooper), London: City of London Corporation (2015).

10 T. Edmonds, *Big Society Bank/Capital*, House of Commons Briefing Paper 05876 (2015); see also: blogs.cabinetoffice.gov.uk.

11 See: data.gov.uk/sib_knowledge_box.

12 C. Wood and D. Leighton, *Measuring Social Value: The Gap Between Policy and Practice*, London: Demos (2010).

13 G8 Social Investment Taskforce, *Impact Investment*, p. 29.

14 Wood and Leighton, *Measuring Social Value*.

15 A. Dear et al., *Social Impact Bonds: The Early Years*, London: Social Finance (2016), p. 58.

16 See: sibdatabase.socialfinance.org.uk (accessed December 2019).

17 A. Fraser et al., *Evaluation of the Social Impact Bond Trailblazers in Health and Social Care Final Report*, London: London School of Hygiene and Tropical Medicine, Policy Innovation Research Unit (2018), researchonline.lshtm.ac.uk, p. 134.

18 R. Horesch, 'Injecting incentives into the solution of social problems: Social Policy Bonds', *Economic Affairs* 20(3) (2000): 39–42, 39.

19 N. Pequeneza, 'The Downside of Social Impact Bonds', *Stanford Social Innovation Review* (31 May 2019), ssir.org.

20 D. Silver and B. Clarke, 'Social Impact Bonds: Profiting from Poverty?' Social Action Research Foundation (2014), the-sarf.org.uk.

21 Fraser et al., *Evaluation of the Social Impact Bond Trailblazers*, p. 14.

22 M. Joy and J. Shields, 'Social Impact Bonds: The Next Phase of Third Sector Marketization?', *Canadian Journal of Nonprofit and Social Economy Research*, 4(2) (2013): 39–55.

23 Fraser et al., *Evaluation of the Social Impact Bond Trailblazers*, p. 13.

24 Ibid., p. 17.

25 R. Ogman, 'Social Impact Bonds: A "Social Neoliberal" Response to the Crisis?', in B. Schönig and S. Schipper (eds), *Urban Austerity: Impacts of the Global Financial Crisis on Cities in Europe*, Berlin: Theater der Zeit (2016), pp. 58–69, 59 and Fraser et al., *Evaluation of the Social Impact Bond Trailblazers*, p. 1.

26 UK Cabinet Office blog on Social Impact Bonds: blogs.cabinetoffice.gov.uk.

27 Fraser, *Evaluation of the Social Impact Bond Trailblazers*, p. 19.
28 S. Fitzpatrick, H. Pawson, G. Bramley, J. Wood, B. Watts, M. Stephens and J. Blenkinsopp, *The Homeless Monitor 2019*, London: Crisis/Joseph Rowntree Foundation (2019), p. xiii.
29 Ibid., p. xix.
30 Ibid., p. xv.
31 Ibid., p. xiii.
32 Ibid.
33 Ibid., p. xx.
34 Ibid., p. xiv.
35 Ibid.
36 Ibid., p. xiv.
37 Ibid.
38 World Health Organisation, 'Depression and Other Common Mental Disorders: Global Health Estimates', Geneva: WHO (2017), p. 5; apps.who.int.
39 Ibid.
40 C. Cooper, C. Graham and D. Himick, 'Social Impact Bonds: The Securitisation of the Homeless', *Accounting, Organisations and Society* 55 (2016): 63–82.
41 Ibid., 71.
42 See: gov.uk/government/publications/life-chances-fund.
43 Silver and Clarke, 'Social Impact Bonds: Profiting from Poverty?'
44 World Health Organisation, 'Noncommunicable Diseases' (2018), who.int.
45 Whitfield, *Alternative to Private Finance of the Welfare State* and Fraser et al., *Evaluation of the Social Impact Bond Trailblazers*, p. 9.
46 Y. Gonen, 'Goldman Gives Up on Jailed Teens After Its Social Program Fails', *New York Post*, 9 July 2015.
47 D. Bryan and M. Rafferty, 'Financial Derivatives as Social Policy Beyond Crisis', *Sociology* 48(5) (2014): 887–903.
48 For a critique of philanthrocapitalism, see L. McGoey, *No Such Thing as a Free Gift*, London/New York: Verso (2016).
49 Fraser et al., *Evaluation of the Social Impact Bond Trailblazers*, p. 19.
50 M. Giddens, 'How Social Impact Bonds Can Confound Their Critics and Create Better Value for Government', *Forbes Magazine*, 3 October 2018, forbes.com.
51 JP Morgan and the Global Impact Investing Network, 'Eyes on the Horizon – The Impact Investor Survey' (2015), thegiin.org, p. 8.
52 City of London Corporation, 'Developing a Global Financial Centre for Social Impact Investment'.
53 Social Investment Research Council, 'The Social Investment

Market Through a Data Lens' (2015), bigsocietycapital.com.

54 S. Foley, 'Impact Investing Must Be More Than a Buzzword', *Financial Times*, 1 November 2015.

55 E. Disley et al., *Lessons Learned from the Planning and Early Implementation of the Social Impact Bond at HMP Peterborough*, RAND Europe, Research Series 5/11, UK Ministry of Justice (2011).

56 Edmonds, *Big Society Bank/Capital*, p. 11.

57 See: bigsocietycapital/social-investment-market.

58 See: socialstockexchange.com/about-ssx/us; E. Kennedy, 'Trading This Market Could Make the World a Better Place', CNNMoney-Invest, 29 November 2017, money.cnn.com; A. Wood, 'How the Market Can Turbo Charge Social Impact Bonds', Social Enterprise Live, 6 September 2011, socialenterpriselive.com.

59 R. Horesch, 'Effective Policy Needs Experiments"', Social Policy Bonds blog, 9 November 2019, socialgoals.blogspot.com.

60 Horesch, 'Injecting incentives into the solution of social problems'; since this time (2000), Horesch has continued to publish on the need to create a secondary market for what he calls Social Policy Bonds.

61 Cf. R. Horesch, 'Make Social Impact Bonds Tradeable', *Alliance Magazine* (2018), alliancemagazine.org.

62 D. Bryan, R. Martin and M. Rafferty, 'Financialization and Marx: Giving Labor and Capital a Financial Makeover', *Review of Radical Political Economics* 41(4) (2009): 58–472.

63 R. Cohen and W. Sahlman, 'Social Impact Investing Will Be the New Venture Capital', *Harvard Business Review*, 17 January 2013.

64 E. Barman, *Caring Capitalism: The Meaning and Measure of Social Value*, Cambridge: Polity Press (2016), p. 16.

65 This slogan was first popularised by M. Bishop and P. Green, *The Road from Ruin: A New Capitalism for a Big Society*, London: A&C Black Publishers Ltd (2011).

66 S. Hall, *Policing the Crisis: Mugging, the State and Law and Order*, New York: Holmes and Meier Publishers Inc. (1978), p. 322.

6. Take Care of You

1 Cf. M. Feher, 'Self-Appreciation, or the Aspirations of Human Capital', *Public Culture* 21(1) (2009): 21–41.

2 Cf. G. Nicolosi, 'Biotechnologies, Alimentary Fears and the

Orthorexic Society', *Tailoring Biotechnologies* 2(3) (2007): 37–56.

3 S. Bratman, 'What Is Orthorexia?' (2014), orthorexia.com.

4 S. Bratman, 'Healthy Eating vs. Orthorexia' (2017), orthorexia. com.

5 M. Benasayag and G. Schmit, *Les Passions Tristes. Souffrance Psychique et Crise Sociale* [*Sad Passions: Psychic Suffering and Social Crisis*], Paris: La Découverte (2006).

6 S. Orbach, *Bodies*, London: Profile Books (2019, revised and updated edition).

7 S. Brown, 'Tracking the Rise of "Clean" Beauty', *Business of Fashion*, 25 July 2017, businessoffashion.com.

8 Ibid.

9 K. Kovac, 'Just the Facts: Natural and Safe Beauty Brands Outperforming Traditional Competitors', *BeautyMatter*, 7 June 2017, beautymatter.com.

10 T. Ahern, 'What is Clean Skincare?' Aú Natural Skinfood, 28 August 2018, archived at: aunaturalskinfood.com.

11 Brown, 'Tracking the Rise of "Clean" Beauty'.

12 E. Burney, 'Clean Beauty: Everything You Need to Know', *Vogue Magazine Online*, Edition Britain, 12 March 2019, vogue.co.uk.

13 F. Hayek, *The Road to Serfdom*, London: Routledge (2001 [1944]), p. 52.

14 In recent years a phenomenon has emerged called 'dry raves', dance parties held from 5 to 9 in the morning on a weekday before work. People can purchase coffee, smoothies or even nutrition supplements (no alcohol allowed) and do yoga alongside dancing to techno. The events are filmed and publicly livestreamed on the internet (see morninggloryville.com).

15 A. Toffler, *The Third Wave*, New York: Bantam Books (1980), p. 387ff.

16 Cf. G. Deleuze, 'Postscript on the Societies of Control', *October* 59 (1992): 3–7.

17 On sugar, see K. Throsby, 'Giving Up Sugar and the Inequalities of Abstinence', *Sociology of Health and Illness* 40 (2018): 954–68, especially 954–5, cited in R. O'Neill, '"Glow From the Inside Out": Deliciously Ella and the Politics of "Healthy Eating"', *European Journal of Cultural Studies* (forthcoming). On positive thinking in connection to health, see B. Ehrenreich, *Bright-sided: How the Relentless Promotion of Positive Thinking Has Undermined America*, New York: Metropolitan Books (2009).

18 N. Pajer, 'What's The Deal With "Clean Sleeping"?', *Huffington Post*, 19 October 2017.

19 Although this cuddle agency is no longer online, its founder has

since set up a training, certification and membership organisation for professional cuddlers, Cuddle Professionals International, which contains much of the same information. See: cuddle-professionals.co.uk.

20 See: cuddle-professionals.co.uk/professional-cuddler-certified-course. For an explanation of cuddling positions, see *Tomorrow Magazine*, 'Cuddling 101 – The Art and Science of How To Cuddle Correctly', 23 July 2018, archived at: tomorrowsleep.com/cuddling.

21 'CPI Member Essentials', cuddle-professionals.co.uk.

22 'Who Books a CPI Certified Cuddler?', cuddle-professionals.co.uk.

23 Ibid.

24 'The Power of Touch', cuddle-professionals.co.uk.

25 J. Evetts, 'The Sociological Analysis of Professionalism: Occupational Change in the Modern World', *International Sociology* 18(2) (2003): 395–415, 400.

26 R. Ratcliffe, 'Thousands Go Online for Therapy, But Does It Work?' *Guardian*, 12 February 2017.

27 See: babylonhealth.com/ai.

28 Babylon Health, 'NHS 111 Powered by Babylon – Outcomes Evaluation', October 2017, assets.babylonhealth.com.

29 See: babylonhealth.com/pricing.

30 S. Duke, 'Cash Injection Gives Helping Hand to Babylon's World-wide Ambitions', *The Times*, 3 August 2019, thetimes.co.uk; I. Lunden, 'Babylon Health Confirms $550M Raise at $2B+ Valuation to Expand Its AI-based Health Services', *Tech Crunch* (2019), techcrunch.com.

31 Ipsos Mori and York Health Economics Consortium, with Prof. Chris Salisbury for NHS Hammersmith and Fulham CCG and NHS England, *Evaluation of Babylon GP at Hand – Final Evaluation Report*, May 2019, London: Ipsos Mori (2019), pp. ii, iii; N. Bostock, 'GP at Hand Now Has Third Largest Patient List in UK', GP Online, 14 November 2019, gponline.com.

32 A. Downey, 'Babylon's GP at Hand Model Risks "Destabilising Care", Professor Warns', *Digital Health News*, 7 August 2019, digitalhealth.net; H. Crouch, 'Doctors' Union Chairman Calls for GP at Hand to Be Scrapped Immediately', *Digital Health News*, 21 June 2018, digitalhealth.net; Press Association, 'Smartphone GP Service "Risks Luring Doctors From Frontline Practice"', *Guardian*, 6 November 2017, theguardian.com/society.

33 See: gpathand.nhs.uk/how-we-work.

34 C. Cederström and A. Spicer, *The Wellness Syndrome*, Cambridge: Polity (2015).

35   N. Rose, *Inventing Ourselves: Psychology, Power and Person-hood, Cambridge*: Cambridge University Press (1998); see also J. Read, 'A Genealogy of Homo-Economicus: Neoliberalism and the Production of Subjectivity', *Foucault Studies* 6 (2009): 25–36.

36   S. Harney, 'Hapticality in the Undercommons: From Operations Management to Black Ops', *Cumma Papers #9* (2013), cummastudies.files.wordpress.com.

37   On anxiety as an affect that shapes contemporary society, see also J. Read, 'The Affective Composition of Labor' (2011), unemployednegativity.com.

38   'What modern management techniques are looking for is for "the worker's soul to become part of the factory".' M. Lazzarato, 'Immaterial Labour' [1996], in P. Virno and M. Hardt (eds), *Radical Thought in Italy: A Potential Politics*, Minneapolis, MN: University of Minnesota Press (2006), pp. 132–47.

39   Google Trends, internet search for 'Self-Care': trends.google.com.

40   See: england.nhs.uk/category/self-care/; rcn.org.uk/clinical-topics/public-health/self-care.

41   S. Graefe, 'Talking About Job Burnout in Germany: The Disappearance and Reemergence of Conflicts in Subjective Narrations', in S. Cassilde and A. Gilson (eds), *Psychosocial Health, Work and Language: International Perspectives Towards Their Categorisations at Work*, Cham: Springer (2017), pp. 113–28, 117.

42   C. Figley, 'Compassion Fatigue Resilience', *The Oxford Handbook of Compassion Science*, Oxford Handbooks Online (2017), DOI: 10.1093/oxfordhb/9780190464684.013.28, p. 5.

43   C. Figley (ed.), *Treating Compassion Fatigue*, London/New York: Routledge (2013), p. 7.

44   C. Hanisch, 'The Personal Is Political', first published in New York Radical Women (eds), *Notes from the Second Year: Women's Liberation* (1970). The essay is archived with an updated introduction at carolhanisch.org.

45   L. Cox, *How Do We Keep Going? Activist Burnout and Personal Sustainability in Social Movements*, Helsinki: Into-ebooks (2011), into-ebooks.com.

46   A. Lorde, 'Epilogue', in *A Burst of Light (Essays)*, New York: Ixia Press (imprint of Dover) (2017 [1988]), p. 130.

47   Talk given at the climate justice conference 'This Changes Everything', Friends Meeting House, Euston Road, London, 28 March 2015.

48   See also S. Ahmed, 'Selfcare as Warfare' (2014), feministkilljoys.com and L. Penny, 'Life Hacks of the Poor and Aimless: On Negotiating the False Idols of Neoliberal Selfcare', *The Baffler*, 8 July 2016.

49 M. Foucault, *The Will to Knowledge: History of Sexuality, Volume 1*, London: Penguin (1976/1998), pp. 100–1.

Conclusion

1 Foundational Economy Collective, *What Comes after the Pandemic? A Ten Point Platform for Foundational Renewal* (2020), foundationaleconomy.com.

2 International Labour Organisation, *Care Work and Care Jobs for the Future of Decent Work*; S. Himmelweit, 'Transforming Care', in L. MacFarlane (ed.), *New Thinking for the British Economy*, Open Democracy (2018): 62–78, 67.

3 M. Schmelzer, 'The Growth Paradigm: History, Hegemony, and the Contested Making of Economic Growthmanship', *Ecological Economics* 118 (2015): 262–71, 266.

4 Rai, S., C. Hoskyns, and D. Thomas, 'Depletion – the Cost of Social Reproduction,' *International Feminist Journal of Politics* 16(1) (2013): 86–105.

5 C. Coffey, *Time to Care: Underpaid and Unpaid Care Work and the Global Inequality Crisis*, Oxfam International (2020), oxfam.org.uk.

6 clapforourcarers.co.uk.

7 C. Higgins, 'Why We Shouldn't Be Calling Our Healthcare Workers "Heroes"', *Guardian*, 27 May 2020, guardian.com.

8 For a concrete proposal and costing for a National Care Service for adult social care, see for example J. Lethbridge, 'The Case for a National Care Service', Working Paper, University of Greenwich (2019), gala.gre.ac.uk; see also Care Commission, *Towards A New Deal for Care and Carers* (2016), carecommission.org and the Women's Budget Group, 'Web Briefing: Social Care and Gender', wbg.org.uk, March 2020.

9 See F. De Ville and G. Siles-Brügge, *TTIP: The Truth About the Transatlantic Trade and Investment Partnership*, Cambridge: Polity (2015).

10 M. A. MacLeod and A. Emejulu, 'Neoliberalism with a Community Face? A Critical Analysis of Asset-Based Community Development in Scotland', *Journal of Community Practice* 22(4) (2014): 430–50.

11 See also International Labour Organisation, *Care Work and Care Jobs for the Future of Decent Work*, Geneva: International Labour Office, ILO (2018).

12 See: savecarenow.org.

13 See for example the Coalition for Collaborative Care, coalition-forcollaborativecare.org.

14 Ibid.

15 See www.buurtzorg.com.

16 M. Waring, *If Women Counted: A New Feminist Economics*, New York: Harper Collins (1988); A. Picchio, *Social Reproduction: The Political Economy of the Labour Market*, Cambridge: Cambridge University Press (1992); D. Elson, 'Integrating Gender Issues into National Budgetary Policies and Procedures: Some Policy Options', *Journal of International Development* 10(7) (1998): 929–41.

17 R. Pearson and D. Elson, 'Transcending the Financial Crisis in the United Kingdom: Towards Plan 7 – a Feminist Economic Strategy', *Feminist Review* 109 (2015): 8–30.

18 L. Toupin, *Wages for Housework: A History of an International Feminist Movement, 1972–1977*, London: Pluto Press (2018).

19 The Care Collective, *The Care Manifesto*, London/New York: Verso (2020), p. 33.

20 M. de Angelis, *Omnia Sunt Communia: On the Commons and the Transformation to Postcapitalism*, London: Zed Books (2017), p. 121 ff.

21 See covidmutualaid.org.

22 P. Beresford, *All Our Welfare: Towards Participatory Social Policy*, Bristol: Policy Press (2016), p. 48ff.

23 J. Tronto, *Caring Democracy: Markets, Equality and Justice*, New York: NYU Press (2013), p. 7.

24 M. Galcerán Huguet, 'Der Kampf und den sozialen Wandel und seine Ankunft in den Institutionen' [The Struggle for Social Change and Its Arrival in the Institutions], in C. Brunner, N. Kubazcek, G. Raunig and K. Mulvaney (eds): *Die neuen Munizipalismen* [The New Municipalisms], Vienna: transversal texts (2017), p. 39.

25 The Foundational Economy Collective, *What Comes after the Pandemic?*, p. 10.

26 M. Pigeon, D. McDonald, O. Hoedeman and S. Kishimoto, *Remunicipalisation: Putting Water Back into Public Hands*, Amsterdam: Transnational Institute (2012), p. 10.

27 O. Reyes and B. Russell, 'Eight lessons from Barcelona en Comú on how to take back control', Open Democracy, 8 March 2017, available at: opendemocracy.net.

28 S. Kishimoto and O. Petitjean, *Reclaiming Public Services: How Cities and Citizens Are Turning Back Privatisation*, Amsterdam: Transnational Institute (2017), p. 159.

29 K. Milburn and B. Russell, *Public–Commons Partnerships: Building New Circuits of Collective Ownership*, 27 June 2019, common-wealth.co.uk.

30 Ibid. See also International Labour Organisation, *Care Work and Care Jobs for the Future of Decent Work*, Geneva: International Labour Office, ILO (2018).

Index